Endorsements

The writing of Greg Asimakoupoulos has the power to move, inspire, amuse and, best of all, to surprise you. His unexpected enlightening connections, in other words, can help the reader see the world with refreshed eyes as we travel the intersections of faith and everyday life with a wise and sympathetic guide.

Michael Medved, nationally syndicated talk radio host;
Author, THE AMERICAN MIRACLE

I have known Greg for three decades; first as my pastor in a tender time of significant spiritual discovery, and then for years as friends who crossed paths at various intersections of life and faith and vocation. I have always admired Greg for the genuine interest he takes in the lives of others. His warm hospitality made a difference in my life. True to his personality, **Intersections** *is a heart-warming collection of stories that are both fun to read and hold poignant truth. Greg's masterful storytelling will make it hard for the reader to put this book down.*

Tammy Swanson-Draheim, President,
The Evangelical Covenant Church

Greg has the gift of seeing wonder in the commonplace. Whether it is the whisper of the wind or the singing of a choir, he finds what he calls "Godwinks" in those moments. Read **Intersections** *to join him on a journey that will lift your spirits and ground your faith.*

Dr. David L. McKenna, past President,
Seattle Pacific University and Asbury Theological Seminary

Greg Asimakoupoulos has a knack for addressing timely topics in a fresh, relatable way that informs and inspires. He continually points us in the right direction, thanks to his warm writing style and his eye on the eternal.

Greg Clugston,
White House correspondent, SRN News

Through the years of reading his beautiful work, it would be hard to estimate how many times the written words of my fellow columnist and poet-extraordinaire, Greg Asimakoupoulos, have brought a smile, a tear, and a nudge towards some deeper pondering. How pleased I am to know his more than two decades of columns are now contained in this book, ready to delight, inspire, and nudge new (and not-so-new) readers with each turn of the page…bravo and happy reading!

Dr. Jodi Detrick, former columnist,
The Seattle Times

Greg Asimakoupoulos has long been a man of the word— preaching and teaching the Bible and telling stories that connect faith to the world around us. A steady, faithful, and insightful writer, Greg is the kind of writer you never forget, someone whose words remain in your heart and your head long after you turn the page.

Bob Smietana, veteran reporter, Religion News Service,
Author, REORGANIZED RELIGION

I'm delighted that Rev. Greg Asimakoupoulos is sharing his wisdom and insights in his book, **Intersections***, based on his newspaper columns. Greg's writing added a positive and hopeful tone for readers of our hometown newspaper, The Wenatchee World, to experience and learn from. He's a gifted writer, a deep thinker and someone who has a gift for helping us appreciate the rich variety of life experiences we encounter every day.*

Rufus Woods, retired editor and publisher,
The Wenatchee World

My friend Greg Asimakoupoulos, captures compelling stories about engaging people in every book he writes. I hope that you will let **Intersections** *take you on a journey of really interesting stories and wonderful characters.*

SQuire Rushnell, Author/TV Producer,
Hallmark Godwink Movies Series

Greg Asimakoupoulos

On the Tracks Media LLC

Intersections: Reflections on Life and Faith
Copyright © 2022 by Greg Asimakoupoulos

All rights reserved. No part of this book may be reproduced or transmitted in any form or by any means, electronic or mechanical, including photocopying, recording, or any information storage and retrieval system, except in the case of brief passages embodied in critical reviews or articles, without permission from the author: awesomerev@aol.com

Printed in the United States of America.
ISBN: 979-8-9869449-2-0

Cover painting: David Marty, used by permission
Cover Design: Joe Yakovetic
Interior Design: Rick Lindholtz for On the Tracks Media

On the Tracks Media LLC
onthetracksmedia.com
10   9   8   7   6   5   4   3   2   1

This volume is dedicated to The Reverend Carl L. Taylor and Captain Stephen E. Stewart (USN Retired).

An Editor's Prayer

"Heavenly Father, I pray Your blessings on Greg – may his book be a safe place where readers can encounter You to find comfort for their sadness, a haven for their anxious hearts, a heavenly perspective for their problems, and reasons to celebrate Your goodness. Please bless Greg for bringing others closer to You at the intersection of life and faith. May his words sing from the pages praises to our Savior and invite others to join in the chorus. I pray this in Jesus' name. Amen."

Table of Contents

Foreword 1
Introduction 3
The Silver Lining of National Sorrow 8
A Classic Movie with a Timeless Message 11
Cultivating a Sense of Wonder 14
At Eastertime a Son Waits in the Shadows 16
A Summer to Remember 18
A Recipe for Graduates 21
The Light Shines Through the Dark 23
Finding God in "It's a Wonderful Life" 25
A Time for Looking Back 27
2 Seahawks 12:48-49 29
Another Bicentennial to Celebrate 31
God Remains Our Source of Courage 33
When Your Presence Is the Best Present 36
Remembering Billy Graham: More Than Memorabilia ... 39
Three Cheers for Liberty! 42
What I Learned from Our Nation's Pastor 45
The Colors of Grief 47
How Silent Night Came to Be 50
O Little Town of Fredericksburg 52
When You Aren't in Kansas Anymore 55
A 70 Year Anniversary 58
A Triangle, a Round Ball and the Shape of Things to Come 60
Holy Week is a Living Icon 63
Oh the Places You Will Go! 65
Lessons from the Resurrection Tree 67
Lessons from a Blackberry Bush 69
Who Are the People in Your Neighborhood? 72
Three Kernels of Popcorn 74
Going Public with Your Love 76

A Prescription for a 20/20 Vision 78
A Prayer for My Home State 80
Pulling Together as a Team 82
COVID Lessons 84
A Step to Follow (Fifty Years Later) 87
Let's Hear It for Bridges! 89
What's in a Name? 92
Love Never Quits! 94
A Thanksgiving to Remember 96
Don't Get Lost in the Hectic Days of Christmas 98
A Prayer for Our New President 100
Dusting for Divine Fingerprints 102
Signs of Hope, Messages of Love 104
When Interruptions Become Opportunities 106
The Universal Message of Easter 108
Rhymes (and Reasons Not To) 110
With Praise for St. Arbucks! 113
A Message to the Class of COVID-19 116
Celebrating Christmas in July 119
Let's Hear It for Anniversaries! 122
9/11 Anniversary Triggers Thoughts on Unity 125
A Tale of Two Hughs 128
Looking for Aslan in Everyday Life 131
Calendars Can Help Us Number Our Days 133
Talking Turkey About Turkeys 135
It's a Wonderful Family Time 137
The Cruising Altitude of Christmas 140
A Date That will Live in Infamy 143
There's No Age Limit on Personal Growth 146
A Monumental Milestone 148
March Madness Remembered 151
The Dash of Life 153
An Unexpected Reminder of Resurrection 156

Seventy Things I've Learned in Seventy Years of Living	159
It's Time to Light the Holiday Candles	162
Wanted Posters Needed in Church	164
The Circle of Life is More Than a Song	166
Pledging Allegiance Through Prayer	169
Finding Common Ground	171
Celebrating the Seniors Among Us	174
A Heated Debate Over Tent City	176
An Uncommon Friendship	178
In Praise of a Winter View	180
Honoring Mother Earth	182
A Son's Tribute on Mother's Day	185
When Faced with Other Faiths	187
Listening to Freedom's Cry	189
Parenting Lessons	191
Becoming Soulmates	193
By George, It's Lent!	195
Praying for Our New President	197
My Favorite Holiday	199
Initial Ponderings of a New Pastor	201
In Search of the Christmas Beast	204
A Recipe for a Grateful Heart	207
Death Reminds Us to Embrace Life	209
Cheap Dates with Rich Rewards	211
On Unexpected Unemployment	214
A Little Piece of Quiet	217
Praying with Our Eyes Open	219
Another Date That will Live in Infamy	222
Goodbye American! A Tribute to Paul Harvey	224
Good Grief Is Not an Oxymoron	226
Tent City: A Personal Reflection	228
How the Church Stole Christmas!	231

An Antidote to Whine Flu 233
Yes, Virginia, There Is a God 235
Remember to Stay Alert to the World Around Us 237
Looking Back and Looking Forward 239
Walk, Pray, Love 241
Caffeinated Faith 243
And the Rest is History! 245
The Blessing 247
The Hallmark of Valentine's Day 249
A Prayer for More Than Lawmakers 251
The Year Thanksgiving Came Early 253
On Giving and Receiving 255
Sharing a Common Cup with the World 257
Reflections on Oso 259
A Christmas Prayer 261
The Lord's Day vs. Game Day 263
When the Parent Becomes the Child 265
Finding Buried Treasure 267
What I've Learned Since High School 269
A Godwink While Hunting for a House 271
Thankful for Normal Days! 273
The Boiling Point 275
The Slippery Slope of Common Ground 277
Confessions of a Streetwalker 279
The ABCs for Graduates 281
Grateful for a Mother's Legacy 283
Now That I'm Sixty-Four! 285
First Impressions Can Be Misleading 287
Lessons I Learned from Bert and Ernie 289
A Letter to the Christ Child 291
A Veteran of Gratitude 293
What's Faith Got to Do with It? 295
The Day Mr. Potter Went to Church 297

A Bittersweet Holiday	299
My Favorite Martin	301
God, Bless America (Revisited)	303
There's No Place Like Nome	306
Reflections on a White House Visit	308
At the Heart of It All	310
Let There be Peace on Earth	312
...and Let It Begin with Me!	314
My Father Was a Failure	316
Hope Is Restored by the Dawn's Early Light	318
The Rest of the Story	320
Making Peace with the Past	322
Baptism on the Ninth Hole	324
Remembering a Life Well-Lived	327
He Was Everything to Me	330
Making the Most of a High School Reunion	334
Learning How to Spell Love	337
The Class of 70 Turns 70	339
The White House or Our House?	341
The Him Behind the Hymn	343
Honoring Our Spiritual Shepherds	346
Home Row of Freedom	348
A Wish Book Christmas	351
A Head of His Time	353
Life Lessons from Mister Rogers	356

Foreword

His name is long and difficult to pronounce. But what isn't difficult to pronounce or read is the wide variety of journalist essays, social commentary, poetry and authorship of his fifteen books. Greg Asimakoupoulos, former pastor and current chaplain at *Covenant Living at the Shores* on Mercer Island, has been at the intersection of life, death and biblical faith for over forty years.

Since marrying our firstborn daughter in 1982, Greg has been at the intersection of our family for over forty years as well. His unique personality and creativity provide the social lubricant to our family gatherings. There is always a lively sense of pleasure and verve when he is with us. As a published author, I was delighted when Greg sought me out for feedback and encouragement when he began to express an interest in writing early on in his pastoral career.

A native of Washington State, Greg with his distinctive artistic flair, brings an everyman approach to his writing. During the dark times when people are trying to piece together the broken parts of their lives, Greg has uniquely allowed us to hear their voices. At the same time, he has offered his unique writing skill and as a comforter through his empathy. Through his voice, he has sung a favorite hymn to a person during the last moments of their life. (Greg is currently the on-call chaplain with the Mercer Island police and fire departments. He is paged whenever there is a tragedy or unexpected death.)

It was in this context; i.e., offering a pastor's perspective on faith and values that Greg became a columnist for the Daily Herald in suburban Chicago more than twenty years ago. The Daily Herald's editor recognized in Greg a Will Rogers-like gift for storytelling and carried Rogers's famous mantle, *"A stranger is just a friend I haven't met yet."*

Thus, like Winston Churchill who believed, *"The further backward you look the further forward you can see,"* Greg's new book, **Intersections: Reflections on Life and Faith**, is more than a historical social commentary of the past twenty years. While dealing with the great questions of our times, climate change, war, global pandemic, cultural shifts, injustices and more, Greg brings to his writings a biblical consolation of hope (and joy) in the dark and confusing times of our lives.

Greg further subscribes to the notion that each generation has a mandate to pass to the next generation the treasure it has inherited. ***Intersections: Reflections on Life and Faith*** is such a treasure.

Hugh Steven
*Retired missionary with Wycliffe Bible Translators
and author of more than forty books including*
I've Been Thinking *and* ***The Nature of Story and Creativity.***

Introduction

This book is unlike any of the others I have written. The contents of this volume are a compilation of columns in newspapers for which I have been privileged to write. I have chosen *Intersections* as the title because these previously published essays seek to speak to the intersection where life and faith meet.

As my best friends know, my writing life began when I was a parish pastor. The people who comprised the congregations I served had fascinating stories begging to be told. Many of these stories were published in our denominational magazine, *The Covenant Companion*. Others appeared in the local newspaper for which I wrote from time to time. My most regular columns, however, were simply published in our in-house church newsletter. I called my monthly contributions *Intersections*.

When my abilities as a writer matured, I was invited by the editor of our local newspaper to submit regular columns with a pastoral perspective. Repeatedly when tragic circumstances dominated the landscape of our community, I was asked to provide a context for hope. Over the past twenty years I have been the featured "Faith and Values" columnist for *The Daily Herald* in suburban Chicago, *The Mercer Island Reporter* in suburban Seattle and *The Wenatchee World* (my hometown paper). I've also been featured in *The Seattle Times* and quoted in *The Wall Street Journal*.

I am dedicating this anthology of my work to two significant mentors in my life, The Reverend Carl L. Taylor and Captain Stephen E. Stewart (USN Retired). Carl was the senior minister at Interbay Covenant Church who hired me as his associate while I was still in seminary. It was in that congregation where I first began to freelance as a writer.

Intersections

Sadly, Carl died during the season I was envisioning this project. Though miles and years separated us, Carl remained a mentor to the end. He encouraged me in my preaching and publishing over four decades.

Steve served as the chair of the leadership team at Crossroads Covenant Church in Concord, California for most of the eleven years I served as pastor. This retired military officer believed in my creative approach to ministry and applauded my attempts to document our success. Steve's encouragement and support continues to be nourishment for my soul.

A book like this is not possible without many special people who have contributed to its creation.

I am indebted to the following editors: Bob Smith and Chris Gerke, (*The Daily Herald*), Marco Martinez (*The Wenatchee World*), David Nelson (*The Kitsap Sun*) and Andy Hobbs (*The Mercer Island Reporter*).

I am grateful to my longtime friend David Marty for giving me permission to use his exquisite painting of an intersection in downtown Seattle for the cover. David was a member of Interbay Covenant Church when I was on the pastoral staff. We were part of a men's discipleship group that found us prayerfully imagining how God would use our gifts in the years to come. His artistic skills regularly contributed to the creative expressions in our congregational worship and outreach. To learn more about this renowned artist's unique style, I encourage you to check out David's website: davidmarty.com

Joe Yakovetic, an artist friend in the Orlando area, designed the cover. His creative eye for detail has benefited me on multiple book projects. I am in his debt. Take a look at his website as well: yakovetic.com

I also want to give a shout-out to Barbara Krieger who was willing to proofread the manuscript. From the time I began publishing my weekly poetry blog (myrhymesandreasons.com) in 2002, Barb has offered her editorial and grammatical expertise without solicitation and without charge.

I am also very appreciative of Rick Lindholtz, founder of On The Tracks Media, for his willingness to serve as my publishing agent once again. Rick's talents in layout and design have made this book possible.

My father-in-law's willingness to write the foreword to this volume is a gift for which I am deeply grateful. Hugh Steven, having written more than forty books, has been a mentor to me ever since his daughter, Wendy, became my wife. Many of his books are available on Amazon.

And speaking of my wife, words are not adequate to thank Wendy for her encouragement to keep writing. She supports me in my efforts to creatively express what I see from my seat on the bus as this journey called life continues. I'm so very grateful for Wendy's signals that caution me to the special opportunities each intersection we encounter offers.

Intersections

Reflections on Life and Faith

Intersections

The Silver Lining of National Sorrow

Where were you when you were told that Pearl Harbor had been bombed? What were you doing when you heard the news that President Kennedy had been assassinated? How about when Neil Armstrong walked on the moon or when the Challenger exploded after lift-off? If you are thirty years old or older, you can't help but recall what you were doing and where you were doing it when the Twin Towers fell in New York City.

And what were you doing when you learned that Queen Elizabeth died? I'm guessing that will be one of those days we will not soon forget. I was at my computer editing my weekly blog post about her amazing life. News that her family was being called to her side alerted me to her imminent death. I wanted to reflect on England's longest ruling monarch who ascended the throne the year I was born.

My fingers found the keys to pound out words about her courageous dignity, poise and grace lived out against the backdrop of family turmoil and tragedy. I remarked on her quiet faith that anchored her soul when her ship of state encountered stormy seas. Even though she stood only sixty-four inches high, the world looked up to Her Highness as a model of humility and perseverance. Elizabeth stood tall. In a reign of seventy years, she showered her subjects with memorable moments irrigating the blooms in their heart.

While I was typing away, my brother texted that Her Majesty had passed away. Even though I was anticipating the news, when the word of her death actually came, I was taken back. As a chaplain in a retirement community, I've learned this lesson well. Since I face death continually, I can attest to the fact that the maxim holds. *Preparing for* the inevitable doesn't preclude the emotional impact when the inevitable arrives.

What we observed in Great Britain recently was nothing less than astounding. Hundreds of thousands filled the streets of London to pay their respects and blanketing the gates of Buckingham Palace with bouquets. Tributes bombarded social media with expressions of love, admiration and grief. The nation came together in an uncanny display of unity.

A Prime Minister who stridently called for the end of the monarchy decades before now celebrated the place of the Crown with gratitude. Ironically, she was the last person to be photographed with the Queen. And King Charles' two sons put their relational struggles aside while focusing on a common goal.

The national response to the death of this much-loved Queen reminded me of the aftermath of September 11, 2001. As you likely recall, the days that followed that tragic Tuesday appeared to play out in slow motion. It was surreal. It was unfamiliar. It was sacred. Paradoxically, it was life-giving.

We learned then what we observed this month. National grief coalesces a country like nothing else save war. Political adversaries call a time out. The wealthy and the poor are united by a common debt of love. National pride undermines any sense of global inadequacy. And God is permitted to take center stage.

Do you recall following 9/11 how impromptu prayer gatherings were held in churches in the middle of the day in the middle of the week? *God Bless America* replaced *Take Me Out to the Ball Game* at the seventh inning stretch of Major League Baseball games. Conservative Republicans and Progressive Democrats stood on the steps on the U.S. Capitol singing patriot songs in unison (in harmony).

If you watched the prayer services that led up to the State Funeral for Queen Elizabeth as well as the funeral itself, you heard more than just mention of the monarch's depth of faith. You heard words from God's Word that comforted and challenged a nation in grief. You witnessed those in leadership calling upon God Almighty for divine help, without concern for being politically correct.

Like the old gospel hymn suggests, *"In times like these, we need a Savior..."* And in times like these, we tend to agree!

A Classic Movie with a Timeless Message

Last month was Breast Cancer Awareness month. But for the last twenty-five years or so, October has also been observed as Pastor Appreciation Month. Churches throughout the country look for tangible ways to recognize pastors and priests for the contribution they make in our lives.

Needless-to-say, clergy serve on the frontlines of warring factors in our culture. They play a significant role in combatting injustice and self-destructive tendencies. Often, however, their efforts are overlooked. Their attempts at compassion are easily camouflaged. At the retirement community where I serve as chaplain, we recently invited area clergy to our campus and honored them with a special lunch and a small gift. They were grateful.

Having been in the ministry for more than four decades, I know firsthand the joys and challenges pastors face week in and week out year after year. Someone has aptly stated that the clergy person's rewards are out of this world. But the struggles he or she faces are very much in the here-and-now.

One of those challenges common to the typical clergyman is taming the inner beast known as ego. What pastor or priest has not wanted to grow his congregation or parish? What person of the cloth has not looked for tangible ways to earn the respect and recognition of his or her peers? Who of them has not known the hunger for power and influence that becomes insatiable at times?

While that unhealthy hunger is hardly abnormal, it is also hardly new.

Intersections

The lust for power and recognition has cost too many celebrity pastors their reputation. The inner conflict that can destroy the gifted has been dramatized on the silver screen over the decades.

One of those films celebrates its 75th anniversary this year. "The Bishop's Wife" starring David Niven, Loretta Young and Cary Grant portrays the inner struggle of an ambition-driven cleric. Although this timeless picture was remade in 1996 as "The Preacher's Wife" (with Whitney Houston and Denzel Washington), there is no replacing the original. I ought to know. "The Bishop's Wife" is this chaplain's wife's favorite Christmas film. We watch it every year.

One of the actors in "The Bishop's Wife" is a friend of mine. Karolyn Grimes, who played the part of Debby (the Bishop's young daughter) is now eighty-two years old. Karolyn was also in "It's a Wonderful Life" (my favorite Christmas movie) as George Bailey's daughter Zuzu. Having spent time with Karolyn, I know that playing the role of the bishop's daughter was a highlight of her young acting career.

Curiously, Karolyn once told me that David Niven (who portrayed the ego-motivated minister in "The Bishop's Wife") had his own struggles as an actor. He didn't like children. Karolyn related much better to Cary Grant, whose angelic role on screen was replicated in real life.

As with Frank Capra's "Wonderful" film about Mary Bailey's husband George, "The Bishop's Wife" deals with a dark plot. In both black-and-white classics, we see desperate men calling on God for guidance. In the underrated movie that exposes the over-ambitious clergyman, the film ends with a redemptive conclusion. The bishop discovers his identity is not tied to the construction of a new cathedral. Instead, he finds (with the help of an angel) that his life and ministry is most fulfilled by serving those most in need of his care. And those include his wife and daughter.

As one who has tasted the sweet (but forbidden) fruit of ambition, I understand the seductive nature of success. A bout with clinical depression thirty years ago proved to be the reality check I needed. An undisciplined ego demands a high cost. Examining my motives, I determined to invest my limited energy in those around me. As a result, this chaplain's wife can attest to my contentment and hers.

And so, I commend to you "The Bishop's Wife." This movie celebrating a milestone anniversary offers a glimpse of the humanity of those clothed in holy garb. But it also reminds us that investing in people (and not brick-and-mortar) results in the most lasting value.

Cultivating a Sense of Wonder

It was the most unusual thing. While vacationing at Lake Chelan, my wife and I took a stroll along the Riverwalk Park. Near the end of our forty-minute walk, I looked up in the trees and saw a sight that surprised me. There, on the trunk of one of the trees, was a face looking at me. Having traversed that path for some thirty summers, I can honestly say I had never seen that face before.

As we walked back to our lake house, I wondered "How many people walk past that countenance day in and day out without even knowing it's there?" It got me thinking of the importance of being aware of unexpected "wonders" in the midst of daily routines.

We all know the expression "You can't see the forest for the trees." More often than not, though, it's the trees we can't see because of the forests on which we are fixated. The big-picture backdrop of daily life can easily divert us from noticing the beauty of a fragrant rose or a brilliant falling leaf. Too often we are oblivious to daily gifts the Creator drops in our path that are ready to be unwrapped and enjoyed. Like the countenance Mother Nature carved on a tree trunk in the Chelan park, they are as plain as noses on our faces. Sadly, we often miss seeing them.

During our courtship, my wife gave me a book that has become one of my all-time favorites. In *A Touch of Wonder*, Arthur Gordon celebrates the poignant serendipities woven into the fabric of human existence. The author's personal accounts of brushing for God's fingerprints inspired me to look for evidence of Providence in my world.

What awaits me can be something as small as the symmetry of a spider's web glistening in the late afternoon sunlight following a rainstorm. Or it could be as large as the profile of President Lincoln naturally sculpted by hundreds of years of erosion in the brown hills near my hometown.

It reminds me of the story I heard about a Native American who ventured from his rural town to visit New York City for the very first time. While walking with a friend in midtown Manhattan, the visitor heard a familiar sound amid the honking of taxis and the hubbub of pedestrians. "I hear a cricket!" he said to his friend.

His friend told him he must be crazy. There was no way anyone could possibly hear a cricket's chirp against the backdrop of such noise. To the friend's amazement, the New York visitor crossed the street and walked to a cement planter where he found a cricket beneath some leaves.

Totally amazed, his friend insisted he must have super-human hearing. "Not so," the Native American replied. *"It all depends on what you're listening for."*

If you know the story, you will recall that the Native American proceeded to drop change from his pocket on the sidewalk. To the surprise of his friend, several people, from as far away as twenty feet, turned toward the sound of the coins.

Even if that anecdote is just urban legend, its moral is memorable. Each of us is the recipient of unexpected "gifts" we can easily overlook. We don't unwrap and enjoy what we do not see.

To paraphrase the words of a first-century rabbi, *"Let he who has eyes to see, enjoy that to which others are blind."*

At Eastertime a Son Waits in the Shadows

"The Lord is my shepherd, I shall not want..."

Jews and Christians alike find comfort in the ancient words of Israel's shepherd-king. In the twenty-third Psalm, David reflects on how the Almighty protected him during times in his life when he was forced to journey through the valley of the shadow of death — times that included facing a giant named Goliath and running from a bloodthirsty evil king named Saul. In such times of despair, David, who had been a shepherd in his youth, discovered the shepherd-like qualities of his Creator.

As Easter approaches, I am celebrating the Christian's hope of life beyond the grave a little earlier and with more personal application than I normally do. Although the several funerals I've recently conducted have been challenging, there is something that has been even more difficult. It is the journey through Death Valley that I am taking with my own family.

There is nothing quite as stressful as watching one of your parents shuffle through the valley of the shadow of death. I know. I am living through that right now. My eighty-two-year-old father, a retired pastor in Wenatchee, is slowly surrendering to the claim that bone cancer has on his body.

Although I have been a shepherd for many in my flock who have faced similar situations, it's different this time. I need someone to shepherd me. My stomach is knotted up. Anxiety surprises me at unexpected times. I see the panic in my mother's face as she gradually comes to terms with the fact that my dad will be dying soon. Seeing her face causes me inner turmoil. I love my parents so much.

The other day as I drove the three hours to visit him in my boyhood home, I stood over his bed while he was sleeping. I found peace in the midst of my emotional storm as I observed him resting. The pain that he has fought was temporarily not an issue for the moment.

I took my pen and a pad of paper and proceeded to write…

I stand beside your bedside, weeping
comforted to see you sleeping.
While awake you're victimized by pain that saps your peace.

I can't help thinking as I stand here
how you rescued me from danger
when my nightmares bucked me off and left me all alone.

I think about when you were standing
by my bed with bars of candy.
I was only six or seven, home from school and sick.

But now it's my turn to be standing
at your bed. It's not demanding.
It's a privilege. Dad, I love you more than you could know.

I stand beside your bedside, weeping
comforted to see you sleeping.
I am asking God to give you dreams of Heaven's joys.

As I read and reread what I had written, the tears flowed, but my anxiety ceased. I realized that my loving Heavenly Father will care for my earthly father right up to the end — and beyond. I was comforted by the knowledge that the same Good Shepherd, who guided a young shepherd through the valley of the shadow of death when he faced his giant, will guide both my dad and me through the dark cold shadows of coming days.

A Summer to Remember

I never will forget the summer of 1969. It was the summer I bought my first car and got my first job. I can remember driving that '59 Studebaker Silverhawk to my job at KPQ radio as though it was yesterday.

The summer of 1969 was also a meaningful one for our nation. Sen. Edward Kennedy was involved in a car accident on Chappaquiddick Island in which a young woman by the name of Mary Jo Kopechne died. Neil Armstrong declared "That's one small step for man, a giant leap for mankind" as Apollo 11 landed on the moon. That same summer nearly half a million fans converged on a dairy farm in upstate New York for a three-day rock concert known as Woodstock.

The summer of 1969 was a significant season for our family as well. On August 13, my brother and I, along with our parents, stood before a Superior Court judge. As he banged his gravel, he declared that the Edwin Smith family would hereafter be known as the Edwin Asimakoupoulos family. Talk about a giant leap!

It all began back in 1906 when a fifteen-year-old boy immigrated to the United States from Greece, never to see his parents again. Haralambos Asimakoupoulos made his way from Ellis Island to Lewiston, Idaho. He was so grateful for his new homeland that he wanted to claim a name that sounded truly American.

In spite of the fact that his complexion was dark and his Greek accent was thick, he was convinced that changing his name would allow him to fit in more easily with the crowd. Since his last name meant silversmith, he had an idea. When he was naturalized as a U.S. citizen, Haralambos Asimakoupoulos became Harry Smith.

Harry married Margaret Turley and they had four girls and two boys. They named their second son Edwin, who, after serving as a Marine in World War II, married Star Birkeland. Edwin and Star Smith had two sons. I was the firstborn, followed two years later by my brother, Marc.

From the time we were little, our father told us about our grandfather's decision to change our ancestral name. While we were called the Smith family, we knew the rest of the story. A few years after my paternal grandpa died, my dad had the opportunity to visit relatives in Greece. He returned home with a renewed sense of ethnic pride. He had discovered an identity he'd not realized previously growing up on a ranch in rural Idaho. He knew he wanted to embrace his Greek culture in a tangible way.

He contemplated his options. What if he undid his father's decades-old decision? It would require a lot of paperwork. It would require legal action. He talked it over with my mom. After much prayer and contemplation, the decision was made.

A lawyer was hired, and the process began. When the appropriate forms were filed and approved, the day of destiny arrived. On that hot Wednesday morning, I entered the Chelan County courthouse Greg Smith. I left Greg Asimakoupoulos. Two weeks later, I began my senior year of high school with a new identity.

As I have reflected on that momentous occasion fifty years ago, I've wondered what Grandpa Harry would have thought. My guess is that he would have been proud of his son's courageous decision. In fact, as I contemplate the rich diversity that punctuates our population as a people, I've come to yet another conclusion. My grandfather likely would have had second thoughts about surrendering a name in the first place that celebrated his ethnic heritage. He would have been proud of his big fat Greek name.

After all, being truly American means a whole lot more than answering to an Anglo-Saxon surname. America is at its best when immigrants are welcomed and the cultures they bring with them are accepted.

Intersections

Over the past four decades, that big fat Greek name has served our family well. It has been a conversation starter as well as the means by which people are more apt to recall having met us. And once someone learns to pronounce it (awesome-ah-COPE-ah-less), they never forget it.

A Recipe for Graduates

It's that time of year once again. Those we love will soon parade on stage, dressed for success in cap and gown, to collect a piece of parchment signifying their academic achievement. If ever there was cause for a celebration feast, this is it! With that in mind, here's a recipe for graduates:

Start with one good egg (that's you) hard boiled by a dozen years of school assignments and life experiences. Carefully remove the outer shell that too easily hides the essence of who you really are. Realizing you have nothing to lose, risk being yourself without the protective pretense you've grown accustomed to projecting.

Then sift through the collection of memories you've preserved in the vacuum-sealed containers located in the pantry of your mind. As you unlock each memory, savor the fragrance of what those memorable moments emit. Take time to simmer.

Stir about the mixed emotions reduced from simmered memories. Take note of what you feel. You will discover that bitter memories and sweet ones blend together into a poignant and profitable picture of the past.

To this mixture of contemplations, combine your abilities and interests along with your hopes and dreams for the future. A focus on what's ahead is the yeast that raises expectations of what in time might be.

Don't forget to add a pinch of pride. Reaching this milestone in your life is a definite cause for feeling good about yourself. Processing reasons why you are "worth your salt" will add to the nutritional value of the feast you are preparing.

Make sure you add a half cup of humility to the aforementioned ingredients. Remember, although you've graduated, you haven't yet arrived. An honest estimation of what you have yet to learn will go a long way in making sure what you eventually dish out to others will be well done.

Pepper your parents with questions about what they wish they'd learned by your age. Their answers might surprise you. The truths they have to offer are nothing to sneeze at. After all, they have actually tasted firsthand what you are currently wondering about.

Extract from your grandparents a splash or two of wisdom from the vat of their fading perspective. Ask questions of those you trust who have a vested interest in your future. The flavors they've tasted aren't easily acquired but will definitely add to the complexity of what you serve as you make your entrée into the adult world.

Make sure you marinate on the meaning of life. This is a step too often neglected. For this purpose, use a brine drawn from the well-seasoned advice of pastors, priests or rabbis. The values articulated by your spiritual mentors will release the potential within you. After all, faith is like chicken stock. It is the foundational ingredient that both flavors and enhances the other ingredients that life's recipe calls for.

Parboil the lessons of life you've learned from the books you have read. In the process of completing school assignments, you've likely encountered authors who have identified a hunger in your soul for knowledge. What did they teach you about suffering, perseverance, forgiveness, acceptance and love? Coat your mind with those insights.

There you go. It's a simple recipe that you won't find in a typical cookbook. But it's a recipe for a successful life that is tried and true. As you continue your educational pursuits on another campus or in a career of your choosing, it's a recipe that will serve you well wherever you go and whatever you do. Bon appétit!

The Light Shines Through the Dark

December 2006 remains frozen in my memory. A freak windstorm toppled trees and power lines, leaving our neighborhood without lights, heat, and electricity for eight consecutive days. It was a week in which darkness dominated our lives. It was an unforgettable week in which we were reminded just how dependent we were on flashlights, candles or the glow of a cell-phone screen to navigate the halls of our frigid homes. In addition to being a major inconvenience, it was eerie. It just wasn't right.

Since the dawn of human history, darkness has been a metaphor of what isn't right. Darkness (as you know) is not a tangible reality in itself. It is simply the lack of light. Thus, it is an appropriate word to reference the absence of virtue, knowledge, and life. The godless deceive beneath the cover of darkness. The uninformed are trapped in the darkness of their ignorance. The dead are said to inhabit the "valley of shadows."

No wonder both Judaism and Christianity approach their holy days in December mindful of light. Hanukkah calls for candles (and for eight nights, no less). Advent and Christmas incorporate candles as well. A flaming wick atop a taper of wax symbolizes God's divine intervention in a dark world of despair and hopelessness.

An ancient Hebrew prophet anticipated the day when light would deny darkness its right to reign. *"The people walking in darkness have seen a great light. On those living in the land of deep darkness a light has dawned."* (Isaiah 9:2 NIV)

For Jews, those words recall countless times God has delivered His captive people and illuminated their future with hope. Christians see the birth of Christ as the fulfillment of Isaiah's prophecy. *"In him was life, and that life was the light of all mankind. The light shines in the darkness, and the darkness has not overcome it."* (John 1:4-5 NIV)

For both Jews and Christians, the Scriptures offer an invitation to look past this present darkness to a future bathed in the light of goodness, justice and peace. The light that has dawned is in the process of dispelling the darkness.

Finding God in "It's a Wonderful Life"

Christmas came early for me this year. In April I was contacted by a publisher asking if I'd be interested in writing a book about a classic Christmas movie. Although they were unaware "It's a Wonderful Life" was my all-time favorite film, they were not unaware of my immediate response.

"Absolutely!"

In the process of writing *Finding God in It's a Wonderful Life*, I discovered there's a George Bailey in each of us. Like the movie's protagonist, it is common for everyone to question the value of having been born. But when we feel like a failure, the back story of *IAWL* just might prompt us to press the pause button and render our self-critique premature.

"It's a Wonderful Life" was nominated for five Academy Awards in 1947: Best Picture, Best Director, Best Actor, Best Editing, and Best Sound Recording. By the time Oscar's long night of celebrating was over, the Capra film had been shut out. It didn't win one little gold statue.

When all the statistics had been tallied, "It's a Wonderful Life" did not have such a wonderful life. Variety's list of movies released in 1946-47 found the Capra castaway in twenty-seventh place. But then something unexpected happened.

In 1974, almost thirty years after its release, the film's copyright protection expired due to a clerical error. As a result, the movie fell into public domain, and television stations were able to show it without any royalty fee. Some seven decades after its debut, "It's a Wonderful Life" was awarded the No. 1 spot on the list of "Most Inspiring Movies of All Time."

Isn't that amazing? The movie, just like the main character of "It's a Wonderful Life," illustrates the value of patience. When tempted to prematurely evaluate the impact or success of our performance on the stage of history, it is easy to jump to less-than-accurate conclusions. And while easy, it is also wrong. The right reaction in times of self-doubt and despair is to take a leap of faith and trust God with the scenes of our lives that are still in the process of being written.

The words of the divine screenwriter recorded in the Old Testament spotlight our cause for optimism. *"I know the plans I have for you ... plans for good and not for evil, to give you a future and a hope."* (Jeremiah 29:11 NIV)

A Time for Looking Back

Seventy-five years ago a worldwide audience fixed its gaze on Tokyo Bay. They'd been promised the performance of a lifetime. The deck of this magnificent ship became a floating stage on which the delicate dance of peace was performed. It would prove to be a dance of destiny choreographed by a five-star general.

Douglas MacArthur's Parker pen became the baton with which he conducted an overture that preceded the opening curtain of an unforgettable scene. It is a scene we recall with grief and gratitude alike this week. The price tag of the performance was the currency of human life. But the curtain call continues after all these years in the land of the free and the home of the brave.

A nineteen-year-old Marine corporal from Arrow, Idaho, stood twenty feet behind MacArthur on September 2, 1945. From his unique perspective, he was an eyewitness to history. But he was not alone. Hundreds of others stood near him in uniformed allegiance. Proudly perched, these sailors and Marines recognized the significance of the drama playing out before them. Autographs on parchment attested to the negotiated peace. These signatures secured a surrender reluctantly offered.

From what I've been told, it was a somber ceremony that efficiently achieved the desired outcome with dignity. It was a moment in time that we remember seventy-five years later while the ghosts of the past look on and salute.

The reason I know so much about that historic occasion is because my late father was that nineteen-year-old corporal. Several famous photographs from the surrender ceremony include my dad. In most of the pictures, he is standing soldier straight with his hands clasped behind his back. But my favorite photo finds my father crouched on his haunches looking back toward a camera that captured his countenance.

My dad didn't even know that photograph existed until twenty years after the fact. One afternoon he was seated in a barbershop, waiting his turn. While browsing an American Legion magazine that chronicled the twentieth anniversary of the surrender, he turned a page and saw himself. He could hardly contain himself.

While showing the magazine photo to family members, my dad explained why he was looking back while everyone else was facing forward. A Russian photographer on the ship was jockeying for position on a makeshift ladder. Losing his balance, he dropped his camera. The crash caused my dad to turn to see where the noise was coming from. At that very moment, another member of the press corps was snapping a photo of the surrender ceremony.

Amid the "noise" of nonstop headlines crashing in on us during this unprecedented season in our nation, this is a time to look back and reflect. We would do well to recall what peace looks like. At the same time, we would benefit from being reminded how costly war really is. Looking back at all the signatures on that peace treaty would be a positive reminder of the strength that is found in working together. We need to be reminded that positive change is possible when allied forces form an alliance against totalitarian terrorism, climate change or a global pandemic.

So much in our world has changed since that September day in Tokyo Bay. But much remains the same. Racism and injustice refuse to surrender. Faith and science continue to pick fights with each other. The threat of nuclear war still successfully fuels a fragile peace. And a commitment to the core values of our democracy remains visible. Liberty's heart continues to beat strong as seen in the tireless demonstrations and protests that freely voice differing opinions.

Yes, this is a time to look back that we might look forward with a focus on a common vision of liberty and justice for all.

2 Seahawks 12:48-49

Have you noticed? The Seahawks' second straight trip to the Super Bowl has a way of energizing our entire state.

This common focus has a way of neutralizing social, political and religious differences that often divide us. We are a united state! You can hardly pass anyone on the street without hearing *"Go 'Hawks!"* to which you'll likely respond *"Go 'Hawks!"* It reminds me of passing the peace in church.

Such unity is nothing short of remarkable. So was that unlikely victory against Green Bay that catapulted the Seahawks into the big game. It was unbelievable! At the end of the first half the score was 16-0. Our team was lifeless.

Ironically, I had to miss the second half to officiate a memorial service at a nearby church. As I contemplated Psalm 23, the shadow of death had multiple meanings. I was mourning the end of an elderly friend's life as well as the end of the post-season that held such promise.

I was dying inside not knowing what was going on in the game. As a colleague eulogized the deceased, I hid my smartphone behind my hymnal to peek at the score. The Packers led 16-7 at the end of the third quarter. In spite of offering hope to the hopeless in the sanctuary, I didn't hold out much hope for the 'Hawks.

Nonetheless, following the benediction, I bolted out the door in search of a television. My heart sank. The score was now 19-7. With three minutes to go, we were down by two touchdowns. Our beloved Seahawks were beaten and all but buried. There was just no way!

And then with you, I witnessed the comeback of the century! It was a resurrection of sorts. The gloom of Good Friday gave way to the glory of Easter Sunday. Sure defeat was trumped by triumph.

Regardless of the outcome of the Super Bowl, I will savor the sweetness of the final few minutes for years to come. Brothers and sisters, I have been to the mountaintop. I have seen the Promised Land. Those two quick scores, the two-point conversion, the onside kick, the successful coin toss and that overtime touchdown — talk about milk and honey!

In a football game we'll not soon forget, I've glimpsed a timeless truth of life. No matter the circumstances, it's always too soon to give up.

That's what a first-century rabbi by the name of Paul was getting at when he penned these familiar words: *"We are hard pressed on every side, but not crushed; perplexed, but not in despair; persecuted, but not abandoned; struck down, but not destroyed ..."* (2 Corinthians 4:8-9 NIV)

As long as time remains on the game clock of life, we have reason to hope. Faith invites us to remain focused. An empty tomb provides pause to consider the possibility of resurrection! Can I get an Amen?

Another Bicentennial to Celebrate

A few weeks ago, my wife and I sat at Century Link Field watching the Seahawks trounce the Chicago Bears in a pre-season contest. Prior to the start of the game, an immense American flag covered the north end of the field as the national anthem was sung. When the soloist reached "the rockets red glare, the bombs bursting in air," flares shot out of the scoreboard on cue. The effect was impressive. Cheers exploded from the enthusiastic crowd.

But it doesn't take pyrotechnics to cause my patriotic heart to maintain a proud cadence. The sight of "Old Glory" painting the breeze is about all that's required. There's just something about the standard of our freedom that reminds me of our God-blessed history and the fact that I share a common identity with a nation of some three-hundred-million people. There was also something about seeing the stars and stripes that kindled an emotional response in a thirty-five-year-old lawyer by the name of Francis Scott Key.

On September 14, 1814, the morning after the British failed in their attempt to take Fort McHenry in Baltimore Harbor, Key spied the flag still flying at the fort. From his position on a ship ten miles out to sea, he scratched out a poem on a piece of paper and titled it "Defence of Fort M'Henry." The rest, as they say, is history!

Several years ago, I saw the original flag on display at the Smithsonian. That tattered and faded fabric measured forty-two feet by thirty feet. It was the immense size of the flag that allowed Key to see it at such a distance from the fort.

Intersections

As I stood in front of the huge flag with its fifteen stars and fifteen stripes, I couldn't help but feel dwarfed. But that's as it should be. The symbol of our freedom represents a dream and a destiny much larger than we can imagine or embrace. It also codifies a common commitment to defend that dream and destiny against acts of terror at home and abroad.

This week also marks the thirteenth anniversary of the events that blindsided our comfortable routines on a typical Tuesday we will forever refer to as 9/11. Who can forget the sight of those three New York firefighters hoisting an American flag amid the rubble of Ground Zero? It's an image that reminds us we live in "the land of the free and the home of the brave."

God Remains Our Source of Courage

For now, darkness dominates both literally and figuratively. This past Wednesday was the shortest day of the year. News headlines are short on hope. Light seems in limited supply. But are you a glass half-empty or half-full person? This season invites you to be the latter. And by the way, if you haven't noticed, the days are already getting longer.

Where were you on September 11, 2001? That's a question the vast majority of Americans can easily answer. On that unforgettable Tuesday morning I was driving to work listening to the radio. The announcer interrupted the music and read a news bulletin. First reports indicated a small single-engine plane had crashed into one of the towers of the World Trade Center. Subsequent reports brought the fuzzy news story into fearful focus. We were a nation under attack.

The magnitude of the tragedy soon became unimaginable. Thousands of lives had been lost. Tens of thousands had been personally impacted. The skyline of New York City had been altered beyond recognition. What was worse, our enemy was unknown. Subsequent attacks were possible. As a result, airports across the country closed down for the better part of a week. Churches opened their doors for spontaneous prayer services. There was a renewed sense of patriotism and dependence on God independent of party lines or religious affiliation.

Although the sudden fervor of faith faded as our nation regained its emotional balance, a haunting fear has dogged us for the past decade. National security remains on most everyone's mind. The increase in terroristic activity overseas, as well as the senseless mass shootings in our country, has left us feeling vulnerable.

Intersections

The tenth anniversary of 9/11 provides us with an opportunity to remember how quick we were willing to turn to God a decade ago. This sad milestone causes us to recall the fragility of life and fleeting nature of peace. It is an invitation to reflect and listen to what our Creator is attempting to say to us in the midst of daily headlines that rob our sense of confidence.

We all reflect and listen differently. Some meditate in silence. Some brush paint on an empty canvas. Others journal their inmost thoughts. Still others go on a contemplative walk through nature. My preference is to write poetry. As the anniversary of 9/11 approached I put pen to paper, reminded that God holds us securely even when the slippery fingers of our faith find it difficult to hang onto hope.

Since September 11 is a Sunday, local clergy can use the following poem as a congregational hymn. (Suggested tunes: "Ode to Joy" and "What a Friend We Have in Jesus")

God remains our source of courage
when we're traumatized by terror.
When we're haunted by the headlines
and the violence everywhere.
Hear God whisper in the silence,
"Don't despair, I'm in control.
Hurting hearts and broken cities
will at last one day be whole."

God recalls that tragic Tuesday
when twin towers disappeared,
when 3,000 people perished
and our hearts were numbed by fear.
Yet God whispers ten years later,
"Justice will in time be done.
I will stand with those who need me
till my Kingdom fully comes."

God invites us to be trusting
when we find that faith is hard.

*When we're fearful for our safety
and our nerves are frayed or jarred.
Still God whispers in the silence,
"Even when your faith is weak,
I will keep your feet from stumbling
when your way is dark and bleak."*

An ancient Hebrew poet composed a hymn for an insecure nation that offers a similar theme. You don't know the tune, but it's likely you know the words:

"God is our refuge and strength, an ever-present help in trouble. Therefore, we will not fear, though the earth give way and the mountains fall into the heart of the sea." (Psalm 46: 1-2 NIV)

Intersections

When Your Presence Is the Best Present

It's called "the Christmas Creep." In an attempt to maximize their holiday sales, retailers start decorating their stores for Christmas long before Halloween. It's so predictable. What is just as predictable is my grousing about this ungodly tendency. What has crept into our culture really bugs me. With Scrooge, I'm tempted to say "Bah, humbug!"

Fortunately, not all stores are so "creepy." I applaud Nordstrom's corporate policy that refuses to allow store managers to "deck the halls" until after Thanksgiving. Christmas shouldn't be unpacked until the ghosts, goblins and pilgrims have been put away. Christmas isn't quite as merry when it's creepy. That said, my annual campaign against "the Christmas Creep" is a bit less vocal this year. I have come to see that there is a time and place to be creepy. Let me explain.

A few months ago my friend, Priscilla, was diagnosed with inoperable cancer. Her doctors gave her a choice. She could endure the consequences of chemotherapy or opt for quality (instead of quantity) of life. She chose the latter.

Recognizing their mom would not likely live to see Christmas, Priscilla's adult children tangibly expressed their gratitude for their mother's love three weeks before Thanksgiving. Hauling down decorations from the attic, they transformed her condo into a Christmas wonderland.

When I stopped by to visit and pray with Priscilla, I had no idea what her kids had done. I was totally surprised to see a Christmas tree trimmed and lighted. My octogenarian friend proudly walked me around her place, showing me her treasured collection. Priscilla beamed like an eight-year-old.

After we prayed, I suggested we stand by the tree and sing some carols. Our voices lacked perfect pitch, but I dare say "Silent Night" never sounded so sweet.

Allowing my friend to celebrate Christmas early was truly a gift. Why shouldn't Priscilla spend her final weeks of life basking in the glow of tree lights and enjoying the soundtrack of her favorite season?

After leaving her condo, I reflected on what I had experienced. A woman stunned by a doctor's unexpected diagnosis was at peace. The message of Emmanuel (God-with-us) had made itself at home in her heart. I realized the truth of Christmas isn't seasonal. It's a truth that is applicable year-round.

Christmas announces that light has invaded darkness, that love overcomes hatred, that reconciliation wins over alienation, that acceptance outlasts prejudice, and that life ultimately defeats death. No wonder at the heart of the Christmas story we find old wise men bowing in submission to a newborn baby.

Calling on Priscilla that day also brought to mind the importance of visiting those whose days on earth are few. The light in Priscilla's eyes conveyed her gratitude for my stopping by long before she thanked me with words as I left.

My presence meant more to my friend than any present I might have given her. When death is drawing near, what tops a person's gift list is time with people they care about. They would rather unwrap memories of shared experiences while sipping a cup of tea than open a box filled with something they won't have time to enjoy.

Chances are you know someone who is in the process of celebrating their last Christmas. Perhaps they won't make it to Christmas Eve. Unlike my friend, your friend or family member may be in a nursing home or a hospital room devoid of decorations. What they long for this Christmas is your presence. A visit from you would likely deck the hallways of their heart with joy.

Intersections

While I still balk at "boughs of holly" in a department store before Halloween, seeing the same in the home of a dying friend is enough to leave me humming "Joy to the World." I'm guessing it will leave you humming, too.

Remembering Billy Graham: More Than Memorabilia

When I was a kid, three Billys defined my life. Uncle Billy was one. My dad's brother lived outside of Lewiston, Idaho. My best friend, Billy Crayton, was another. And then there was Billy Graham. According to a radio broadcast our family listened to every Sunday night in our home, the famous preacher could be reached in Minneapolis, Minnesota. The announcer reminded us "that's all the address you need."

As one destined for ministry in an evangelical denomination, I looked up to Billy Graham as a role model. I took my cues from him. Billy Graham was a larger-than-life figure for me. In addition to tuning in "The Hour of Decision" each week, our family subscribed to Decision Magazine published by the Billy Graham Evangelistic Association. My pastor-father subscribed to Christianity Today, a magazine of evangelical theology and thought founded by Billy Graham.

Like many families throughout America, we watched Billy Graham's crusades on television religiously. I could mimic the evangelist's familiar phrases framed in his signature southern dialect. *"The Bible says ... " "God loves you ... " "The buses will wait ... "*

When I was a senior in high school nearly half a century ago, I was given a scrapbook designed to collect classroom memories. Each page had a theme. One page was titled, "The Influencers." Beneath the headline at the top of the page were these words: "Quite a few friends have helped you become the person you are now. Your parents, teachers and friends, local, national and world leaders. You've learned from them and been influenced by them. Here's your chance to give them credit ... "

Intersections

This seventeen-year-old knew exactly who he wanted to credit. The page is pasted with pictures of my dad, my sixth-grade teacher, my maternal grandfather, a favorite uncle, Jesus Christ and Billy Graham. Each one had been a key influencer in my personal development, although Billy Graham's role had been indirect.

It was about this time that I received a copy of *Living Letters*, a portion of the New Testament in everyday language. This special edition of Ken Taylor's paraphrase of St. Paul's epistles (the first installment of what would become *The Living Bible*) was distributed through the ministry of the Graham Association. Thanks to Billy, the word of God came alive to me. Reading it more frequently than my King James Version, I began to sense a call to pastoral ministry.

As a young pastor with a penchant for writing, I submitted one of my first faith-oriented articles to Billy Graham's nationally syndicated periodical. Imagine my delight when I received a letter from the editor of Decision magazine indicating my piece had been accepted for publication.

In one of my first ministry assignments, I served a church that was in the same area where Billy Graham's nephew was a youth pastor. Kevin and I spent time together. His references to his famous uncle only served to validate my respect for "a friend I had never met."

Through the years, I began collecting memorabilia related to my ministry mentor. My collection includes an original portrait taken of Mr. Graham by a Seattle photographer the year I was born, a Christmas card sent by the Graham family, vintage news magazines with Billy on the cover, an autographed copy of *Living Letters*, a program from the famous Madison Square Garden Crusade in 1957 (that lasted sixteen weeks), a crusade songbook and an 8x10" color photograph of Billy preaching at the funeral of President Nixon with the living Presidents and their wives hanging on his every word.

When word of Billy Graham's death was announced, I retrieved my collection from storage. I was invited to display it in the lobby of the retirement home where I currently work.

As I arranged the memorabilia related to Billy's life and ministry in the display case, it occurred to me that the most significant part of my collection is not behind glass. It is in my heart.

Thanks to this man I never had the privilege of meeting, I have a settled assurance that God loves me "just as I am."

Three Cheers for Liberty!

This is the time of the year when we wax poetic celebrating our love of country. Familiar songs leap from our lips because we know them by heart. Tangible expressions of our national pride are exploded in the sky.

But not all fireworks are limited to displays after dark. The fire over which we grill hamburgers and hotdogs is also a ritual we gladly embrace.

My two grandfathers helped me appreciate how blessed we are to live in America. Both sailed into New York harbor about the same time. One was from Greece and one was from Norway. The sight of the Statue of Liberty left a lump in each of their throats. Neither could ever get over how blessed they were to be called "nephews" of Uncle Sam.

This week, as I contemplated my grandfathers' first impressions of what they saw arriving in America, I scratched the following in my journal.

There's a statue in a harbor
and her name is Liberty.
She stands tall for all the things that we hold dear.
A government of people
who (by rule of law) decide
what's permitted, what is not and what to fear.

And she symbolizes freedom
in a world that's torn by terror.
She stands up for peace enlightening the world
for the torch within her right hand

dispels darkness and helps guide
those who pledge allegiance to our flag unfurled.

She stands tall and (though she's silent),
she invites the poor and tired
to breathe new air and dream of being free.
Like the cross, she stands triumphant
as a picture of new life
purchased by the blood that bought our liberty.

For people who share my Christian faith, the cross on which my Savior died does convey a similar message to that of the Statue of Liberty. It calls to mind the sacrifice that opened the door to a new way of life and new opportunities for embracing an unblemished future.

As a Christian and as an American, I am free to pursue my God-given dreams. I love to spell American this way: Amer-I-CAN.

Yes, the theme of liberty is the focus of my thoughts as I write this column. It's the key to the lyrics Francis Scott Key used to unlock our gratitude for Old Glory. It's the essence of Independence Day.

Liberty has factored into my life since I was a kid. I went to Liberty Elementary School. In addition to steel pennies and buffalo nickels, I collected Liberty dimes as a boy. The Liberty Theater was where I made my debut in stand-up comedy. (It was a short-lived career.)

But those experiences of my youth pale in significance to the Liberty our immigrant parents and grandparents celebrated as they sailed beneath the outstretched torch of the Lady in New York harbor. The sight of that celebrated landmark triggered tears of gratitude and joy for many more than my grandfathers.

That lovely lady, and what she stood for, stimulated a similar response in all those who dreamed of the land of the free and the home of the brave. As they looked up into Liberty's countenance, they knew they were home. A home where courage is born and heroes are nurtured. It's a home where opportunity is given the run of the house.

And we, too, are grateful for this nation we call home. In light of that, let's not limit our expression of gratitude for America to one day a year. Let's regularly pause to check our patriotic pulse and reflect on the blessings we too often take for granted as Mother Liberty's offspring.

What I Learned from Our Nation's Pastor

On a hill not far from the White House stands an imposing granite building where the daily proceedings are opened with prayer. The members are concerned with both world and personal affairs. The chambers are visited by thousands of tourists each year.

No, I'm not referring to Capitol Hill. Rather, I have in mind St. Alban's Hill on which is perched Washington National Cathedral. The lesser-known hill that shadows our nation's capital is nonetheless significant given our country's highly politicized environment.

While vacationing in Washington, D.C., this summer, my wife and I had the privilege of worshiping at the cathedral. The preacher of the morning was Randy Hollerith, the fifty-five-year-old dean of the cathedral. His message was based on the Old Testament account of David being confronted by Nathan the Prophet following the king's adulterous relationship with Bathsheba. I found the dean's application, in which he called for leadership to be held accountable, especially timely.

When I was invited to conduct a funeral in Arlington Cemetery several weeks later, I contacted the National Cathedral to see if I could interview Hollerith. To my delight, my request was granted.

Curiously, the day before the Senate Judiciary Committee heard testimony from Dr. Ford and Judge Kavanaugh, I sat down with the dean of our nation's most well-known church.

Like Father Tim in the Mitford Series novels, this Episcopal priest shared office space with his dog. Lady, the dean's black lab, welcomed me with a well-lubricated tongue and a waving tail.

Intersections

When I asked Randy about his most memorable experience as leader of the National Cathedral, he referred to Sen. John McCain's Memorial Service a few weeks before. So far, it's the highlight of his two years in the position.

He mused, "As I officiated a service watched by millions, I stood directly in front of three former presidents and their wives. It was a picture of the potential unity that exists in a sadly divided country."

Following an hour-long visit, I left the Dean's office pondering his description of McCain's service. It occurred to me that looking for signs of unity is not the exclusive purview of a D.C. cleric whose office overlooks the White House. It doesn't take the elevated location of the National Cathedral to be given a perspective by which to see signs of hope. It is an opportunity extended to each of us.

I determined to start looking for encouraging signs from my vantage point. I thought of the multi-faith clergy association in the community where I live. Pastors, priests and rabbis focus on what we share in common as we sponsor an ecumenical Thanksgiving celebration each fall, as well as the high school baccalaureate service in the spring.

I see signs of hope in residents of the retirement community where I work who annually walk side-by-side to raise money for breast-cancer research regardless of their political persuasion or religious label.

I see signs of unity among our state and national politicians who reach across the aisle to engage in weekly prayer groups. I see hope in a well-known conservative pastor publicly calling on the President to apologize for the insensitive way he mocked the accuser of Judge Kavanaugh. And I see a sign of optimism in the ten-year-old daughter of Judge Kavanaugh suggesting her family pray for the alleged victim. My list of signs is growing.

Although permitted the privilege of sitting in the office of the cathedral dean, I will likely never stand at the Canterbury pulpit in the cathedral nave. All the same, I have an unobstructed view of ways people around me are choosing to cooperate. I'm guessing you do, too. The key is focusing on what's before us and determining to fixate on the positive.

The Colors of Grief

November 4, 2008 was a red-letter day for our nation ... and for me. That was the day the first Black American was elected to the White House. It was also the day my eighty-two-year-old dad died.

As I stood by his bedside and watched the color fade from his face, I held his lifeless hand as it grew cold. Nausea filled my gut as tears rolled down my cheeks. The father who had introduced me to baseball, basketball and golf was the same one who had taught me how to pray. My father's death changed my life forever.

On the tenth anniversary of my dad's passing, I can personally attest to the profound impact of a father's death. I can easily recall the spectrum of emotions associated with what I have termed "the colors of grief."

The Green of Envy

After my dad died, I was more keenly aware than I had previously been of men sitting at a sporting event with someone whose physical characteristics indicated this was definitely his dad. I would become momentarily overcome by a strong desire to be sharing my life with the one who helped bring it about.

Although my relationship with my dad was not perfect, it was close. My dad served as my financial adviser and spiritual mentor. He celebrated my gifts and took pride in my accomplishments as a writer and pastor. I could talk to him about almost anything. Seeing others with their dad caused me to long for what I can't have.

The Purple of the Early Morning

One of the colors of the rainbow that overarched my grief was purple. It is the dark, purplish color that emerges from the dark horizon just before dawn. As I navigated life without my dad, the early morning hours would remind me of him. For as long as I can remember, my dad greeted the day by communing with his Heavenly Father.

My dad spent the first hour of every day with an open Bible in his lap and a pen in his hand. His example of a non-compromised quiet time motivated me to take my relationship with God seriously. At his memorial service, I preached from that well-marked volume that documented his life.

The Gray of Everyday

My spectrum of grief also included gray. When I lost my dad, there were so many details to take care of; I was numb to what I was feeling inside. But soon the normalcy of daily routines returned. The fog of grief lifted only to reveal a dull overcast overhead. Something wasn't the same and I sadly recognized it never would be.

When you lose your dad, life seems drab and colorless. The person you looked to for affirmation is gone. That person who cheered you from the sidelines is missing. The one you could always call for advice will never answer the phone again.

An old Swedish proverb states, *"A shared joy is a doubled joy."* That's so true. What brings happiness to you is amplified when you can share that special joy with someone you are close to. When a man loses a dad, one of the significant "joy sharers" in his life can no longer be a means of multiplication. The brilliance of a once-blue sky becomes a boring gray.

The Gold of Heaven

Gratefully, the colors of my grief are not limited to green, purple and gray. They include a golden hue. While there are no words that can adequately describe the unique grief men experience when their fathers die, there are three words that describe the hope men have when their fathers were followers of Jesus — streets of gold. The Book of

Revelation describes the city streets of Heaven as being paved with pure gold (Revelation 21:21).

While there is not a day that goes by that I don't miss my dad, I have to admit that I am more fascinated in the topic of Heaven than ever before. Knowing that I will see my dad again, dulls the ache. The gold of what's to come overshadows all the other colors my dad's death brought to mind.

How Silent Night Came to Be

The week before Christmas 1818 found the pastor of St. Nicholas Church in the little village of Oberndorf, Austria, making final preparations for the Christmas Eve service. Joseph Mohr loved all the elements of the midnight service — the Scripture readings, the traditional hymns and the lighting of the candles. Celebrating the nativity of his Lord was a highlight of his year.

As the twenty-six-year-old bachelor pastor contemplated how he might conclude his sermon, he had an idea. What if he introduced the congregation to a Christmas hymn never before sung? The one he had in mind was a hymn deeply personal to him. Before moving to his current church a year earlier, he had written a poem that celebrated the birth of Christ. Joseph titled his verse (written in German) "Stille Nacht, Heilige Nacht."

Although his words were not initially written as a hymn, the meter of the lyrics lent themselves to be sung. The more he thought about the idea, the more he liked it. A new carol accompanied by a solo guitar would add a special touch to the traditional service.

Mohr consulted his good friend, Franz Gruber, a local school teacher who was also the church organist and a gifted musician. Could he compose a sing-able melody for the pastor's Christmas poem? Could he arrange it in such a way that the pastor could accompany the new hymn on his guitar? Gruber assured the young minister that he would do his best.

And his best resulted in a melody that has proven timeless. With a touch of inspiration, the church organist came up with a tune he deemed appropriate within a few hours. The handwritten score was delivered in time. On December 24, Pastor Mohr and Franz Gruber sang the lyrics to the accompaniment of the guitar as St. Nicholas' small choir joined them. Based on a description of the carol's debut performance written by Gruber, after hearing "Silent Night" the congregation erupted into applause.

Within a year, the collaborative work of Mohr and Gruber began to take on a life of its own. The Rainers, a famous Austrian family of traveling musicians, performed "Silent Night" at their home church in Fugen on Christmas Eve 1819. Three years later, they sang the new carol for the Russian Czar and the Emperor of Austria. In 1839, The Rainers traveled to New York City, where they performed "Silent Night" for the first time ever in the United States.

In addition, The Strassers, a family of glove makers also known for their singing, traveled to annual village fairs in Germany. In 1832, the singing glove makers included "Silent Night" in their repertoire as they entertained the shoppers. By the 1840s, the song had become so popular that the King of Prussia considered it among his favorites. In 1863, the hymn was translated into English and by 1871 the English translation made its way to the United States and was included in Charles Hutchins' "Sunday School Hymnal."

As you may be aware, some fictionalized accounts of "the rest of the story" suggest that the reason Pastor Mohr resorted to using his guitar was that the church organ was not working. Some accounts even go as far as suggesting that church mice had gotten into the works of the instrument, rendering it disabled. But there is no actual documentation of that fact.

What is known is this: Some months following the premier performance of "Silent Night" at the 1818 Christmas Eve service, Karl Marcher, a master organ builder, worked on the St. Nicholas instrument. He likely saw a copy of the Christmas hymn and took it with him as he returned to his home near Innsbruck. Much like the message of Christmas, he knew it was too wonderful not to share.

Intersections

O Little Town of Fredericksburg

I began celebrating Christmas four months early this year. While visiting relatives in Fredericksburg, Virginia, my sister-in-law gave my wife and me a tour of the historic downtown. The little town of Fredericksburg on the Rappahannock River is rich in history, having played a role in both the Revolutionary War and the Civil War.

Although I couldn't recall the details, something in the back of my head suggested that this quaint Virginia town somehow factored into the writing of one of my favorite Christmas carols. While stopping for a famous frozen custard cone at Carl's Drive-In, I did some research on my iPhone. And to my delight, I was right.

I asked my sister-in-law if we could stop at St. George's Episcopal Church. She agreed. Together, we climbed the steps to the historic church and entered the sanctuary. Except for a custodian working on a piece of carpet and docent seated in the back pew, the church was empty.

"I understand this is the church where The Rev. Phillips Brooks preached his first sermon!" I announced excitedly to the docent. *"He's the man who wrote 'O Little Town of Bethlehem.'"*

To my chagrin, the tour guide stared blankly at me. Looking at her notes, she indicated that this indeed was a very famous church. George Washington's mother had been a member of the congregation. John Paul Jones' brother was buried in the church graveyard. She pointed to a couple of Louis Comfort Tiffany stained-glass windows that graced the worship space. But sadly, she could not confirm what I had been told years ago and what I had confirmed on the internet.

I assumed there had to be a plaque of some sort somewhere documenting Phillips Brooks' connection to this church. I investigated the walls of the narthex. I walked around the sanctuary. I scoured the chancel area by the ornate pulpit. And then I saw it. A bronze plaque to the side of the altar contained these words: Bishop Phillips Brooks preached his first sermon in this church on July 3, 1859 following his ordination as a Deacon.

Although no mention was made of his famous carol, I knew him to be the author from previous research I had done as an amateur hymnologist. Taking a hymnal from the pew rack, I opened to the page containing "O Little Town of Bethlehem" and showed the docent Phillips Brooks' name. She assured me she would add this fascinating fact to her future tours.

That's when I asked her a favor. Would she also be willing to use my iPhone to shoot a video of me singing "O Little Town of Bethlehem" from the pulpit where Brooks preached his first sermon? She agreed. Standing behind Phillips Brooks' pulpit, wearing my Seahawks jersey and jeans, I sang from the St. George's hymnal to an empty church.

As my eyes focused on the lyrics, I noticed the date at the bottom of the page. It was then I realized that this year is the one-hundred-fiftieth anniversary of Brooks' carol. And it dawned on me that the message of this hymn is just as timely today as when it was written. His words and phrases gripped me.

In his carol, Brooks speaks of the hopes and fears of all the years. He underscores a town marked by deep and dreamless sleep. How appropriate, I thought. In a world punctuated by Black Lives Matter and the Me-Too Movement and mass shootings, there are fears in spite of hopes. Our longings for peace on earth are often dreamless. Our world of sin is marked by dark streets in need of a shining light. Not much has changed since a young, unknown deacon in Fredericksburg became the beloved bishop of Boston. We desperately need the Christ of Christmas.

Intersections

This Christmas as I sing "O Little Town of Bethlehem," I will recall my visit to Fredericksburg. I will also visualize Bishop Brooks' words, especially the last verse of the carol that evolves into a prayer. *"O holy Child of Bethlehem descend to us, we pray. Cast out our sin and enter in. Be born to us today. We hear the Christmas angels the great glad tidings tell. O, come to us. Abide with us, our Lord, Emmanuel."*

When You Aren't in Kansas Anymore

I've been thinking a lot about "The Wizard of Oz" recently. For one thing, this year marks the eightieth anniversary of that timeless film. Although the movie didn't garner an Oscar for Best Picture, it was nominated for five Academy Awards. As you may recall, it won the Best Original Song category with "Somewhere Over the Rainbow."

There's another reason I have "Oz" on my mind. One of the residents at the retirement community where I work was actually in the movie. Meredythe Glass was only eighteen years old when the producer, Mervyn LeRoy, found a part for her in the film. She was a "green lady" in the Emerald City scenes.

Her big break came about because she was LeRoy's cousin. Although she didn't have a huge part, Meredythe never tires of talking about her experiences on the MGM soundstage with Judy Garland.

The silver screen's entertaining adaptation of Frank Baum's tale of Dorothy Gale and her adventures in the Land of Oz never seems to grow old. One of the reasons may be the fact that the 1939 movie portrays a gripping picture of the human condition.

The tornado that catapulted the Kansas farm girl into the imaginary kingdom is more than just a tornadic wind. We all face storms in life. Some gale-force winds are worse than others. They are clocked with varying velocities. But we all face them. A health crisis. Unexpected unemployment. A car accident. The death of a marriage. The death of a child or a spouse. Perhaps the death of a dream.

Such ill breezes can blow us off course or knock us off balance. When our worlds spin out of control, our confidence is shaken. We aren't sure where to turn or who to turn to. About the only thing of which we are certain is that we aren't in "Kansas" anymore.

It's at times like this we discover what Dorothy did. We need a company of committed friends to keep on going. When she first met the scarecrow, the tin man and the lion, there's no way the young girl from Kansas could have known just how much they would help her survive.

Nearly thirty years ago, I was knocked off my feet by a psychological cyclone called clinical depression. It was an unanticipated storm the local weatherman could never have predicted. For nine months I was trapped in a dark storm cellar of despair. But gratefully I was not alone.

Three friends walked beside me as I gradually found my way out of that emotional basement. Each made time for me. Without judgment they listened to my heart. Their presence reminded me I wasn't alone.

These who journeyed with me were not professional counselors. And they did not have their "acts" entirely together. Each limped along, crippled by their own individual struggles.

One was dealing with the emotional pain associated with parenting a child with special needs. Another was attempting to dance with a difficult marriage. The third was a retired military officer who was rebounding from his own personal (and painful) bout with depression.

As we shared our lives together, we helped each other shoulder a burden that was too heavy for any one of us to carry alone. Thankfully, the dark clouds eventually lifted and I walked out into the sunlight once again.

Through it all I discovered, like Dorothy did, that the most helpful companions are those who live with unmet expectations of their own.

In the longing for what is lacking in our own lives, we develop a capacity for showing compassion to others.

What makes "The Wizard of Oz" the timeless classic that it is has to do with the unlikely fellowship of friends who travel the yellow brick road together. What makes the difficult journey of life meaningful is the privilege of sharing the road with those we encounter on the way.

A 70 Year Anniversary

Certain dates punctuate our history as Americans – November 11, 1918; December 7, 1941; June 6, 1944; November 22, 1963; and September 11, 2001. My late father engraved an additional date on the cortex of my memory. Because he was an eyewitness to the surrender ceremony in Tokyo Bay that ended World War II, Dad would not let my brother and me forget September 2, 1945. Because of his willingness to recall details of that decisive day aboard the USS Missouri, the anniversary of that historical event provides me with a tangible connection to my father six years after his death.

This week calls to mind yet another significant date that we dare not forget. Today is the seventieth anniversary of V-E Day. On May 8, 1945, just days after Hitler committed suicide in the Battle of Berlin, the Allied Forces accepted Germany's unconditional surrender. This victory in Europe allowed the world to breathe a unifying sigh of relief.

As Harry Truman blew out sixty-one candles on his birthday cake that day, he was grateful the anniversary of his birth would be overshadowed by the announcement across the Atlantic. While American flags would continue to fly at half-staff for another week (to mourn FDR's death April 12), the patriotic hearts of Americans proudly beat in unison.

All the same, because the curtain had not yet fallen on the conflict in the South Pacific Theater, the Truman show prevented a full-scale celebration. Four more months of conflict would have to be waged before the concluding credits would be screened.

Reflections on Life and Faith

Just as President Truman's birthday was overshadowed by V-E Day, so V-E Day was eclipsed by V-J Day in my family. My dad's personal experience influenced which date on the calendar we honored. But had my dad fought in the Battle of the Bulge, such would not have been the case. For many of my college classmates, the European Theater of World War II was the context for their fathers' contribution to the protection of our freedoms. As such, V-E Day gave them pause for appropriate pride and grateful reflection.

Ironically, when my parents purchased vacation property in the resort community of Chelan, Washington thirty-five years ago, the lakeside home included an indelible reminder of the Second World War. But it wasn't the exact sentiment my father would have chosen had it been left up to him. Herb Hamel, who built the home seven decades ago, had his own idea. He made sure his neighbors would never forget the theater in which his friends had fought. In the cement breakwater, Mr. Hamel engraved V-E Day 1945.

Whenever our family enjoys time at Lake Chelan, I am reminded of the anniversary we celebrate this week. But I am also provided an opportunity to reflect on the fact that one person's experience of life does not define another's. Patriotism comes in a variety of colors.

What was important to Herb Hamel was not identical to what mattered most to Edwin Asimakoupoulos. The same is true for you and me. My religious persuasion may differ from yours. My political perspective won't likely line up with yours. Unique experiences each of us has had shape the way we view the world. Our families of origin influence the values that in turn filter our choices.

This week I am thankful for those Americans who sacrificed their lives in Europe and in the South Pacific. Because of the blood they shed, you and I have the freedom to express our personal opinions and celebrate our differences. The flag that continues to fly over our fifty United States grants us permission to disagree.

It was a demonic demagogue in Europe who tried his best to eliminate diversity. Hitler's war on humanity will haunt the history books for centuries to come. But V-E Day is a lasting reminder that we won that war seventy years ago.

A Triangle, a Round Ball and the Shape of Things to Come

It's that time of year when "roundball" finds our favorite teams squaring off as bracket-filled rectangles call to mind an annual mental illness that plagues our country. It's a malady we welcome known as March Madness.

On a recent trip to Israel, I was reminded that not all madness associated with competing entities is limited to the month of March or concerns collegiate basketball. The craziness that has characterized the attempts of Jews, Muslims, and Christians to live together in cooperative ventures is continuous. The full-court press of ongoing tension is put on temporary hold with the occasional timeout only for the benefit of tourists. I was reminded there are no fast breaks in the game of international peace.

The graphic evidence of rival loyalties was huge in the little town of Bethlehem. In this sacred place revered by Christians, a graffiti-covered wall keeps Jews out while Palestinian Muslims seek to eke out a living. I was struck by the haunting irony of a welcome mat opposite the slogan-laden barrier wall.

But against the backdrop of hostility and division, I also witnessed a reason for hope. The shape of what's to come included a triangular sign and a rectangular basketball court where "roundball" brings kids of all faiths together. The hope I detected was housed in the historic Jerusalem International YMCA.

Since our hotel was a five-minute walk from the JIY, my wife and I decided to explore. A staff member, Ra'ed, agreed to give us a tour of the complex. The familiar triangle logo greeted us, reminding us of the

YMCA's commitment to body, mind and spirit. Our host told us that the facility's original design of three distinct structures (including a one-hundred-seventy-five-foot tower that dominates the skyline) symbolized the tri-part motto of the institution. I was intrigued to learn that the JIY was completed in 1933 and designed by the same architect who built the Empire State Building two years earlier.

As I walked through the decades-old facility — it includes a fifty-room hotel and restaurant — I was amazed at the timeless beauty. The architecture is an intentional blend of motifs and symbols borrowed from the three Abrahamic faiths. It was obvious this was a place where Christians, Jews and Muslims were welcome. There was a place to pray. There was also a place to play.

The original design included a basketball court and swimming pool (the first in Jerusalem), offering a safe place to exercise the essentials of teamwork as well as strengthen the muscles of friendship. And today, an extensive swim program and a thirty-two-team basketball league continue to build on that original foundation. Teams include participants from all faiths (and no faith). There is no attempt at proselytizing. There is only an attempt to model love, tolerance and acceptance in a part of the world that is deficient in all three.

At the end of the guided tour, Ra'ed escorted us up to the top of the tower. The view of old Jerusalem was breathtaking. But so was my view of the future. Having been shown how Christians, Jews and Muslims are free to celebrate their beliefs side-by-side intentionally, I was hopeful. What I had just witnessed was music to my ears.

And speaking of music ... Before we descended from the "upper room," the staff member pointed out the carillon bells that crown the imposing tower. He opened the door to a small chamber that shelters the carillon keyboard. Ra'ed insisted I sit down and play something.

I froze. Having taken piano lessons as a kid, my skills are still quite elementary. There was no sheet music and I had nothing memorized. And then out of the blue a melody flowed out of my heart.

Pushing the large levers that strike the huge bells, I managed to play the first line to "Jesus Loves Me." I'm guessing it was the first time ever that old Sunday school tune rang out over Jerusalem. Wondering if my choice was an acceptable one, I looked up to Ra'ed.

Our Muslim host's smile reassured me. After all, I was in a place where my faith was as welcomed as his.

Holy Week is a Living Icon

I am proud of my Greek ancestry, but I did not grow up in an Orthodox home. Rural Idaho where my paternal grandfather settled after emigrating from Greece, was not near a Greek Orthodox church. My father and his siblings were raised in an Evangelical congregation. As a result, my brother and I grew up in a home that did not include an appreciation of icons.

Sadly, (and ignorantly) I was led to believe that sacred art (such as icons) fostered something akin to idol worship. It wasn't until I began studying for the ministry that I discovered the meaning and beauty of these miniature religious paintings. And then I was blown away by their significance as an aid to worship.

The icons on my computer desktop help illustrate what I came to see. Those images are symbols you click to open a program that you can engage more fully. Those icons are not an end in themselves, but windows (literally) that open to a deeper reality than the graphic image on which you initially glimpse.

In addition to my computer, I have icons on my actual desktop in my office. One of them was given to me by my father before he died. (Like me, he came to appreciate his Orthodox heritage later in life.) Another icon was recently painted by my son-in-law. These symbols of my faith invite my prayerful meditation.

In this week before Easter, Christians around the world are contemplating the good that resulted from a bad Friday. Because of our familiarity with the Gospel accounts, the events surrounding the passion of our Lord are engraved on our minds and hearts but can easily be ignored. Like icons on a computer, they must be purposely accessed.

The events we commemorate this week are "living icons" of the soul. When we virtually click on them, they open up to reveal the virtues of our faith. For example, that final supper in the upper room on Thursday is a scene that recalls the power of humility. We can picture a young rabbi stooping to wash his students' feet while modeling a humble spirit.

When we click on Friday, what pops up is the image of a bruised and bleeding scapegoat unjustly hung out to die. You can almost hear his bleating whimper as he gives us an example of laying down our lives for another.

And then there is that fateful Saturday. It is the icon that calls to mind a "black Sabbath" in which the followers of Jesus hide behind locked doors fearing for their lives. It is an image that reminds us that doubt is part of the faith journey. That group of grieving disciples couldn't imagine how the valley of death's shadows would ever succumb to the dawn's early light of Sunday.

And speaking of Sunday, Easter is an icon not unlike the Microsoft Word icon on my computer screen. As I click on that icon, a blank page appears. It provides the means by which I can compose something new. It is the invitation to begin again and start over.

As we Christians believe, Easter is the ultimate reboot. Death and regret have given way to life and hope.

In the events of Holy Week, we are given "living icons" on which to click in order to contemplate what the culmination of the Lenten season is all about. These days are an opportunity to fix our gaze on what we see in order to focus on what those familiar images mean for us today.

Oh the Places You Will Go!
Advice to graduates, with apologies to Dr. Seuss

The world's your oyster. The world's your stage.
Your time has come. You've reached the age.
The Lord will guide you. So, trust His plans.
Just say "Your wish is my command."
Look in your heart. What brings delight?
Embrace your gift. Turn on the light.
God made you just the way you are.
So go with that and you'll go far.

But far begins with one small step.
So lace your shoes and then expect
to run your race at your own speed.
Don't fret about who's in the lead.
This thing called life's a marathon.
It's not a sprint. So, carry on!

Along the way, you'll trip and fall.
You'll bruise your knees and that's not all.
Your pride will smart, but that's okay.
That's how you learn to make your way.
So, each new day look in the mirror.
Confront yourself and what you fear.

Look deep inside at what you see.
Reflect on who you long to be.
Don't overlook what you don't like.
Tell bents you hate to take a hike.

Intersections

*Be honest with the one you face
embracing God's amazing grace.
It covers all you dare confess
and undermines perfection's stress.*

*Be sure to give yourself a smile.
It's good to celebrate each mile.
Along the path that you will go,
who cares if you go fast or slow.*

*The speed that marks your upward climb
means not so much so never mind.
The trek you take is most unique
So, too, the plans you aim to seek.*

*Dream big. Imagine. Go for broke.
While some may laugh, it is no joke.
Remind yourself God's in control
and He will help you reach your goals.*

*You will achieve more than you know.
The many places you will go
cannot be seen from where you sit.
You have to move out bit by bit.*

*Make every day your chance to start
to live your dream and own your part
in what the good Lord longs to bless
including you and your success.*

*What matters most is making time
to pace yourself and read the signs
of where to go and what to do.
The future does depend on you!*

Lessons from the Resurrection Tree

For the past five years, I have been a faith and values columnist for The Wenatchee World. As such, I have reflected on the meaning infused within the mileposts on life's journey. I've touched on such things as births, graduations, career achievements, sports accomplishments and family struggles. A frequent theme has been the fleeting and fragile nature of the human experience.

As a chaplain at a retirement community, anticipated death is a common occurrence for me. Unexpected death, on the other hand, takes your breath away. That was the situation when Bud Palmberg, my dear friend and ministry colleague, died a few weeks ago while on a preaching mission in Bali.

This much-loved resident at Covenant Shores lost his balance on the way to dinner, fell and hit his head. The resulting brain injury proved fatal.

Since Bud has been a fixture in my life for forty years, his sudden death hit me harder than normal. As a fellow pastor seventeen years my senior, he mentored me when I was called to my first church out of seminary. We regularly played golf on Mondays. He even provided premarital counseling when Wendy and I got engaged.

I never could have guessed that twenty-five years later I would have the privilege of being called to lead the church on Mercer Island he served for a quarter of a century. Neither could I have anticipated I would be his chaplain the last several years of his life.

Dealing with my friend's unexpected death was made a bit easier knowing he was ready to go. Whereas a significant part of my job description is helping residents "pack their bags for Heaven," Bud's bags were tagged and waiting for pick up. A sermon he gave at church a year ago called attention to his anticipation of death and his hope of resurrection. That audio clip was played at his memorial service.

About the time Bud preached on his readiness to die, another unexpected death occurred at Covenant Shores. It was a giant willow tree that has guarded our lakefront for more than one hundred years. This much-loved fixture to our campus has provided shelter for many an outdoor concert.

Last July, five days following a performance by the seventy-five-piece Bellevue Community Band, the giant tree collapsed in the middle of the night. Although we were grateful the willow had not fallen on any unsuspecting individuals, we were deeply saddened to lose a friend.

The sudden loss of what we had taken for granted was devastating. The arborists were called and came to remove the limbs we had grown to love. The emotional impact was such that we even held a memorial service for the tree.

This past Easter Sunday as I prepared to lead our annual sunrise service on the lakeshore, I walked by the stump of the old willow tree and marveled at what I saw. In the dawn's early light was a picture of resurrection. New life was growing from what had died. Unexpected death had given way to signs of hope.

The "resurrection tree" has become a source of comfort to me as I grieve those in my life who have been taken from me unexpectedly. It is a beautiful reminder that people of faith do not grieve as those who have no hope.

Obviously, we grieve. Grief is an indicator that we have loved. Grief is proof of the fact that we have shared life and made memories with someone of significance to us. But as St. Paul reminds us, an empty first-century grave empties grief of its hopelessness. I guess you could call that "good grief."

Lessons from a Blackberry Bush

I've always been inspired by Elizabeth Barrett Browning's timeless verse that celebrates the fingerprints of the Creator in creation.

"Earth's crammed with heaven,
And every common bush afire with God,
but only he who sees takes off his shoes;
The rest sit round and pluck blackberries."

The artistic beauty and symmetrical precision of nature point to a Grand Designer. A glorious morning sunrise is a call to worship. A breathtaking sunset inspires wonder. The impressive parade of tulips in the spring trumpets praise of God. And the colors of autumn trigger a sense of awe.

But I do have a bone to pick with Ms. Browning when it comes to picking blackberries. In my experience, there is something sacred about that end-of-summer ritual. It is a holy endeavor. For me, the process of berry picking is nothing less than a parable of life.

The celebration of simplicity

Because blackberries grow rampant in our neighborhood, gathering the wild fruit has become an after-dinner activity on our long summer nights. I pick the succulent purple treasure and my wife bakes them into a pie.

This farm-to-table exercise in the middle of suburbia is an opportunity to "simply" get back to basics. Gathering food is a possibility without the need for running an engine or staffing a factory.

Returning to our ancestral roots (literally) is a reminder that our lives are linked to those who first populated this part of the country. It's an invitation to remember that a life that matters demands de-cluttering and finding joy in what is simple. That value does not always have a price tag.

The importance of silence

While thrusting my arm into the thorny vines to reach for those plump (at times elusive) berries, I choose not to listen to the Mariners, my playlist or a podcast. I am content to enjoy the sounds of silence. The quiet of the early morning or early evening is a welcomed "interruption" in an otherwise noisy distracting day.

Being alone with nature (and myself) provides the atmosphere to reboot my internal computer and sense God's presence. A meaningful life demands we unplug and "play," even if our definition of play was once considered work. What's important is to make time to be quiet and get away from the crowd.

The importance of patience

After years of harvesting wild blackberries, I've learned to recognize which ones are past their prime (I generally pick and eat those) and which ones are pie-worthy.

It's also interesting to see how many are not quite ready. What is even more amazing to me is how many berries ripen within a twenty-four-hour period. Often I'll return to my favorite patch within a day or two of my last berry hunt and find a whole new crop from which to choose.

Sixty-seven years of living have convinced me that patience is a virtue. What we long for can't be achieved in the short term. Goals and dreams take time. Learning to wait is a key to success.

The reward of persistence

There is nothing quite like a warm slice of freshly baked blackberry pie with a scoop of ice cream. To this man of the cloth, what I've just described is heaven on a plate. It's divine!

But it didn't just appear out of nowhere. It took effort and it took time. It also took a partnership. There would be nothing on my plate if my wife, Wendy, wasn't willing to take what I'd gathered and complete the task.

In life — and in berry picking— that for which you are working is what keeps you going. Visualizing the end result is what motivates the effort. And working together as a team is the ice cream on the pie.

As my Swedish friends like to say, *"A shared joy is a doubled joy!"* Yes, Ms. Browning, there is something sacred about picking blackberries after all.

Who Are the People in Your Neighborhood?

Fifty years ago, I was living on Gellatly Street in Wenatchee. That same year there was a new street that everyone was talking about in our town. In fact, most every city and town in the nation boasted having a new street by the same name.

"Sesame Street" debuted in 1969. To celebrate this milestone in children's television programming, the place I work has an elaborate display of Sesame Street memorabilia. Even though the residents on our campus are now senior adults, they were parents of preschoolers when Sesame Street took to the airwaves of Public Television.

Because I was a senior in high school, I wasn't one of Jim Henson's disciples. But I was aware enough of what was going on in popular culture to recognize the names of his Muppets who were making news. There was Kermit the Frog, Big Bird and Oscar the Grouch, in addition to Bert and Ernie.

I also was clued in to some of the music associated with the residents on Sesame Street. The lyrics of one of the songs asked "Who are the people in your neighborhood?" As with Mister Rogers, Jim Henson and his writers and puppeteers were concerned with helping children recognize and appreciate the various people that contributed to their lives. Both "Mister Rogers' Neighborhood" and "Sesame Street" introduced their viewers to vocations that help make our world go 'round.

Having an appreciation for those "people in our neighborhood" is just as important to us as to our children or grandchildren. And yet it is easy to take such people for granted. With a month to go before our nation celebrates Thanksgiving, I'm all for getting an early start and finding ways to express gratitude to those individuals who make life meaningful to us every day. Here's hoping you're willing to join me.

Make a list of those professions without which your little world would not turn as smoothly? There's your mail carrier, FedEx driver and Amazon Prime delivery person. There's your barista, the person who does your nails and your hair stylist. There's your landscaper, your housecleaner and pizza-delivery guy. There's your pastor, priest or rabbi. How about your doctor, pharmacist and therapist?

Life is a challenge to be sure. But can you imagine how much more challenging your life would be if these people were not in your neighborhood? And most of them are not accustomed to being thanked for the necessary — often overlooked — work they do.

Because there are so many, it's unrealistic to give each person on your list a Starbucks gift card. But you could write a handwritten note and leave it where they could find it. Personal expressions of thanks are not as common as they once were, but you likely can personally attest to how an unexpected note of appreciation makes you feel.

There's only one holiday that even comes close to honoring the jobs people do that make the world a better place. But since Labor Day is considered the unofficial end of summer, we tend to spend that day coupled with two other days and celebrate ourselves. Labor Day is typically observed at the beach or the lake or grilling in our backyard. We enjoy a long weekend, but we come up short when it comes to showing thanks to people who most deserve it.

Maybe we need a new national holiday called "People in Our Neighborhood Day." Since Bert and Ernie could help us get started, perhaps they can tell us how to get to Sesame Street.

Intersections

Three Kernels of Popcorn

We have a Thanksgiving Day tradition in our home. We place three kernels of un-popped popcorn to the side of each person's plate at the family table. The kernels symbolize the corn the Native Americans provided the pilgrims at that first Thanksgiving potluck.

Following our dinner of roast turkey and trimmings, and before the pumpkin pie, we go around the table and (holding the kernels of popcorn) verbalize three things for which we are grateful this past year.

This year, my top three reasons for thanksgiving are quite obvious. I will finger my first kernel of corn with gratitude for our second grandchild born this past April. A healthy Ivy Joy Anderson joined her big sister, Imogen, who will turn three in January. Cradling that miniature human being for the first time called to mind the miracle of birth. The gift of new life has a way of rebooting one's operating system. It gives us a fresh perspective of what's going on and what really matters. As someone once said, "Babies are God's way of saying He hasn't given up on the world."

Looking back on this year, I will hold up my second kernel of popcorn grateful for my mom. The star of our family (my mom's name actually was Star) died in July at the age of ninety-two. Although dementia had diminished the quality of my mom's life in recent years, it had not robbed her of an ability to love music, her family or her God. My heart is filled with gratitude as I celebrate having this special person in my life for sixty-seven years. My mother's death has unlocked a treasure trove of special memories that sweetens the bitterness of sorrow.

My third kernel of corn concerns a unique experience I had not long ago. It was a weekend trip I took to Washington, D.C., with one of our residents at "The Shores," the retirement community where I work. Because Zip's only family lives in Singapore, I was invited to be the chaperone for this Korean War veteran. Zip and I traveled with the Puget Sound Honor Flight organization that allows veterans in our area the opportunity to visit the military memorials in our nation's capital, all-expenses paid. I continue to be impressed by this amazing program that pays tribute to "the greatest generation" who paid freedom's price tag.

It was not only Zip's first opportunity to visit the memorials, it was the first time this eighty-eight-year-old had ever been to Washington, D.C. Because of Zip's limitations, I pushed him in a wheelchair all three days. In addition to the Korean and World War II memorials, we visited the Vietnam Wall and the impressive remembrances to FDR and MLK.

But the highlight of the trip for me was the half hour we spent at the Lincoln Memorial. The view of the National Mall from Mr. Lincoln's throne was breathtaking. But what was just as breathtaking for me was seeing my elderly friend seated in his wheelchair facing the likeness of our sixteenth president. I couldn't resist taking a photo with my iPhone.

Upon returning home, I had a canvas enlargement made of that image of Zip in his wheeled throne in front of Lincoln on his stone throne. It is a poignant picture of a grateful American sitting in the presence of one who influenced our country for good. It is as if Zip is thanking Mr. Lincoln for his courageous contributions that have compounded into a growing endowment of liberty. It is a reminder for me to be grateful to God for the privilege of living in a nation He has blessed in countless ways. It is a reminder that Thanksgiving is more than a day. Gratitude is an attitude we can choose all year long.

Intersections

Going Public with Your Love

I recently met Kelly Andrews and Ethan Lynette while spending a day off with my wife poking around in Bellingham. Driving through the Fairhaven district, I happened upon an old brick office building that caught my attention. The sign above the front door read Bailey Brothers Building and Loan.

Anyone familiar with Frank Capra's timeless movie "It's a Wonderful Life," recognizes it as the family business that Jimmy Stewart's character operated after his father's untimely death. Because I am a huge IAWL fan and have written a few books and several articles about this inspirational film, I had to stop and take a photo of the building with the sign.

While I was snapping a couple pictures, Kelly came to the door. I asked the obvious question. *"Is this really a building and loan business?"*

With a smile, Kelly told me that the building actually housed a fertility clinic. He quickly added that the professional signage was simply an homage to a movie he and his business partner loved. He offered to give me a tour of the building and introduced me to his business partner, Ethan.

I learned that Kelly and Ethan met in second grade, became close friends in high school and went into business together in 2007. Because they both loved "It's a Wonderful Life," (watching it with their families each Christmas) they would often throw around quotes from the movie at work just for fun. When they bought the historic brick building five years ago, it just seemed right to name it Bailey Brothers Building and Loan. The sign was a tangible expression of their love.

Since meeting Kelly and Ethan a couple months ago, I've reflected on the concept of going public with what you love. We do it with our favorite NFL team. The Seahawks flag that flies in front of our home makes it clear to all who drive by who we cheer for each weekend. During election season, the signs planted in our front yard provide tangible proof as to who we want to win.

This month marks the thirty-eighth anniversary of when I went public with my love for my wife. Two days after Christmas in 1981, I asked Wendy's father for his firstborn's hand in marriage. That very afternoon, while playing a game of Scrabble in a park, I popped the question and placed a ring on her finger. That diamond ring was a visible sign of who I loved.

The Christmas season, celebrated the world over, is based on the central truth of the Christian faith. It asserts that by being born as one of us, the Creator went public with His love for His creation. Rather than simply conveying His desire for a relationship with those made in His image through parchments and prophets, God provided a sign. In the birth of Jesus, we are given a gift that conveys the love of the Giver. Like the diamond ring I gave Wendy, that baby is proof that God's love for the world is unmistakable and unconditional.

Speaking of babies, all three of our daughters were born in Concord, California. That's the same town where jazz great Dave Brubeck began running the human race. I really like the contemporary Christmas carol in our church hymnal written by Dave Brubeck and his wife. In addition to its haunting melody and syncopated rhythm, the title says it all — "God's Love Made Visible."

And that, my friends, is what Christmas is all about. In the Bethlehem baby, we are given the ultimate sign. It is proof of how He feels about you and me.

A Prescription for a 20/20 Vision

In addition to this being the start of a new year, it is the beginning of a brand-new decade. This year also marks the commencement of my fifth decade as a pastor. In every church I have served over the past forty years, the leadership team would conduct the arduous work of casting a vision for the congregation. A carefully crafted vision pictured a preferred future for which goals and objectives became stepping stones. A vision serves as a vehicle to get you where you want to go. A vision is crucial for a church, an organization, a nation, as well as an individual.

Crossing the threshold of this New Year, I'm in the process of formulating a vision for this season of my life. Perhaps my "work in progress" will prompt you to initiate or personalize your own. Although my eyesight has diminished with age, when it comes to the next twelve months my vision this year is definitely 2020.

Because seeing is believing, visualizing desired change is the first stage in realizing what you long for. Picturing a preferred future can be translated into goals or resolves. I believe my New Year's resolutions will motivate me to become more effective as a husband, father, grandfather and pastor.

This year I resolve to glance back while gazing forward. Lessons learned this past year are worth reflecting on. Embracing nostalgic moments has a way of softening the hardship of current realities. But too much past-pondering can be counterproductive. The operative words are glance and gazing.

My 2020 vision invites me to spend more time contemplating the future than considering the past.

This year I also resolve to focus on what is right with our world instead of being so quick to identify the issues that bother me. The headlines of national and world events can coax us into thinking crime, scandal and injustice dominate human existence. I am determined to look for the good and decent in every day. Godwinks, generosity and random acts-of-kindness are more common than we realize.

I also resolve to engage people who think differently than I do when it comes to matters of faith, political perspectives and cultural values. While I treasure what I believe to be true, I want to esteem people created in the image of our Creator even more. In this current milieu of hate speech and adversarial-ism, I refuse to give in to us-versus-them ideology.

Furthermore, I resolve to look inside myself when my sense of worth starts to blur and I have a hard time remembering what I am skilled at doing. Focusing on what others affirm in me can silence my doubts and clarify my calling in life. Reviewing past achievements (and failures) serves to remind me of what I can easily forget. Watching "film" is not just the prerogative of NFL players.

Finally, I resolve to look up when I start to lose my focus on matters of the heart. I determine to always admit my need for help no matter how many candles will adorn my next birthday cake. Even though I've been a man of the cloth since 1979, I first learned the importance of admitting my helplessness when the cloth that defined my position in life was a security blanket I pulled across the playroom. Requesting a helping hand from a parent paved the way for acknowledging one's need for God. And that need to look up never goes away.

So, there's my 2020 vision. My picture of a preferred future is still a work in process, but it's something tangible on which to focus. Here's hoping you'll discover the wide-eyed wonder of picturing your dreams for the coming year.

* How was I to know that, within two months of writing this optimistic forecast for 2020, COVID-19 would mask our hopes and dreams for the new year and send us to our bedrooms for an unanticipated time-out?

A Prayer for My Home State

Fifteen years ago this month, I flew to Seattle from Chicago to interview with a church that proceeded to hire me as their lead pastor. Although I'd been raised in Washington State, it had been a quarter of a century since I'd lived here. That unusually warm and sunny February weekend revealed the amazing beauty of the Pacific Northwest I'd forgotten. I realized how much I loved Washington.

It is that love of our state I celebrated recently. Whereas Valentine's Day tends to bring out the poet in many a romantic, I found myself waxing poetic. Having been invited to give the opening invocation at the State Capitol in Olympia, I decided to pen my prayer in rhyme. What follows is my Valentine's Prayer with gratitude for our beloved state.

Creator God, we render thanks
for salmon grilled on cedar planks.
For snow-capped mountains, tulip fields
and rivers cold and clean.

We love our state of Washington
where millions come to share our fun
at ski resorts and Lake Chelan
and in the San Juans, too.

Good Lord, there can be no mistake.
Our hearts beat proudly for a state
that woos us with her endless charm
and beauty that won't quit.

Reflections on Life and Faith

*For public markets by the Bay
and venues where our sports teams play,
for landmarks needling the sky
and piers where cruise ships dock.*

*We give You thanks for Mount Rainier
that symbolizes You are near.
Its awesome wonder we behold
speaks grace we can't ignore.*

*For businesses of which we boast,
we offer prayers and make a toast
that they will prosper and succeed
within this new decade.*

*For Starbucks, Costco, Amazon,
Microsoft, the list goes on
including Nordstrom, REI,
Expedia and more.*

*Potatoes, orchards, vineyards, wheat
help feed our world and offer drink
to celebrate that life's a gift
we unwrap every day.*

*For those who hunger without homes,
who struggle daily on their own,
we pray protection even as
we seek to end their plight.*

*Most gracious God, as we confess
our need for You, would You please bless
the ones who lead us. Help them strive
to serve with dignity.*

*So in this week of Valentine's,
our love's expressed with words that rhyme
as we commit to care for this
great state we call our home.*

Intersections

Pulling Together as a Team

Within the past few days, this year's Iditarod Trail Sled Dog Race made national news. The winning musher from Norway with his team passed beneath the famous burl arch on Front Street in Nome that serves as the finish line. As fans cheered, that old gold-rush town on the Bering Sea came to life.

Believe it or not, ninety-five years ago, Nome had an even more significant reason to celebrate. In January 1925 the lives of countless children in Nome were at stake. Although not as widespread as the coronavirus, an epidemic of diphtheria threatened the entire town. Because Nome did not have a sufficient amount of antitoxin, fears grew. Dr. Curtis Welch, the local physician, telegraphed Fairbanks, Anchorage, Seward and Juneau asking for help. Three-hundred-thousand units of serum were located at a hospital in Anchorage. It was the only supply in the entire state.

But a major obstacle yet remained. How would the needed medicine get to Nome to stave off the epidemic? Since the Bering Sea was frozen and there were no railroad tracks or roads that led to Nome, dog teams were the only solution. Scott Bone, Alaska's territorial governor (who would later become editor of the Seattle Post-Intelligencer), authorized the time-sensitive operation.

The three-hundred-thousand units were packed in a cylinder and wrapped in fur and canvas. The precious cargo was transported from Anchorage to Nenana on an overnight train. The serum arrived at 11:00 p.m. on January 27. From there, it would need to be transported six hundred seventy-four miles by a sled dog relay in a race against time. It was a distance that mushers who delivered the mail normally covered in a month. But the dying children needed the antitoxin much sooner than that.

The first musher took the insulated cylinder fifty-two miles and passed it to the second musher who traveled thirty-one miles. From musher to musher, the relay continued involving a score of sled dog drivers and their teams. The needed medicine arrived in Nome on February 2, just one hundred twenty-seven hours after the life-saving mission began.

The cooperative effort of twenty mushers and one- hundred-fifty dogs that braved sub-zero temperatures and blinding blizzards accomplished the desired outcome. The lives of Nome's children were saved.

The Iditarod Trail Sled Dog Race was established in 1973 as an annual means of commemorating "The Serum Run of '25." Each year after a ceremonial start in Anchorage, dog mushers and their teams leave Wasilla on their one-thousand-forty-nine-mile trek that culminates in Nome. Although there are other sled dog races in the country, this particular one is the most popular. No wonder "The Last Great Race" is the most popular sporting event in the forty-ninth state.

Since learning that the Serum Run of '25 is what inspired the Iditarod, I've had the opportunity to cover the event as a member of the media. I've also written a book about this amazing race. Although I've never been as cold as the night I stood at the finish line, I was warmed by what I witnessed. Those lean and fit canines are devotedly cared for by their loyal and loving masters. They are masters who know it takes a team to reach a desired goal.

As our communities continue to face the unknown consequences associated with the coronavirus, may the events of what took place in Nome ninety-five years ago inspire us to do our best. Let us not forget what can be accomplished when we pull together as a team and keep our eyes on a common goal.

What it takes to save lives (or to win first place) has not changed. Reaching the destination of our dreams requires racing against time and believing we can win.

COVID Lessons

To invert and borrow from Dickens, "It is the worst of times. It is the best of times." The coronavirus pandemic that continues to impact our lives has presented us with unprecedented challenges. All the same, it has provided us with remarkable opportunities.

Reflecting on the checklist of behaviors we've been given to flatten the curve and stop the spread of COVID-19, I realized such instructions relate to more than just this virus. Against the backdrop of this health crisis, I've been reminded of timeless life lessons.

Remember to wash your hands

In addition to the hygienic benefits of literally scrubbing our digits for twenty seconds, there is symbolic value. Historically speaking, "washing your hands" of a given situation means putting something behind you. Too often we hang on to regrets of the past we can't do anything about. We need to learn to forgive ourselves. Christianity celebrates the concept of grace. And grace allows us to follow Princess Elsa's lead and "let it go!"

Give each other space

Social-distancing has become a new addition to our English vocabulary. We've been told that maintaining a six-foot distance can prevent unnecessary burials six-feet under. But giving another adequate space has other benefits as well. It is important to give those with whom we interact the freedom to espouse and act on their own perspective. Insisting others see things "our way" crowds creativity and selfishly suffocates.

Stay at home

In our state, Governor Inslee has instructed us to stay home to stay healthy. And "sheltering in place" has largely accomplished that goal. In the process, however, we have rediscovered the value of balance in our lives. If we're honest, I think we'd have to admit the "old normal" of daily life found us spending too much time at work and investing in pursuits that took us away from our families. Having rebooted our home page, I'm hoping the "new normal" will find us recognizing the importance of staying home more often.

Wear a mask

Speaking of the "new normal," it appears that face coverings will be part of our daily wardrobe for the foreseeable future. My Seahawks mask will allow me to express my allegiance as a "12" on more than just Blue Fridays. It will also provide others with protection should I unknowingly transmit a virus that finds me asymptomatic. But there are also times in life when it is most appropriate to wear masks as well. I'm thinking of those times when another's painful situation calls us to hide our personal emotions. In such settings, we are not denying our own plight. Rather, masking our issues allows us to focus on the needs of someone else that are more critical at the moment.

Meet up creatively

Back when I was a kid, Zoom was a hot cereal. Not anymore. Those Brady Bunch screenshots are everywhere. Gratefully, social-distancing does not mean being socially disconnected. As human beings, we are created for community. As such, we can't help but find ways to interact. Even though we are "sheltering in place" alone, we take comfort that we are alone together. More than that, we find ways to comfort one another by reaching out. In sickness and in health, we are social beings who cannot neglect the assembling of ourselves albeit creative.

Bottom line?

We virtually cannot live without each other. And gratefully we are finding ways to connect virtually. Companies are conducting virtual staff meetings. Churches are congregating remotely. My musician daughter is teaching flute lessons via Skype and my youth pastor son-in-law is interacting with students via FaceTime. Don't you love the video clips we see on the nightly news of drive-by birthday parties and balcony concerts in apartment complexes?

All this to say, when the pandemic has finally passed, I'm convinced the future will find us all present and accounted for — still washing our hands, giving each other space, staying at home, wearing masks and meeting up creatively.

A Step to Follow (Fifty Years Later)

It was fifty years ago this week I spoke at graduation as the senior class president of Wenatchee High School. Recently I came across the speech I gave to my classmates and our parents. What follows are excerpts from that address. Although I'm a bit embarrassed at the lofty language I attempted to employ, the dream I articulated remains a call to action. After half a century, the homework I gave our class has yet to be completed.

As graduates we are faced with the growing complexities of social injustice, racial inequality, protests, demonstrations and bloody wars. They are problems that are products of jealousy and hate handed down to us by preceding generations who sought in vain for solutions. If we are to be the ones that find the answers to the world's ever-growing needs, we must find "a step to follow."

Many have gone from ceremonies such as these to commence and exercise ideas conceived within themselves to aid in the cause for world peace, hope and prosperity. Footprints planted by those who have gone on before us present incentives and initiatives to seek for the glory of success, the truth of reality and goals that now seem impossible.

Thousands left such impressions upon the soil of history for us to follow. Thousands more did not. As we endeavor to calculate our course towards the destination of success and fulfillment, let us step forward behind such persons who dedicated their lives for the opportunities and freedoms we now cherish, realizing the great dilemma yet to be resolved.

In our day and age when revolutions are in the making and campus disorders misconstrue the real meaning of democracy, thoughts go back to a certain young man who (as a revolutionary) charted a course for each of us to consider. Instead of violent upheavals, massive rebellions and militant advocations, this man propagated love, equality, beauty, honesty ... life in its fullest meaning. Truly something our society hasn't given much of a chance.

He stood for what he believed in beckoning others to follow. He was a bridge over troubled waters spanning the gap between an omnipotent God and imperfect man. He gave his life for a purpose and took a giant step. And for us, a step to follow.

Impossible? Well, something else was considered just as impossible until a little less than a year ago when Neil Armstrong, flag in hand, opened the hatch of Apollo 11 and planted his foot on an impossible dream come true. He said, "One small step for man, a giant leap for mankind."

The world is pleading for answers, pleading to the greatest country in the world, our own United States, pleading to Wenatchee High School, more importantly, pleading to the senior class of 1970. Tattered and undone, the world is seeking for cures to cancer, ways to world peace and solutions for survival.

The commission rests on our shoulders to do with what we will. And in such an uncertainty, the questions arise once again, "Just where do we go from here and just what will we do?" But I contend that we will accept the challenge. We will find the cures, the ways and the solutions no matter what the price. We will give our lives for a purpose. Why? Because we have faith in God, because we have faith in others and because we have faith in ourselves. We, the Wenatchee High School Class of 1970, hold the key. We have a step to follow and from this point on a giant step to take.

Reflections on Life and Faith

Let's Hear It for Bridges!

Once a long upon ago, in a place not so very far away, a foot-shaped island floated in the middle of Lake Washington. Like a severed appendage, it was disconnected from Seattle, Bellevue and Renton. Accessibility was limited. For the longest time, the only way the people of Mercer Island could connect with family and friends who lived on the mainland was by boat.

In November 1923, a drawbridge was constructed linking the Eastside with a pristine forested island named for a Seattle pioneer. Seventeen years later, the foot-shaped community took a major step forward. A two-mile stretch of floating concrete pontoons resulted in the first and longest floating bridge of its kind anywhere. Commerce kicked in at an impressive new level. Residential housing grew by leaps and bounds.

Lacey V. Murrow, the thirty-six-year-old head of our state's highway department, was the main motivation behind the Mercer Island Bridge (later named in his honor). Murrow, the older brother of broadcaster Edward R. Murrow, was also the impetus behind the Tacoma Narrows Bridge.

While the younger Murrow was in London to cover the Battle of Britain, Lacey was making news of his own. Amazingly, both the Narrows Bridge and the Mercer Island Bridge were dedicated the first week of July 1940. Younger brother Ed sent a telegram conveying his congratulations. Against the backdrop of war across the pond, impressive bridges were spanning Washington waters.

Because this week marks the eightieth anniversary of a bridge that connects the community where I live and work to downtown Seattle,

Intersections

I've been contemplating the difference such a connection has made and continues to make. That engineering wonder does more than keep a floating highway afloat on which tens of thousands drive each day. It also floats dreams and transactions that impact millions. Not to have access to the Mercer Island floating bridge would be a nightmare. When bridges fail, those who depend on them suffer greatly.

Ironically, four months after the Tacoma Narrows Bridge was dedicated on July 1, 1940, "Galloping Gertie" collapsed. But she was not alone. Fifty years after the ribbon was cut on July 2, 1940 opening the Mercer Island Floating Bridge, it, too, sank. Perhaps you remember the storm that took it down during the Thanksgiving holiday of 1990. In both instances, people were inconvenienced and alienated. The importance of connectivity was underscored.

But, broken bridges aren't the only things that leave us stranded. The current coronavirus pandemic also has me thinking about other connections we take for granted until they are denied us.

COVID-19, without notice, undermined the reliability of the "bridges" on which we depend on a daily basis. Contact with family and loved ones was suddenly disabled. Personal communication with clients and vendors was cut off without notice.

As the chaplain at Covenant Living at the Shores retirement community, I've observed the impact "sheltering in place" has on seniors when they are denied visits from children and grandchildren. The emotional toll on persons separated from their spouses quarantined in memory care is immense. Those who have not been able to hug their mate for twelve weeks struggle big time. Losing access to the "bridge of touch" is debilitating.

Now that our communities are beginning to reopen, we are realizing how important contact with others really is. Cabin fever was not one of the COVID-19 symptoms. But it certainly is one of the outcomes. As social beings, we were created for community. When we are isolated, we atrophy and fail to thrive. Our hospitality muscles lose body mass.

A bridge failure, much like a "sheltering in place" order, can catch us unaware. But now that we have been through it, we can better prepare for next time. Knowing how vital connections with family and friends are, isn't this a good time to discover new ways to improve how we connect with each other? Isn't it time to fix "bridges" that have fallen into disrepair and access relationships while we can?

What's in a Name?

I love the month of August. It's when summer days truly live up to their name. Right? But have you ever wondered where the name August comes from? Would you believe the eighth month of the year is in honor of Caesar Augustus?

According to St. Luke's Gospel, Augustus was emperor of the Roman Empire when Jesus was born. (And just for the record, July is named for Julius Caesar, the general and Roman statesman who lived just prior to Augustus.)

I like the name Augustus. It has a regal sound to it. It means majestic or venerable. Curiously, it's a family name. My paternal grandmother's older brother was Thomas Augustus Turley.

I met my Uncle Tom when I was twelve. This grocer-turned-farmer and his wife, Miss Mae, traveled from their home in Wytheville, Virginia, to Spaulding, Idaho, for a visit with my grandmother.

I was impressed with my great-uncle. He was kind. He was debonair. And I loved his Southern drawl. Even though he was a rather short man, there was much about him to love. Like his middle name implied, Uncle Tom was a noble, respectable Southern gentleman.

I learned that Thomas Augustus Turley served in World War I. He lived through the Spanish Flu epidemic. He married his boss' daughter, raised five children and lost one in a tragic car accident. In spite of that indescribable sorrow, Tom trusted God and became a leader in community of Wytheville, Virginia.

While doing some research on my uncle after his death, I realized that at the time I was receiving my college diploma in 1974, Tom was being presented a forty-year perfect attendance award from his Rotary club.

I would not join my local Rotary club until thirty years later. But now, as a member, I recognize what that major accomplishment represents. It stands for determination and persistence in service-above-self. It stands for commitment to the Rotary four-way test that affirms honesty, integrity and the welfare of others.

My uncle lived up to his name. He was an august leader who led by serving. Sadly, I met this remarkable man only one time. He died thirty-five years ago.

I'm grateful, however, that I had the opportunity to get to know a few of Uncle Tom's adult children, including his namesake, Thomas Augustus Turley, Jr. Cousin "T. A.", as we called him, lived and worked in Oakridge, Tennessee. He was a patriotic citizen, a faithful husband and a loving dad. I could see in my uncle's son the reflection of his father's admirable character.

This August I've got Augustus on my mind. I want to live up to what that name represents in my family. I want to live up to the name Rotarian and the virtues it suggests. And as a follower of Christ, I want to define the meaning of the name "Christian" (little Christ) by the way I live rather than letting the term Christian be simply defined by popular culture or social media.

Sadly, in these days in which we find ourselves fighting a coronavirus as well as the virus of racism, referring to an Uncle Tom can easily be misinterpreted. Nonetheless, I am grateful I can take pride in referring to my Uncle Thomas Augustus Turley. I, for one, want to continue to learn from his life and example.

Love Never Quits!

It wasn't COVID, but the scenario was eerily similar to what we've read about for the last seven months. A near-death experience would change the direction of my life. Although it was forty years ago this week, I remember it as if it were yesterday.

A close friend, Wendy, was intubated and on life support in Southern California. She had gone into anaphylactic shock and her lungs had collapsed. The doctors told Wendy's dad and mom they'd done all they could and she wasn't responding as they'd hoped. Discovering they were religious people, the staff encouraged the twenty-eight-year-old's parents to pray.

Because I was a pastor in Seattle, Wendy's family called me to ask if members of my congregation would also pray for her recovery. Because I had recently started reconnecting with Wendy (a college friend), the family added something else. They said if I wanted to see Wendy again, I should consider making plans to come down.

The thought that Wendy might not pull through was a game-changer. I realized that I wasn't content with our casual, long-distance dating relationship. I wanted her to live. I wanted a future with her.

Gratefully, as I would soon learn, Wendy felt the same way. More importantly, God answered prayers on her behalf. Although her full recovery would take several weeks, there was a glimmer of hope. A few days after I was notified of her critical situation, Wendy turned the corner. She was taken off life support by the end of the week and was discharged soon thereafter.

A couple months later, I flew down to be with her and to take her to the Rose Bowl football game between Washington and Michigan. Although the Huskies lost 23-6, I felt I had won. Within the year, I asked Wendy to be my wife and she said "yes."

What I experienced four decades ago brought into focus a bottom-line truth. It's a truth that has been reinforced by what I've observed all around me recently. When life is threatened, love finds a way.

The current COVID crisis has resulted in more than two hundred thousand people in the U.S. dying from this invisible enemy that has invaded our country. Countless families have been rocked by the real possibility of losing a grandparent, a parent, a sibling or a child. Fortunately, the vast majority of individuals who have contracted the disease have recovered. But through it all we have seen love in action. Against the backdrop of uncertainty, one thing is certain — crises crystallize core commitments.

At the senior-home campus where I am employed as a chaplain, family members have been separated by quarantine restrictions. Lack of contact and touch has been brutal. But the strict protocols have paid off. To date, we have been minimally impacted by the coronavirus. Still, the emotional pain of separation has been difficult to observe.

Nonetheless, I've seen loved ones creatively find a way to communicate with their love through window visits and FaceTime chats. I've even been asked to video a greeting on my phone that I can play for the spouse in lockdown. There is no end to the way loving acts are expressed.

A first-century rabbi put it this way: *"Love never gives up!"* And the pandemic that has punctuated this past year has illustrated that maxim time and time again. When push comes to shove, love bubbles to the surface. And even when a loving glance is framed by an unwanted windowpane, love shows up and makes its presence known. That same rabbi is also credited with saying, *"Faith, hope and love abide. But the greatest of these is love."*

Intersections

A Thanksgiving to Remember

"Pass the yams! And pass the turkey!
Pass the iPad, too!
I want to FaceTime with my fam-i-ly.
Though quarantined from loved ones,
I am grateful I'm not sick.
And I'm thanking God I have technology."

In a challenging year in which you may be struggling to come up with things for which to be grateful, don't forget Wi-Fi, Zoom and FaceTime. While pumpkin pie remains our go-to dessert, technology unquestionably takes the cake!

Without doubt, this Thanksgiving will be one to remember. The protocols in place mean restrictions on travel, smaller gatherings at home, and separation from extended family members. It's all designed to curb the ravenous appetite of an uninvited houseguest that refuses to get the hint.

In the past ten months, COVID has eaten our nation out of house and home. This rude intruder has devoured happy times and created sad ones. In-person learning has been postponed for many, bars and restaurants have been closed, religious services have been reduced and stores have gone out of business. All the same, this unwelcomed visitor is now taking even bigger bites out of a much-loved holiday.

But, Thanksgiving has not been canceled. May I repeat … COVID cannot cancel Thanksgiving! Remember, Thanksgiving is not defined by who's at our table but by what's in our heart.

Unlike any previous year, this Thanksgiving will be different. But in spite of the restrictions, there is still the opportunity to gather. There is still the opportunity to reflect. And, if we are willing to do the research, there are countless reasons to be grateful. I'm convinced that the key to salvaging this pandemic-plagued holiday is remembering.

"Remember to say thanks!" From the time I was a toddler, my mother's words have rung in my ears. But her desire to instruct her firstborn in good behavior resulted in more than what she hoped for. Those four little words continue to inform me as an adult. As I've contemplated my mom's advice, I've come to see they contain the secret to cultivating a grateful heart.

We recognize those things for which we have to be thankful when we take time to remember. Memory is a wonderful gift we too often take for granted. If Alzheimer's disease has impacted your family as it has mine, memory is on your short list of things for which you thank God.

If ever there was a time to make withdrawals from our memory banks, this is it. Recall your last visit with your parents. Reflect on an unforgettable trip with siblings. Savor the memory of recent conversations with grandchildren. Instead of mourning the fact that you can't be with family members this week, remember special times you shared with them. Take time to reflect on those who will miss being with you this Thursday. Remember how much they have contributed to your life.

And while this will definitely be a Thanksgiving to remember, make sure to take time to remember. And be grateful!

Intersections

Don't Get Lost in the Hectic Days of Christmas

While clearing out and boxing up my parents' home recently, I discovered a few items I didn't know existed. In the bottom of a cedar chest, I found the infant blanket in which I was brought home from the hospital sixty-eight years ago.

Amazingly, my mom had also saved my schoolwork from my elementary years. In a stack of yellowed papers, I found the very first poem I ever composed. It was a Christmas rhyme I penned in second grade. Since I've published four books of poetry as an adult, I was thrilled to find my first poetic work.

And then I saw it. I could hardly believe my eyes. Before me was a Christmas card that my mom had addressed back in December 1956 to close family friends. The envelope was sealed and stamped. But for some reason it had never been mailed.

The wife of the couple, for whom the card was intended died a few years ago. Her husband, a retired minister, remains a friend of mine on Facebook. Ironically, I'd forgotten to acknowledge Wayne's ninety-first birthday that very week. So, in addition to sending him a belated birthday greeting, I texted him a photo of the unmailed Christmas card. I joked that one of these two belated greetings was a bit more belated than the other. His response was priceless.

I began to speculate why the Christmas card to Wayne and Pat Adams had been misplaced. My dad was the pastor of a growing church in suburban Portland, Oregon. Crafting countless sermons that made the ancient message of Christmas culturally relevant was time consuming. My mom was challenged by the demands of a four-year-old (me) and my two-year-old brother. In addition, as a traditional pastor's wife, our mother was rehearsing for the Christmas Eve pageant at church, organizing the women's program as well as being the church pianist.

Nonetheless, my folks' busy schedule back then is not all that different from the typical family today. This time of the year is filled with all kinds of commitments at work and at home. Even COVID-19 cannot diminish the demands of the holiday season. To the routine task of trimming the tree and decorating the interior of our homes, add stringing lights on the outside.

Then there's addressing cards, writing year-in-review family letters, shopping for gifts, attending virtual concerts, hosting family get-togethers for those in your bubble, not to mention organizing a household schedule of individuals each of whom has their own commitments. Christmas is a maze of expectations more often than it is an amazing season of celebration.

Year after year, we enter the month of December with the best of intentions. We promise ourselves we are going to cut back on spending, minimize gift giving, limit social engagements and maximize time at home with those we love. This year, COVID restrictions have encouraged sheltering in place and in the process graced our intentions with a better chance of success. Still, the reason for the season can be masked by our many traditions.

Back to the misplaced Christmas greeting. I decided to open the envelope and see what my mom had written in the card. To my surprise it was a note of congratulations related to the safe arrival of the Adams' newborn daughter. How ironic, I mused. The craziness surrounding a holiday that celebrates the birth of a baby had prevented my folks from sending a Christmas greeting and acknowledgement of their friends' addition.

And unless I'm careful, the hectic trappings of this holy season can keep me from acknowledging what the Bethlehem baby continues to offer. Lest the meaning behind our traditions gets lost in our nonstop activity, we need to take time to ponder why Christmas continues to be the most popular holiday in Western civilization.

A Prayer for Our New President

Once a year, for the past decade, I have given the invocation in our state Senate or House of Representatives in Olympia. The closest I've ever come to offering a prayer over a President took place when our family lived in the Land of Lincoln. To my delight, I was invited to give the opening prayer in the chambers of the Illinois state Senate.

When I referenced the Chicago Cubs in my invocation, I had no idea that one of those listening to my prayer would be elected President within several years. I also was unaware that as a southsider, Barack Obama was a Chicago White Sox fan.

I doubt I'm the only person of the cloth who has ever pictured what it would be like to be clothed with the privilege of praying at the inauguration of a new President. All the same, it doesn't take an invitation from POTUS to seek the face of the Creator on behalf of our commander in chief.

Here's my prayer as this country prepares to inaugurate its forty-sixth president on January 20.

Almighty God,

In this pivotal season in the history of our nation, we come before You with gratitude and anticipation. Thank You, sovereign Lord, for a glimmer of light in the corridor of darkness that has defined the past year. For the long-awaited vaccine, we give You thanks. Please make the distribution of it efficient and its impact efficacious. Temper our enthusiastic hopes with guarded realism as we give ourselves permission to picture a more normal way of life.

Reflections on Life and Faith

As we inaugurate our forty-sixth President, we celebrate a peaceful transition of power. It is our desire, O God, that divisions among us would morph into a spirit of cooperation, compromise and unity. Would You orchestrate the soundtrack of our lives so that the symphony of unity and cooperation will once again be heard in the chambers of Congress? Would you cause the hallways and mess halls of office buildings on Capitol Hill to be abuzz with the sounds of civility, friendship and laughter?

We are grateful that the one we elected to serve us for the next four years is one who takes his faith seriously. Cover Joseph R. Biden with Your hand of protection. Grant him health and energy for the task before him. Infuse him with skillful insight and measured determination to face the challenges that await. Give him wisdom. Guard his heart. Guide his choices. Strengthen his resolve to resist temptations to short-circuit the lengthy and cumbersome process of bipartisan engagement. Imbue him with patience to trust the DNA of our democracy.

God, bless America. Not because we deserve Your blessings, but because we stand in need of that which You alone can provide: forgiveness for past wrongs, a sense of Your presence today and faith in what the future holds.

In the meantime, would You teach us how to balance the virtues of unconditional tolerance and unconditional love with the conditions and consequences associated with Your principles and Your blessings?

Remind us once again that the direction of our nation is not as dependent on the one who inhabits the White House as it is on those who live in our homes.

Remind us, as well, of the lessons we learned this past year in the vice grip of the virus. May we never forget how much more meaningful relationships are in comparison to riches. Or how much more valuable opportunities are when compared to objects that gather dust or start to rust. Or how fragile health is even in a country marked by world-class medical care.

Lord, would you give us the courage we need to make necessary changes in worn-out routines and self-destructive patterns of behavior. Continue to be our help and our hope for our good and Your glory. This we pray in Your holy name. Amen.

Intersections

Dusting for Divine Fingerprints

Have you ever heard the term "Godwink"? Several years ago I was given a book titled *Divine Alignments: How Godwink Moments Guide Your Journey*.

As a pastor, the word "Godwink" intrigued me. I added it to my growing stack of books-to-read beside my bed. Because I'm a slow reader, I didn't get to the "Godwink" book for a couple years.

I loved the concept of God "winking" at us through unexpected random experiences that we often refer to as coincidences. Prior to hearing the word "Godwink," I'd called such holy happenstances "God-incidences." Like a detective dusting for divine fingerprints, I have always been aware of the fact that evidences of God's presence are more prevalent than we think.

One case in point was a situation that took place recently at a retirement community on Mercer Island where I have been a full-time chaplain for the past eight years. A one-hundred-ten-year-old willow tree collapsed in the middle of the night. Arborists arrived the next day and removed everything but an eight-foot stump. Because the landmark tree had been a gathering place for our residents for decades, we felt a deep sense of loss. We even held a memorial service in honor of our fallen friend.

Amazingly, within a few months green shoots began to emanate from the stump. What we had grieved as gone was returning to life. Within a year, the tree had returned to its previous glory. I took a photo of the tree to document what I viewed as a "Godwink." The reborn tree was God's way of reminding me that it is always too soon to give up.

When I snapped that picture of the fully restored willow tree, I had no idea that our campus (and nation) would be living through a cataclysmic pandemic. Neither did I have any idea that I would write a book about the coronavirus in which I would document various "Godwinks" (like the tree) I'd encountered during my research and writing.

Looking up contact information for author of the "Godwinks" book I'd read, I discovered SQuire Rushnell had written six other books on the topic. Three Hallmark movies have also been produced with the "Godwinks" theme. I opted to email SQuire a few of my "Godwink" sightings. To my delight, SQuire asked permission to post my "Godwinks" on his website. When I told him I was writing a book that included my "Godwinks," he graciously offered to write an endorsement.

And speaking of "Godwinks," when it came time to design a cover of my new book, the photo of the "tree that refused to die" seemed the perfect choice. How could I have known when I took that picture it would end up on the cover of a book.

Signs of Hope, Messages of Love

It's true! Valentine's Day is not for lovers alone. Long ago, greeting-card companies created printed expressions for family members and friends to share with each other. I remember taking Valentines to school as an elementary-age student for each one of my classmates. My wife has routinely purchased cards for our three grown daughters. And now Wendy has started giving heart-shaped Valentines to our two granddaughters.

Valentine's Day is for everyone. Married or not, we all need to be reminded we are loved. Alone or sharing life with a significant other, we never tire of being told our lives matter to someone else. Never have we been more aware of that need for affirmation and encouragement than during the past eleven months.

The social distancing and separation from family and loved ones have taken an emotional toll. Lack of hugs and lack of smiles (hidden by face coverings) have drained our joy reservoir. While Zoom meetings and virtual family visits help bandage a bad situation, nothing can take the place of person-to-person encounters. All the same, when such are not possible, creative expressions of hope and love can keep us counting our blessings.

A couple weeks into the pandemic, I was walking in a wooded park in our community. Out of nowhere, I saw a red rock that someone had painted with white letters. It was a creative call to obey COVID guidelines. It said, "Keep calm and social distance." In the midst of dead leaves and brown twigs on a muddy path, this beautiful rock stood out in bold relief. Since I had my iPhone in my pocket, I snapped a photo of it.

A week or so later, I noticed another painted stone. It pictured a puppy with its face looking upward. I began purposely looking for more rocks on my regular walks. One day I saw a stone with a balloon on a string. Another intricately painted stone featured a delicate bird and the word "BREATHE." These messages and images provided a much-needed invitation to think positively.

One day I encountered a painted rock that was so beautiful I picked it up and carried it home. Seeing the word "HOPE" painted reminded me that the dark time we were living through as a nation would not last indefinitely.

For months, painted rocks with encouraging messages would appear without notice in different places. Sometimes they would be placed in the knothole of tree trunk. Sometimes they would be at the base of a resting bench. I began taking photos as a way of documenting the causes of my Kodak smiles. I wondered who the artist was. Was there more than one? What prompted them to begin their creative communications to passersby?

As the one-year anniversary of the pandemic drew near, I found another stone wedged in a hollow of a decaying tree. Its message was simple but profound. "You are loved!" Against the backdrop of a global pandemic, racial injustice, job insecurities, emotional despair and a politically divided nation, if ever there was a Valentine's Day to consider the fact that we are loved by God and others, this is it. If ever there was a time to be alert to signs of hope and messages of love in unexpected places, this is it.

When Interruptions Become Opportunities

The Chinese character for the word "crisis" is actually the linkage of two Chinese characters. One character signifies "danger" and the other that indicates "opportunity." Living through the past year of a crisis known as COVID, I experienced the reality of that play on words quite literally and deeply personally.

A year ago, when the coronavirus first invaded our country, I was spending several days in Wenatchee helping my brother dismantle the family home. Several months earlier our mother died, ending a chapter in our lives that had been long in coming. Our much-loved mother had lived with dementia for a decade following our father's death. In response to Dad's request, Marc and I promised him we would not sell the home of our childhood until Mom was gone.

The task of sorting through the stuff my folks had collected living in one place more than fifty years was arduous. I realized — in the midst of tossing and sorting — that the possessions we think worth hanging onto do not compare with having time with those we love. Dismantling a family home triggers precious memories of shared moments. It reminded me of how much I valued being in the presence of those people I most love. I had no idea I was about to help shepherd a group of three-hundred-fifty people (with whom I work) through an extended time of forced separation from their family members.

My work in Wenatchee was interrupted by restrictions that were being put into place by our governor. Businesses and eating establishments were shut down. The senior-adult community where I am employed as a full-time chaplain was in the process of putting strict protocols into place. The dining room was closed. Residents were being asked to "shelter in place." The CEO of our national organization requested that the chaplains at each of our twelve campuses begin producing meditations to be broadcast each day on our closed-circuit TV channel.

The purpose of the daily five-minute broadcasts was to encourage individuals blindsided by a pandemic that had caught us mostly unaware. But writing daily devotions was not the only content that was called for. Since in-person worship services were not permitted in our chapel, for ten months I was forced to preach to empty seats in an empty chapel. Thanks to technology, we were still able to have "church" each week. My prerecorded daily devotions and weekly sermons were also broadcast virtually on our closed-circuit TV system.

Having written a newspaper column for twenty years and having authored a dozen books during my four decades as a pastor, I had an idea. Why not edit the content of the messages I delivered during COVID into a volume for family, friends and residents of our campus? *Sheltering in Grace: Hopeful Insights for Uncertain Times* was published just after Thanksgiving.

An interruption to my personal life and my work life resulted in an opportunity I never would have anticipated a year ago. But that is not unique to my situation. Interruptions and complications have long been viewed as blessings in disguise. It's a truism that has become cliché for a reason. Like the framed needlepoint quote I came across in my sorting of belongings claims, "When God closes a door, He opens a window."

The Universal Message of Easter

This is the weekend that Christians around the globe celebrate the resurrection of Jesus. It recalls a weekend two millennia ago when the followers of the rabbi from Nazareth were sheltering in place, fearing for their lives. Behind closed doors, the eleven were devastated that their twelfth man had been silenced.

Their friend and teacher was dead and buried. So, too, were their hopes and dreams. A pandemic of paranoia and disillusionment imprisoned their emotions. They had given up everything to follow him and now all seemed in vain. What they'd considered normal would never be the same. Or so they thought.

What Jesus' followers experienced for a weekend, much of the world has experienced for a year. In spite of being masked and maintaining a social distance separated by six feet, upwards of six hundred thousand in our country have ended up six feet under.

In a post-pandemic parade, fear and depression have joined the ranks of the grieving and the unemployed. Exhaustion and frustration have taken up the rear along with reluctant virtual learners and faithful virtual worshipers.

For the early Christians, the despair and disillusionment they experienced that three-day weekend was nothing less than gut-wrenching. What began Thursday evening was a portent of something ominous. The traditional Seder supper was less than satisfying. While Jesus had modeled humility by washing their feet, clean feet were not enough to compensate for what followed the meal. There was talk of death. There was talk of treason.

As Thursday morphed into Friday, it was anything but good. There was betrayal, cowardice, a kangaroo court and ultimately crucifixion. A public execution witnessed by family and friends. The grief was intense.

And then there was a self-enforced lockdown. Fearing guilt by association, the followers of Jesus quarantined in that familiar upper room. For how long? They had no clue. After all, that first Easter weekend there was no way of knowing Friday would one day be labeled "Good." Neither did anyone know that the events of Sunday morning would redefine the significance of what had taken place.

Even as the restrictions under which we have lived as a nation are beginning to be lifted, the pandemic of fear that paralyzed the early Christian disciples was not permanent. An unexpected discovery early Sunday morning proved monumental.

A sealed tomb was accessible. A corpse was missing. Jesus' followers could not locate him but the face covering and the strips of cloth that had been wrapped mummy-like around their friend were only too visible. The nightmare through which they had lived for three days was over. Sleepless nights of agonizing despair gave way to dreaming of what yet might be.

For Christians down through the centuries, a vacant grave became a virtual vaccination of sorts. What once was dreaded can now be embraced as a necessary part of life. What once was viewed as a death sentence is seen from a new perspective. Life is no longer punctuated by a period but rather by a semicolon. For his followers, Jesus' defeat of death has taken the fear of our own mortality away.

The fear that has held us hostage for more than a year is beginning to evaporate like mist in the morning sun. Increased vaccinations and decreased hospitalizations find us dreaming of brighter, happier days. Death is being swallowed up in life. The joy of restored normality cannot be masked by face coverings. By the dawn's early light, hope can be detected on the horizon of tomorrow.

Intersections

Rhymes (and Reasons Not To)

April is National Poetry Month. It was established twenty-five years ago this month by the Academy of American Poets. Having observed the success of Black History Month each February and Women's History Month in March, the group opted to create a month dedicated to poets and their work in hopes of increasing the public's awareness and appreciation of poetry.

My mom and dad's generation studied poems in school as part of their exposure to the classics. Poems like "I Wandered Lonely as a Cloud," "Invictus," "Thanatopsis," "The Road Not Taken" and "Jabberwocky" stretched their minds and capacity for memorization. Sadly, today's school curriculums don't introduce our kids to such a treasure trove of verse.

However, given the recent popularity of rap music and spoken-word poetry, both appreciation and awareness of verbal artistry has been on the increase. Twenty-three-year-old Amanda Gorman's poem, "The Hill We Climb," gave poetry a major plug at President Biden's inauguration a few months ago.

Seven years before April was designated "the rhyming month" in 1996, a Robin Williams movie captured the heart of our nation. "Dead Poets' Society" celebrated the time-honored role poetry has played in our culture. In that memorable classroom speech by Mr. Keating (Williams' character in the film), we were reminded that poetry and the arts are *"what we stay alive for."*

While many poignant poems are not dependent on rhyming meters, that is not true for all. One of my favorite poems of all time was written by eight-year-old Fanny Crosby in 1828. The rhyme is not all that remarkable, but the meaning conveyed in the poem certainly is. Fanny was permanently blinded by an inept doctor's treatment for an eye infection when she was six weeks of age. Her simple verse exhibited maturity beyond her years as she celebrated acceptance of misfortune rather than harboring resentment. She wrote:

Oh, what a happy soul I am, although I cannot see!
I am resolved that in this world contented I will be.
How many blessings I enjoy that other people don't,
to weep and sigh because I'm blind I cannot, and I won't!

That was the first of more than eight thousand poems that Fanny Crosby wrote in a lifetime that spanned ninety-five years. Many of her lyrics were set to music and published in hymnals throughout the world.

Speaking of poetry penned by eight-year-olds, while cleaning out my parents' home last fall, I made an interesting discovery. Buried in an old chest of drawers was a file of my elementary school work my mother had saved. To my amazement, I uncovered the first poem I ever wrote. I had no idea the original still existed. I was over the moon. It was a Christmas rhyme I wrote in second grade and dedicated to my dad.

I've written hundreds of poems since I was eight (including four published volumes of poetry), but for some reason I've always remembered the first one. Maybe it was the joy I felt inside being able to express a thought with the additional element of rhyming words. Lines that rhyme are like musical chords that resolve. There's a sense of rightness.

But here's the curious thing — in sixty years of writing poetry, when faced with tragic circumstances or attempting to comfort victims of despair, poetry that doesn't rhyme seems more appropriate. Perhaps "blank verse" (as non-rhyming poetry is called) inherently speaks to a reality we all have come to realize in the past year: Life doesn't always rhyme.

Intersections

Ours is a world where unexpected hurt and pain often undermine the predictable (and comfortable) meter of daily routines. But it is against the backdrop of an injustice, heartache and confusion that the poet finds a voice as well as a receptive audience.

With Praise for St. Arbucks!

A milestone worthy of celebrating recently came and went and hardly anyone noticed. Because of our preoccupation with finding vaccination sites and monitoring the gradual evaporation of the COVID cloud, you likely missed it. I certainly did. Starbucks just celebrated its fiftieth birthday.

I was also totally unaware when the very first Starbucks opened its doors in the historic Pike Place Market on the Seattle waterfront. On the last day of March in 1971, I had just begun classes in the final quarter of my freshman year in college. As I prepared to write a term paper on the letters of St. Paul, I was clueless as to what was taking place not more than five miles from my dorm room on Queen Anne Hill.

A storefront with a sandwich board sign announcing the sale of premium coffee beans and the brewing of grounds would prove to be nothing less than holy ground. It truly was a groundbreaking occasion.

Fast forward four decades. About the time our firstborn daughter began working at the local Starbucks, I began referring to the caffeine commissary down the street as "St. Arbucks." Although my play on words prompted predictable chuckles, from what I'd observed in my career as a clergyman, the correlation seemed appropriate.

Starbucks, like a local church or synagogue, is a gathering place. It's a place where people commune with a cup in hand and share life. Prior to COVID, coffee drinkers would meet religiously for fellowship. Small groups would gather to discuss the Scriptures, to dialogue about an inspirational book or to debrief the Sunday sermon.

In addition, youth mentors would find sacred space in front of outdoor fireplaces to spark discussions or kindle conversations about college choices or career options. Pastors would meet with starry-eyed couples for premarital counseling.

Maybe it's just my faith-based bias, but I see baristas behind the counter akin to preachers behind their pulpits. They take delight in serving up what is bound to warm and refresh those who are thirsty. Because of the loyalty of regular customers, baristas know the faithful by name and greet them accordingly. They take interest in your families. They give attention to your pets. In addition to being served your beverage or food item of choice, you feel cared for. Baristas are twenty-first-century shepherds of their flock.

It's the Gospel truth. St. Arbucks has truly ministered to the needs of our community during the past year. And that includes our family. When COVID restrictions kept houses of worship shuttered and favorite eateries from opening, our local Starbucks provided a place of belonging.

In a confusing, year-long journey amid all its unexpected twists and turns, St. Arbucks (or "Our Lady of Lattes" as some might say) has been a point of reference. Even when indoor seating was not permitted, those who communed daily found their jolt of joy in more than a high-octane brew. The ritual of conversation proved to be much-needed good news (no matter how brief).

They say that confession is good for the soul, so let me confess that my devotion to St. Arbucks is grounded in more than my obsession with iced non-sweetened passion tea. The reason I can't seem to stay away from our local coffee cathedral is because our youngest daughter has followed in her older sister's footsteps and donned the green apron. And so I faithfully pay homage to my favorite saint as a way of supporting her.

Not only did COVID undermine churches, schools and restaurants, it caused small-business owners and self-employed contractors to lose work. Many lost hope. More than a few lost faith. Our daughter, a classical musician and private flute instructor, lost students. Like others, she sought part-time employment to make ends meet. St.

Arbucks blessed her with supplementary income. And as a result, the popular saint graced our daughter with new friendships and new connections in our community.

Yes, I have good reason for being grateful for St. Arbucks. No wonder I am singing his praises!

A Message to the Class of COVID-19

Dear class, congratulations on surviving the coronavirus pandemic. In many ways you are like a graduating class in high school. You've proved yourselves. You've passed the test. You've made the grade. Yes, you have every right to feel a sense of accomplishment.

In this season of graduations and celebrations, allow me to offer you some "give and take" as you commence with getting on with your lives. Here are six suggestions to consider:

1. Give thanks to God for surviving this crisis. Acknowledge God's provision. There is nothing quite like a crisis to bring us to our knees. Pandemics remind us we are not in control of our own destinies. If ever there was a time to express gratitude to the Creator for the privilege of being alive, it's now. In your own way, according to your own tradition, verbalize your dependence on your Creator and be grateful to the One from whom all blessings flow.

2. Give your loved ones a hug. Your family and friends have helped you maintain your focus. They encouraged you when you felt down and wondered if you could go on. While sheltering in place, those you love (who love you) gave you a reason to honor the rules that kept us distanced from one another. In addition, they found creative ways to communicate and keep in touch even when actual touch was not possible.

3. Give normal a chance to catch up with us. I can't predict when returning to what we once called our normal lives will take place. But it's likely to be awhile (if it ever will). If ever there was a time to be patient, it is now.

Several years ago, a friend of mine was planning a trip to Illinois. He knew my wife and I had raised our family in Chicagoland. Ken called me to ask how long it would take from Chicago to get to Normal (where Illinois State University is located). While I could confidently tell my friend it would take about two and one-half hours to get to Normal by car, I can't predict when we will arrive at normal or by what means.

4. *Take off your masks and take a breath.* I mean take a really deep breath. The face coverings we've worn for more than a year not only hid our faces, they altered our breathing patterns. We longed to be in the safety of our own space where we could unmask and breathe. What was necessary was nonetheless a nuisance.

But it's a new day. Try breathing purposely when you wake up each morning. As you inhale, remind yourself that God's Spirit (the Creator's breath) is what keeps you alive. As you exhale, surrender to God your worries and your fears. Breathe in your hopes for the day. Breathe out your doubts.

5. *Take a break.* Although we have been on an involuntary break from familiar and cherished routines for more than a year, we all need a break from COVID. Even before we arrive at normal, we'd do well to plan excursions that allow for much-needed rest stops.

In the midst of this unwelcomed detour on life's journey called COVID, take a car trip. Take in a movie at a local theater. Go on a weekend hike. Pack a picnic and head to the beach. Visit elderly friends in a nursing home who've been relationally starved.

6. *Take time to reflect.* Even though graduation ceremonies typically mean no more exams, I'd like to challenge you to take this one final quiz as you commence to embrace the future that awaits. Don't worry. Your answers won't be graded. But they will definitely impact your future both short term and long term.

- What life lessons have you learned over the past sixteen months?
- How are you a different person because of COVID?

- In what ways is your life actually better because of COVID?
- What have you begun doing during the pandemic that you desire to continue?
- Who helped you the most during the lockdown?
- How can you best express your appreciation to them?
- In light of COVID, what and/or whom mean more to you than they used to?

Reflections on Life and Faith

Celebrating Christmas in July

Seventy-five years ago this month, Hollywood Director Frank Capra was filming "It's a Wonderful Life" in Bedford Falls. Did you know an increasing number of movie buffs believe that Bedford Falls, the fictional town Capra created for his timeless Christmas classic, was based on Seneca Falls in Upstate New York?

After numerous visits to the town that also boasts the birthplace of the Women's Rights Movement, I am among those who believe Seneca Falls is the real Bedford Falls. Even though some aren't sure, the evidence seems to lead to that logical conclusion.

There is no doubt, however, as to where the Bedford Falls created for the movie was constructed. Frank Capra used the RKO ranch in Encino, California, for the charming town in which George and Mary Bailey raised their four children and where they fended off the evil influence of Old Man Potter.

The massive outdoor set covered four acres with the main street stretching three-hundred yards (the equivalent of three city blocks). The imaginary town included seventy-five stores and buildings, as well as a residential neighborhood. And it wasn't just the buildings that looked realistic. Because the climax of the movie took place on Christmas Eve, Capra went to great lengths to find a new form of artificial snow that wouldn't look fake. The result was a product called foamite.

While researching the backstory to "It's a Wonderful Life," I was struck by the irony of filming a Christmas movie in the middle of summer. I discovered a major heat wave crippled Southern California in the midst of the final weeks of production during July 1946. At one point, Frank Capra actually shut down production to allow the cast and crew to recover from heat exhaustion.

The unbearable heat explains why Jimmy Stewart appears to be perspiring in that pivotal scene on the Bedford Falls Bridge when he is contemplating suicide. Well, who wouldn't sweat while wearing a heavy wool overcoat on a one-hundred-degree day? All the same, the unintentional perspiration on the protagonist's face made the poignant close-up all the more believable.

Contemplating the making of a Christmas movie in the middle of summer has me thinking. Even though I've never sat in a director's chair on a Hollywood movie set, I've had to "think winter" when it's not. Like you, I've had the opportunity on more than one occasion to live out the storyline of my faith when the circumstances around me seemed counter-intuitive.

In other words, there are times in our lives when we are called upon to choose to act in accordance with our belief system even when we don't feel like following the script. When tempted to cave to what is convenient, it is easy to let outside conditions threaten our inner values. What's at stake is nothing less than our integrity.

In "It's a Wonderful Life," there is a scene that reminds me of Jesus' temptation by Satan in the wilderness following His baptism. You know the one I mean. Mr. Potter offers George Bailey a job with a lucrative salary in exchange for walking away from his family's building and loan business.

In the heat of a financial crisis, Jimmy Stewart's character is tempted to sell his soul. Fortunately, he realizes his personal wealth is worth more than the benefits Mr. Potter is offering. In the heat of the moment, George keeps his cool.

What we do and say on the stage of life is a dress rehearsal for what's to come. We are called to study our lines and take the director's cues to heart in anticipation of a time when our faith will become sight. Our choices and actions are made against the backdrop of a reality that is yet to be fully realized.

That's what people of faith are called to. We sing lyrics of hymns that celebrate the premier of love, justice and peace that is still in production. We look at present-day circumstances through the lens of a promised future. We start with the end in mind in order to keep from making ill-advised choices. We sing Christmas carols while those around us are complaining of the heat.

Let's Hear It for Anniversaries!

Our journey through life is marked by milestones. This year my progress on the road that leads to the future has been slowed a bit by acknowledging several such milestones. For one thing, 2021 has been the year of anniversaries.

My maternal grandparents were married one hundred years ago this year. Both my parents and my wife's parents were married seventy years ago. My middle daughter and her husband recently celebrated their tenth wedding anniversary.

On a personal note, I began my divinity studies forty-five years ago. This summer, I celebrate sixteen years as the faith and values columnist for our local newspaper as well as eight years as the full-time chaplain at a nearby retirement community.

Anniversaries are noteworthy. Like milestones on a highway, they provide perspective. They invite us to slow down and reflect on the past. Looking back allows us the means to recall God's hand in our lives. I like to think of such glances in the rearview mirror as "dusting for Divine fingerprints."

My friend SQuire Rushnell is a fellow detective. This former network television executive, who now writes books and produces movies for the Hallmark channel, first coined the word "Godwinks." For SQuire, the thought of the Almighty "winking in our direction" captures the Creator's joy in aligning the circumstances of our lives in delightfully unexpected ways.

Since being introduced to the term "Godwinks," I've been more apt to recognize them. But I've also discovered that God's hand in my life is easier seen after the fact when I've taken time to look back.

Anniversaries give us permission to call a timeout and savor the special moments of our past as we relive them in slow motion. When viewed intentionally, anniversaries frame the yesterdays of our lives with purpose and meaning.

Anniversaries are also signposts that point ahead. They provide the means to look forward through the windshield. Anniversaries offer a reality check on how things are progressing when compared to an anticipated destination. In most jobs, performance reviews occur on the anniversary of being hired or the anniversary of a new budget cycle. In keeping with yearly evaluations, goals are tweaked, abandoned or rewritten. Such revising of goals applies to marriages, too.

I've lost count of how many times I've led couples through a renewal of wedding vows on the occasion of their anniversary. This special ritual refocuses a commitment. It serves to reboot the operating system of a relationship for which worn-out routines have resulted in undesired drag. It's a way of joyfully re-upping for the long haul. It's a time for couples to recommit so as to eventually reach the desired port of "till death us do part."

But anniversaries are also rest stops on the highway of life. They give us cause to stop, stretch our legs and smell the roses. They are occasions to pull out all the stops and celebrate in the moment. Anniversaries call attention to the fact that we need to take time to count our blessings.

I love that Family Circus cartoon strip in which Bil Keane reminds us of a timeless truth. *"Yesterday is the past. Tomorrow's the future. But today is a GIFT. That's why it's called 'the present.'"*

As one who finds great satisfaction in marking milestones historically and personally, I love anniversaries. I enjoy finding reasons to have a good time. I love to party.

Intersections

This month will find me partying at a family reunion in Southern California. My wife's relatives are converging on the family homestead to celebrate my in-law's seventieth wedding anniversary this year.

But I won't be the resident pastor at this Steven Family Reunion. If there is a renewal of wedding vows, officiating that ceremony will likely fall to my brother-in-law (a pastor from Florida). My role will be having a good time!

9/11 Anniversary Triggers Thoughts on Unity

Recently I was reflecting on where I was and what I was doing when I learned of the terrorist attacks on the Twin Towers in New York City. For whatever reason, I added 9 and 11 in my head. I had never thought to total those two familiar numbers before. But this year the sum total is most appropriate.

Unbelievably, it's already the twentieth anniversary of that tragic Tuesday we simply refer to as 9/11. On that unforgettable day, those three familiar digits became more than numbers you call in case of an emergency. Those three numbers will forever signify an emergency that called into action all the paramedics and first responders our nation's largest city could provide.

Looking back, 9/11 was a dress rehearsal for dealing with a national crisis. We learned how to pull together when blindsided by an unforeseen invasion. We discovered how to set aside our own desires to serve the needs of those around us. Although we were not concerned with social distancing at that time, we found ways to creatively "shelter in place" as we called out to our Higher Power. Twenty years ago, we were reminded rather dramatically that we are still "one nation under God."

I was also reminded how unanticipated heartache is only a heartbeat away — how a dream summer can quickly turn into a season of sorrow. It was twenty years ago I experienced St. Paul's words from 1 Corinthians 10:12 in a deeply personal way: *"So, if you think you are standing firm, be careful that you don't fall!"* That verse came to life through an unexpected death.

Intersections

The summer of 2001 had been a series of celebrations for our family. Our oldest daughter, Kristin, graduated from high school. And then we commemorated my parents' fiftieth anniversary as they renewed their vows. A couple weeks later, my brother and I accompanied Mom and Dad to Norway to trace ancestral roots as countless cousins feted our folks as American royalty.

That same summer we celebrated my in-laws' fiftieth anniversary in a resort town on the Oregon Coast where they'd honeymooned. They had not returned to Seaside since 1951. Because my father-in-law is a lover of C.S. Lewis, he asked us to read "The Last Battle" (one of the Chronicles of Narnia) prior to our gathering. Our week-long family reunion ended with a discussion of Lewis' views on death. Our verbalized hopes were grounded in our Christian faith.

As we packed up and left for our various homes in Illinois, Virginia, Florida and California, we had no idea how timely our book discussion had been. On August 13, our extended family was rocked with news that my sister-in-law's mother had been killed in a car accident while driving to a meeting at church. Jinx was a beautiful seventy-year-old woman with movie-star looks and creative abilities to envy. We were stunned, but our recent interaction about death had focused our faith and proceeded to guide our grief.

Less than a month later, four planes became flying missiles. Ground Zero found us embracing the "Ground of All Being." Our family (along with every family) recognized our sense of helplessness. We looked to God and we looked to each other. Our common belief and our common plight drew us close as Americans and strengthened our resolve to hope.

When I think of the days immediately following 9/11, I will never forget seeing members of Congress gathered on the steps of the U.S. Capitol Building singing "God Bless America" in unison (in harmony). That harmonious image is a screensaver on the monitor of my mind. Against the backdrop of recent rancor and political polarization, the singing congressmen and congresswomen give me cause to pause and pray.

And what is my prayer? My prayer is that what unified us as a nation twenty years ago, in the aftermath of inexplicable sorrow, will bind us together in the midst of intolerable division. That which we hold in common will not be toppled by issues on which we don't agree. God, bless America once again!

Intersections

A Tale of Two Hughs

This month marks the ninetieth anniversary of an event that put my hometown on the map (literally). On October 3, 1931, Clyde Pangborn and Hugh Herndon took off from Misawa, Aomori, Japan, flying four-thousand-five-hundred miles in forty-one hours before safely landing near present-day Fancher Heights in East Wenatchee on October 5.

In the process, the duo completed the first trans-Pacific flight. It was an historic accomplishment for Pangborn, the middle-class barnstormer pilot raised in Douglas County. To honor his achievement, the regional airport in North Central Washington was named Pangborn Field when it opened in 1941. Clyde's copilot, however, was not similarly honored. Hugh, the playboy son of an heiress to an oil fortune, was disgraced by the journey's end.

The two had begun their flight from Roosevelt Field in New York on July 28 aboard a Bellanca Skyrocket named Miss Veedol. Their goal was to break the world record for circumnavigating the globe in the shortest amount of time.

But early on, Herndon's missteps and miscalculations found them stuck in the mud (literally). Hugh's repeated errors nearly cost the two their lives. His failure to pump fuel from an auxiliary tank forced Pangborn to put the plane into a nosedive over the Pacific in an attempt to windmill the propeller. The stalled engine restarted just before Miss Veedol crashed.

While Pangborn caught a cat nap prior to the much-anticipated landing in Seattle, Herndon struggled to maintain direction. They overshot the intended destination. As Pangborn awoke, the plane was approaching Mount Rainier.

The veteran pilot made a course correction and headed the plane toward Spokane. But due to cloud cover, the two made their unintended landing across the river from Wenatchee. Upon arrival, Pangborn expressed his displeasure with his copilot. Headlines in the Albany Times Union announced the "crash landing" of a former friendship — HERNDON INCOMPTETENT SAYS PANGBORN.

Raised with more opportunity than he knew what to do with, Hugh Herndon ended his life in relative obscurity. It is Clyde Pangborn who continues to be recalled.

Yet another Hugh stepped onto the world's stage about the time Hugh Herndon was making history with Pangborn. In October 1931, Hugh Steven was a six-month-old baby. Unable to care for her child, Hugh's unmarried mother surrendered him to the Children's Aid Society in Vancouver, B.C.

Adopted from the orphanage at age two, Hugh never met either of his birth parents. When his adoptive parents brought Hugh into their home, they were under the impression they could not have children of their own. Time proved them wrong. When a son was born to the couple less than two years later, Hugh became a kind of "cinderfella." Overlooked and underappreciated, he spent much of his time alone dreaming of taking flight in a world of opportunity.

Hugh refused to let setbacks and challenges ground him. Employment at a large department store in Vancouver provided him a sense of pride and self-worth. He found faith at a neighborhood church and with it a sense of direction. Hugh married in 1951 and began to taxi down the tarmac of life. A call to make a difference in the lives of others found him gaining altitude on what would be the adventure of a lifetime.

An assignment in Mexico working with Wycliffe Bible Translators found Hugh exploring new opportunities. In addition to providing translators with supplies and medicines for the various villages, he began to write articles for magazines. His family began to grow, as did

129

his reputation. A move to Chicago to become regional representative for Wycliffe found him trying his hand at writing books.

Now, fifty years later, Hugh Steven has published forty books and countless articles. His four children have married and provided him and his wife with eleven grandchildren and five great-grandchildren. Among them are three pastors, three educators, two classical musicians, a mortgage banker, an international lawyer, a professional basketball player and a Hollywood producer.

It truly is a tale of two Hughs. One was born with opportunity and died in obscurity. The other was born in obscurity but continues to embrace opportunities at the age of ninety. I ought to know. I married Hugh Steven's oldest daughter.

Looking for Aslan in Everyday Life

Long before "The Lion King" was released as an animated movie or a Broadway musical, another lion reigned in the hearts of children in the English-speaking world. His name was Aslan, a Christ-like figure who ruled an imaginary kingdom in *The Chronicles of Narnia*.

Seventy-one years ago, a British novelist by the name of C.S. Lewis first introduced the world to a lion that was good but not always safe. On October 16, 1950, Lewis published *The Lion, the Witch and the Wardrobe* in which Aslan was the ever-present guardian and provider. It was the first of eight books in which the kingly lion pointed the reader to a benevolent Creator.

My introduction to Aslan was in the form of a play performed by a drama troupe from Seattle Pacific University in the fall of 1974. I had just graduated from this outstanding Christian liberal arts institution and accepted a position in the university-relations office. My job found me arranging tours for various performing groups on campus. When the Chancel Players were presented the opportunity to perform *The Lion, the Witch and the Wardrobe* by C.S. Lewis at Expo '74 in Spokane, I traveled with them.

Never having read any of *The Chronicles of Narnia* in my youth, I was intrigued by the character known as Aslan as presented in the Lewis story.

Thirty-five years later I found myself depositing two of my daughters on the campus of Wheaton College in suburban Chicago. Having helped them unload their belongings, I went about exploring the campus.

Intersections

I was delighted to discover the Wade Center named for the founder of ServiceMaster Company. Within this attractive brick building is contained archived materials and memorabilia related to C.S. Lewis, J.R.R. Tolkien, Dorothy Sayers and G.K. Chesterton. The writing desks of Tolkien and Lewis are displayed along with the wardrobe from Lewis' childhood home after which his most famous of all the Narnia chronicles is named. I was thrilled by what I saw.

I looked beyond Lewis' wardrobe to see a beautiful framed painting of Aslan hanging on a wall. It reminded me of the lion sculpture that graces my desk in my office. By now I had come to an informed understanding of Lewis' symbol. The lion is a powerful reminder of an ever-present God who was committed to my well-being. I loved the fact that Aslan was capable of making appearances without fanfare. It seemed as though he was always present even when not visible. He was a means of salvation when all seemed lost.

A dozen years after that self-guided tour of the Wade Center on the campus of Wheaton College, COVID threatened our world. During this time of lockdown and restrictions — as well as fear and anxiety — I noted a number of coincidences that focused my perspective in a heavenly direction. These happenstances reminded me that in spite of being socially distanced, I was not on my own.

My friend SQuire Rushnell refers to such serendipities as Godwinks. In fact, SQuire is the one who coined the term. And during the difficult months of COVID, God, like Aslan, made His presence known at just the right time in unanticipated ways. I began observing Godwinks all around me. I started to sense the hot breath of an un-caged lion on my neck. I knew Aslan was near.

During lockdown, I resorted to my favorite pastime. Sitting at my laptop, I painted word pictures while dusting for divine fingerprints. The result is a collection of poetry in which I celebrate the presence of God in our everyday lives. I've called this volume *When God Speaks: Listening for Aslan in Everyday Life*. It's an interactive workbook in which each poem is paired with a prompt or question and space for the reader to reflect and respond.

Calendars Can Help Us Number Our Days

It wasn't until I was out of seminary and serving my first congregation that I realized that Moses wrote a psalm. Because I had grown up in the church and was the son of a pastor, I knew the "Prince of Egypt" had stood up to Pharaoh and led the ancient Israelites out of bondage. As the publisher of the Ten Commandments, I knew he was known as the "law giver." But I didn't realize he had written Psalm 90. That's the one that begins with the familiar words, *"Lord, you have been our dwelling place through all generations..."*

As I read and reread that well-known song in Israel's hymnal, I could detect Moses' fingerprints all over the parchment. Moses had experienced the all-consuming nature of God's presence from the time he was hidden away in a makeshift cradle among the bulrushes of the Nile River. During his three distinct careers he had tasted the highs and lows of the human experience. He also recognized the brevity of life. In light of Psalm 90, it's Moses who should be credited with that bumper sticker slogan, *"Life is hard and then you die."*

So, when's the last time you read Moses' reflections? Why not Google Psalm 90? As you read his words, be mindful of his bottom-line takeaway tucked in those ancient lyrics. *"Teach us to number our days that we might gain a heart of wisdom."*

Against the backdrop of the speed at which time flies and the modern-day plagues that imprison our dreams, such is a perfect prayer. Lord, help me to make my life count. Keep me from wasting even one precious day.

Indeed, calendars are a great tool with which to be proactive in the way we spend the inheritance the Creator bequeathed us at birth. They help us plan. They provide us perspective. They give us reason to hope for better days ahead. Those blank squares on the wall remind us that we have a choice in how those days will be filled in. So, whether we use old-fashioned paper calendars or chart our appointments on our smartphones or laptops, calendars are a gift.

Sadly, not every person who would like a calendar has access to one. And I'm not referring to folks in Third World countries. I'm thinking about those incarcerated in penal institutions less than an hour from where we live. The Reverend Dale Sewall, a retired pastor in the community where I live, brought this situation to my attention a few years ago. As one who visits prisoners, Dale became aware of the huge need of providing those separated from the outside world with a tool to track their days. And my friend is a man of action.

So, Dale challenged his former congregation to collect calendars from congregants. He also extended the invitation to me as chaplain at a continuing-care retirement community to mobilize our residents to collect as many "days" as we could.

Ever since, we've been "numbering our days." In other words, residents on our campus have been collecting the free calendars that are sent in the mail from various organizations and nonprofits.

Every fall I deposit several hundred at one of the two churches Dale Sewall identified. And every December, Dale delivers the calendars to area detention facilities. And the response has been heartwarming.

With that in mind, if you have been wondering what to do with those calendars that show up in your mailbox unbidden, don't throw them away. Why not contact your minister, priest or rabbi and ask them to serve as a collection site for those in your community who have the same passion my friend Dale has. Think of it as giving someone who has reason to regret their yesterdays the gift of tomorrows. It's a way to help many of them number their days until they're home with loved ones.

Talking Turkey About Turkeys

When I was twelve, turkey was not my favorite food. Since it was typically served only on Thanksgiving Day, I could deal with it. I found that I could mask the taste with mashed potatoes and gravy. Lots of gravy!

When I got into high school and was part of a bowling league on Saturday mornings at Columbia Lanes, I grew to love turkeys. If you're a bowler, you know that a "turkey" isn't something to eat. Rather it's what you get when you roll three consecutive strikes. I couldn't get enough of those.

As an adult, when our family moved to the Midwest, we lived at a distance from the city. I found myself dodging the gobblers on my drive to the office. I discovered that wild turkeys can be a real nuisance.

The same is true of those other turkeys in our lives. You know the ones I mean. I call them "joy thieves." They steal your sense of wellbeing and rob you of your peace of mind. Just being around them stresses you out. They question your motives. They're jealous of your successes. They delight in your setbacks. Gobbling gossip, they can unfairly stain your reputation. These turkeys definitely make life difficult.

The turkeys in our lives are the source of much anxiety and perhaps even deep-seated resentment. In response, we find ourselves basting these birds with negative thoughts while our anger simmers. Ironically, the people to whom we don't want to give the time of day occupy our constant attention. But what can we do?

Many years ago, I heard one of Billy Graham's daughters make a statement that challenged my tendency to let the difficult people in my life dominate my emotions. Ruth Graham, who had suffered much hurt in her life as an adult, discovered that refusing to forgive those who complicate our lives is like drinking poison and hoping the other person dies.

It's an axiom that remains true. In fact, I think it is a fail-proof recipe that provides us a way to deal with the turkeys in our lives before the impact of their hurtful actions results in cooking our goose. It's a recipe that calls for forgiving the offender instead of being held hostage by feelings of hurt and hatred. Or as one first-century rabbi suggested, *"Let us forgive one another as God has forgiven us."*

It's just possible that a forgiving heart may be that secret sauce you need to make your Thanksgiving less bitter. Reading the recipe closely will clarify that forgiveness does not mean forgetting what those turkeys have done to us. Rather, it is choosing not to let them control our emotions.

After all, this is the season for setting turkeys free. Ever since George H.W. Bush's administration, the President has pardoned a turkey at Thanksgiving. Actually, Mr. Bush wasn't the first to commute a death sentence to such a beast destined for the dinner table. History records that Abraham Lincoln freed a turkey someone had given to the White House that one of his sons had adopted as a pet.

And President Kennedy pardoned a White House turkey near the end of his life. In fact, that act of mercy was one of the last public acts JFK did just three days before he died. In the midst of the tragedy that defined his fateful trip to Dallas, that little-known fact has been lost on most historians.

But it isn't simply the purview of Presidents to pardon turkeys. Each of us has the power to grant the irregular people in our lives room to roam. Each of us has the ability to forgive. And by offering forgiveness (undeserved as it might be), we give ourselves a gift. We free ourselves from the prison of resentment and stress.

It's a Wonderful Family Time

One of the most wonderful parts of the Christmas season is getting together with family. One of the hardest parts of the Christmas season is getting together with family.

If you have a great relationship with your clan, Christmas provides an opportunity to maximize your joy. But if your family is divided or dysfunctional, the obligatory gathering can often impersonate the Grinch and steal your Christmas peace.

As a chaplain at a retirement community, I have observed how time and distance can redefine a family's identity. The death of a spouse, a sibling or a child can rob you of branches that used to characterize your family tree. And when miles separate you from those with whom you regularly used to share special times, traditions change.

So, what do you do when you don't have any family (or don't want to be around members of your family) at Christmas? The simple answer is this: Family can be more than just those individuals with whom you share your DNA.

I've seen that in a rather winsome way the past several Christmases. Each December since 2015, I've participated in the "It's a Wonderful Life" Festival in Seneca Falls, New York. Every year I look forward to renewing my friendship with the surviving cast members from the 1946 movie who regularly attend the festival. Carol Coombs Mueller, Karolyn Grimes and Jimmy Hawkins (together with Jimmy Stewart and Donna Reed) comprised the George Bailey family Frank Capra created when he directed the classic film seventy-five years ago. And they remain a family. But it wasn't always that way.

Intersections

After a couple of weeks of filming, the three child actors went their separate ways. The challenges of marriage, divorce, children, and death visited them. They didn't see each other for almost fifty years. And then in 1993, the Target Corporation decided to feature "It's a Wonderful Life" memorabilia in its stores for Christmas. As part of their IAWL focus, the executives of Target decided to reunite the Bailey kids and send them around the country on a promotional tour. That goodwill tour resulted in a reunion and began a connection that continues to this day.

As the actors began to spend time with each other, they shared memories of their time on the set of a timeless movie that they hadn't actually seen themselves until they'd grown up. The memories they'd made during the summer of 1946 (and the memories they've made since) have bonded them in a rather remarkable way.

Today when I see the three together, I see a family. The Bailey kids, now in their eighties, are a "family of friends" whose bonds are stronger than many biological families. They love each other and they love being with each other. As then, still now. It's a wonderful family! And they aren't even related.

There is a passage in the Gospels that troubles some people. It's that scene when Jesus' disciples interrupt his teaching with news that his mother and siblings are waiting for him. To the surprise of the disciples and those listening to him, Jesus asks *"Who is my mother? Who are my brothers?"* He then goes on to answer the question he's posed. *"Whoever does the will of my Father in Heaven is my family."*

While Jesus is making a case for the fact that those who heed his teaching comprise his true family, he is also implying that family units can be defined by more than asking "Who's your mother?"

So, as we prepare to celebrate his birth, it seems quite possible that the Savior would give us permission to redefine family as we contemplate with whom we'd like to gather to party.

This month, as I return to upstate New York to sign copies of my book, *Finding God in It's a Wonderful Life*, I look forward to seeing Carol, Karolyn and Jimmy. Together we will celebrate the message of

Christmas as well as the movie that brought us together in the first place. I can honestly say they have become like family to me. And I can pretty much guarantee it will be a wonderful time!

Intersections

The Cruising Altitude of Christmas

While flying back east over the holidays to speak at a church, I made note of the different stages passengers experience in a typical takeoff. There are the preflight announcements from the cockpit and the safety instructions from the flight attendants. There's the reminder to turn our cell phones to airplane mode and to make sure our seatbelts are fastened and that our tray tables are in their upright and locked position.

When the plane reaches ten-thousand-feet altitude, a bell rings. And whereas I didn't get my angel wings like Clarence Odbody, I did get permission to open my laptop. That ringing chime is an indicator that I can safely jettison the gum I started to chew at takeoff to keep my ears from plugging.

When the plane reaches a cruising altitude, a voice comes over the intercom indicating it is okay to unbuckle seat belts and walk around. At that point in the flight, I tend to take a deep breath and relax. Reaching the cruising altitude is an invitation to enjoy the balance of the flight, barring any unexpected turbulence.

The Christmas season reminds me of a typical plane trip. Leading up to the holiday we're stressed by all the preparations: decorating the house, trimming the tree, shopping for gifts, attending concerts and parties, baking cookies and cooking meals. By the time we get to the day after Christmas, many families are ready to start packing up everything and putting the house back to normal.

For our family, Christmas Day is when we have finally reached our cruising altitude. It's finally time to sit back, relax and enjoy a journey that includes listening to carols, watching Christmas movies or simply enjoying quiet evenings in front of the twinkling tree. The days after Christmas are a perfect time to reread holiday letters and cards and write some thank-you notes.

One of the carols that plays in our home throughout December is "The Twelve Days of Christmas." That classic song is rooted in the way our culture used to view the holiday. Traditionally the season began four weeks before Christmas Day with the start of Advent and continued on until Epiphany (January 6). The twelve days that connect Christmas Day with Epiphany provided the opportunity to unpack the reason for the season before packing up the decorations.

When our kids were little, we intentionally extended our celebration of the holiday. For a pastor's family, it wasn't the Grinch who stole Christmas; it was the church. All the activities and services a pastor is expected to attend kept our family from having the relaxed time others were enjoying. Rather than blaming the church, we opted to underscore the fact that Christmas was a season rather than a day. We created unique traditions to compensate.

Four weeks before Christmas, three little ceramic wisemen began making a slow deliberate journey from our family room throughout the house ending up at the Nativity scene atop our piano in the living room. But the magi didn't arrive at the manger on December 25. They don't get there until January 6.

As with most families, there is the typical emotional letdown for kids after gifts are opened on Christmas Day. In our family, we attempted to upend the letdown with the promise of gifts that would be given twelve days later. We called it our Day of the Kings celebration.

On Epiphany, we would have a dinner that reflected the Eastern culture from which the magi came. In our case, it was Chinese food. At the table there were quilted crowns at each place setting. And in each crown were three wrapped gifts for each family member to open. The number of gifts represented the three gifts the visitors from the East gave the Christ child. We sang special songs and read special stories at the table.

Our strategy worked. A less-hurried after-Christmas celebration became something our family cherished. We still do. The cruising altitude of Christmas provides a wonderful perspective from which to see what really matters this time of year. Why not unbuckle your seatbelt, push your seat back and enjoy the season?

Reflections on Life and Faith

A Date That will Live in Infamy

January 6, 2021. Sadly, for most Americans that date has become one of those squares on our calendars that call to mind a dizzying circle of events we will not soon forget. It joins other dates that will live in infamy — dates like December 7, 1941, June 6, 1944, September 2, 1945, November 22, 1963, and September 11, 2001.

January 6 of last year interrupted our extended New Year's celebrations in which we were dreaming of a COVID-free world. Our hopes that 2020 would find our vision for the future less blurry and less bleary were blindsided. Seemingly without notice, the twelfth day of Christmas gave way to the deafening sound of much more than twelve drummers drumming. The audio that accompanied images on the nightly news that unforgettable day was more akin to the sounds of anarchy.

How ironic that the events in our nation's Capitol building last January occurred on the day Christ followers around the world know as Epiphany. It is that day Orthodox Christians have historically observed as the birth of Christ. It is the day western believers have identified as the day when the magi from the East arrived in Bethlehem to present gifts to the infant Jesus. It is a day that acknowledges the universal nature of God's love and the Creator's blueprint for peace on earth displayed against the backdrop of power grabs, deceit and human suffering.

When the stargazers neared their destination, they conferred with King Herod. This ego-driven monarch, drunk on power and intimidated by their mission, misled the magi. Feigning sincerity, Israel's king proceeded to marshal his jealous rage from the capital city of Jerusalem

143

to the unsuspecting babies in Bethlehem. The result was what history records as "the slaughter of the innocents."

Although Herod had entreated the magi to report back to him when they had delivered their gifts to the holy family, they disregarded his instructions. Instead, as the Gospel account indicates, *"they went back home by another road." (St. Matthew 2:12 CEV)*

That verse reminds me of a traditional way our family would spend New Year's Eve when I was a boy. Each December 31, my pastor-father conducted a "watch night" service in our little church. We would gather as a congregation about an hour before midnight. Following the singing of hymns and prayer, Dad would summarize the story of the magi and underscore the fact that they returned to their homeland in a way differently than they had approached Bethlehem.

My father loved to point out that "having encountered the love of God in human form, their lives were changed. As such, they went home differently." Dad invited his flock to consider what changes they might commit to for the coming year before returning home following the late-night service.

To help members of the congregation tangibly express their resolve for change, my dad would have the ushers distribute stamped envelopes, a sheet of paper and a ballpoint pen. Individuals were then invited to write a letter to themselves verbalizing changes they desired to make in the coming year. They then were asked to seal the envelope and address it to themselves.

Dad would keep the letters locked in his office for the year and then mail them to the parish members a week before the following New Year's Eve service. Such an exercise proved to be a helpful source of accountability and motivation.

As we revisit what occurred in our country a year ago, I'm wondering what letter we might consider writing to ourselves as this new year commences. What did we learn from what we witnessed that we never want to see again? What are we willing to do to prevent history repeating itself? What did we discover from our own reactions to the events of January 6, 2021 that require ongoing reflection and dialogue?

My hope is that January 6 will continue to be primarily recognized as the adoration of One many acknowledge as the Prince of Peace. A prince whose values and teachings will topple kings, prime ministers and presidents who serve themselves rather than those they are called to represent.

Intersections

There's No Age Limit on Personal Growth

A few years ago, I attended a clergy retreat nestled up against the entrance to Saguaro National Park in Tucson, Arizona. It was the first time I'd ever experienced this part of the desert southwest. With spring blossoms and bird migration, I was drinking in the beauty (and some facts) like a thirsty sponge.

With a friend, I took a nature walk among the cacti. Thanks to signs posted on the trail, I discovered that the saguaro cactus grows only in this part of the United States. This familiar species most often associated with Western movies is generally recognized by the arms that grow from its prickly tubular trunk. Another factoid I discovered is that saguaros do not start out with appendages. Up until the time a saguaro produces a limb, it looks like a gigantic prickly cucumber.

What truly amazed me is the length of time it takes for the cactus' signature branches to appear. According to park officials, the average saguaro does not grow "arms" until it is between fifty and seventy years of age. In areas of lower precipitation, it may take up to one hundred years before arms appear.

As I reflected on my newly acquired knowledge, I realized cacti aren't the only living organisms on earth capable of growth as they age. People are, too. Having just celebrated yet another birthday the week before my Tucson retreat, I was living proof that it's never too late to grow and reach. It was not too late to grow in my understanding of the world around me.

Having been a chaplain in a senior-adult community for the past nine years, I have witnessed the capacity for growing "arms of understanding" on a daily basis. Those who are learning how to embrace social media. Those who are reaching to grasp new technologies. Those who are just discovering that their maturity of years qualifies them to speak into the lives of younger people and that those younger actually want to hear what they have to say.

I guess I shouldn't be surprised. The Scriptures provide case study after case study of senior adults who maximized their productivity after the age of sixty-five. For example, Moses was eighty years old before God deemed him ready to lead the Israelites out of Egyptian bondage. The first forty years of his life were invested in being trained in leadership in the courts of Pharaoh. The second forty years provided him with knowledge of the Sinai wilderness where he would be called to shepherd God's people. By the time he turned eighty, he was ready for a new assignment.

In three-month's time, I will begin my eighth decade of life and my fifth decade of marriage. As I approach my seventieth birthday, I have a renewed appreciation for the unique challenges and privileges this season of life offers. I, for one, am grateful for a job that allows me to contribute beyond what we used to consider "retirement age." Experience and lessons learned from it are valuable companions on this stretch of life's journey.

Perhaps we all need to learn the lesson of the cactus. There are opportunities to grow and reach regardless of how many candles will adorn our birthday cake this year.

A Monumental Milestone

The Lincoln Memorial celebrates its one-hundredth birthday this year and I'm recalling my first visit to that elegant limestone house in which our sixteenth president continues to hold court.

It was the summer of 1969, just a couple months before beginning my senior year of high school. I traveled with a choir under the direction of Bob Stone, who had been my youth pastor at First Assembly of God Church in Wenatchee. Our East Coast itinerary included a stop in Washington, D.C., because we had been invited to sing in the rotunda of the U.S. Capitol. As Sen. Henry M. (Scoop) Jackson looked on with his signature smile, we sang "God Bless America."

Following that memorable performance, I visited the Lincoln Memorial with Pastor Bob and his wife, Nancy. Excitedly climbing the steps to view Mr. Lincoln caused my heart to beat in double time. Looking into the marble face of my favorite president was a personal thrill that defied words.

At the time I was oblivious to what it must have been like that warm day in May 1922 when a former president, who was now Chief Justice of the Supreme Court, spoke to the fifty thousand in attendance. William Howard Taft, who had been head of the Lincoln Memorial Commission, formally presented the monument to President Warren G. Harding.

Harding accepted the gift on behalf of the American people. Among the crowd gathered at the memorial that had taken eight years to construct, was President Lincoln's seventy-eight-year-old son, Robert Todd. Ironically, a monument that celebrated the memory of his father who had signed the Emancipation Proclamation was christened by a segregated audience.

I am embarrassed to admit that I also was oblivious the day of my first visit to what had occurred at the Lincoln Memorial just six years before. In retrospect, I wish I had realized what it must have been like for a thirty-four-year-old preacher from Atlanta as he stood on that pillared platform. What I wouldn't give for a chance to travel back in history and hear Dr. King's "I Have a Dream" speech among the integrated crowd of two hundred fifty thousand who culminated their March on Washington at the famous monument.

Preparing to celebrate Presidents' Day Weekend, I'm grateful for those two chief executives whose birthdays fall within this month. While an unvarnished read of history reveals that Washington and Lincoln were less than perfect specimens of humanity, their courageous contributions to our democracy are undeniable.

In recent time, Presidents' Day has become more than a combined celebration of Washington and Lincoln's births. It provides an opportunity to reflect on the legacy of all our Presidents. It gives students a chance to memorize trivia about past and present occupants of the White House should our children and grandchildren ever appear on "Jeopardy."

As a person of the cloth, I'd like to suggest that Presidents' Day can also have a more practical application. It provides a tangible reminder for people of faith to pray for our current President. A little more than a year into his presidency, Mr. Biden finds himself wrestling a pandemic that refuses to be pinned down. His agenda is frustrated by a divided Congress, a complicated economy marked by a spike in inflation and global unrest.

The current occupant of the White House is also beset by the ongoing plight of blacks who visit the Lincoln Memorial wondering when Dr. King's dream will finally be realized. Whether you voted for him or not, our President needs our prayers. To that end, I offer this supplication as a starting point.

God, bless America. Not because we deserve Your blessing, but because we acknowledge our need of You. Please grace our President with insight, understanding, courage and a spirit of cooperation. May President Biden reflect the humility of Mr. Lincoln who governed with a team of rivals. Surround our Chief Executive with a company of wise counselors who will help to guide the decisions he must make on our behalf. This we pray in Your name. Amen.

March Madness Remembered

It has been a crazy couple of years, right? We were all ready to fill out our brackets back in 2020, but the March Madness we banked on being able to follow rimmed out. Roundball took an indefinite intermission. It was we who ended up on the hardwood of hard times, giving and taking shots. Shots from Pfizer, Moderna and Johnson & Johnson. There were no easy layups. It proved to be a March Madness of another kind.

Can you believe it? It was two years ago this week when our normal lives went on vacation. And in response we were called to "shelter in place." Socially distanced, we stocked the toolboxes of our lives with masks, gloves, hand sanitizer and tape measures. Our daily routines consisted of window visits, drive-by birthday greetings, Zoom meetings, virtual classrooms, virtual worship services and working from home.

While normalcy took a vacation, we found ourselves on a journey of our own without a compass or a map. It was an unplanned road trip through seemingly endless restrictions. It was a nonstop flight into fear. The coronavirus cruise on which we found ourselves ticketed made ports-of-call to places we'd never dreamed of or imagined.

And when we docked, the excursions offered were anything but entertaining. Because of the contagious nature of the virus, the voyage we were journaling turned out to be a round-the-world cruise. COVID was everywhere!

Yes, the pandemic made for pandemonium and the restrictions seemed insane. Truly, March Madness became monthly madness. I don't know about you, but I nearly went berserk masking up day after day. And that wasn't the half of it. With people wearing hats, sunglasses and masks, it was easy to pass friends on the street without recognizing them.

We couldn't help but feel for those frontline workers whose jobs demanded they work among those infected. As a chaplain for a retirement community, my visits to residents in our health center made me keenly aware of the acute challenges we were hearing about in the news. The stress was accumulative in nature to more than just senior adults living in vulnerable settings.

With nearly one million people having died in our country from COVID-related complications, I'm guessing most of us know the name of someone on that tragic list. And the mounting toll of deaths has maintained the momentum of anxiety. It has exacerbated the plight of the lonely. Depression rates have increased. Alcohol abuse has, as well.

But two years have passed, and we survived. While it was enough to drive us mad, this March we are less crazy. Mask mandates are being relaxed (if not rescinded). We are more inclined to breathe deeply and think clearly. My hope is that we are more sensitive to the spiritual dimension of our tired souls.

The full-court press of the pandemic has found us tasting flavors of God's grace we didn't even know existed. We discovered how much we need each other. We have learned not to take a handshake or a hug for granted. We came to a new understanding of how precious an average ordinary day really is.

And though it took being in a state of virtual madness, I'm glad for what we've learned. My prayer is that the lessons we gleaned will impact the way we see ourselves and each other as we navigate our way back to what the experts are referring to as a new normal.

The Dash of Life

Walking is good for your health, and I believe that strolling through cemeteries helps one maintain a healthy perspective on life. Headstones can be a most effective means of calibrating one's attitude about what's really important this side of the grave.

While on a speaking engagement in central Indiana some years back, I made an intentional detour off Interstate 69 to get to the little town of Fairmount. That's where Jim Davis, the creator of the Garfield comic strip, grew up. It is better known, however, as the hometown of Hollywood legend James Dean. Fairmount is where the perpetual twenty-four-year-old is buried. He was born February 8, 1931, and died September 30, 1955.

Since I was only three when the '50s heartthrob died, I have not been overly preoccupied with his life. But after watching a television documentary on James Dean, I'd become intrigued with his cult-like following. Because I was traveling so close to where he grew up and was buried, I decided to take some time and check out Fairmount. I wanted to walk around the sleepy Midwest town and soak in some of the ambiance that contributed to the life of the person that millions still praise long after his death.

A grocery checkout clerk gave me directions to the home of one of Dean's high school friends. When I stated the purpose of my spontaneous visit, Bob Pulley invited me into his farmhouse on the edge of town.

Bob had a lot of memories of Dean. He pulled out his 1949 high school yearbook and showed me photographs of the two of them in a school play and on the track team. He smiled as he recounted their senior trip to Washington, D.C. For Bob, it was as if it were only a few years ago.

I asked him about his last visit with his famous friend. Dean had returned home for a photo shoot a few months before his untimely death. According to Bob, he was still the same old "Jimmy." He told me about the funeral. He was one of the pallbearers.

I drove to the Fairmount cemetery and stood in front of Dean's grave. Fresh flowers graced his final resting place. Photographs and cigarettes were strewn at the foot of his headstone. Fans had left them there to commemorate the late actor's birthday.

As I stared at the grave marker, I was impressed by its simplicity. James B. Dean 1931 – 1955. How quickly his life was over. I looked to the left of his grave to see his father and stepmother's marker. I looked to the right to see the marker of the uncle and aunt who raised him after his mother died when he was only nine.

Although the names and dates were different, each gravestone had something in common: between the birth date and death date, each had a small dash. The dash represents a person's life, with all the happiness and heartache that come our way. It stands for the failures and successes we achieve. It stands for what we do with the opportunities God gives us.

The fact that it is a dash is most appropriate. Whether we live twenty-four years or ninety-four, our lives speed by like the time it takes to run a one-hundred-yard dash.

Next time you take a walk through your local cemetery, look at the names. Look at the dates. Consider the dashes.

As you do, think about this: We can't control the date we're born. We can't control the date we die. But we can decide what we will do with our dash. To that end, determine to make the most of your dash as you re-evaluate your purpose in the world. Don't take it for granted. Resist the temptation to run away from the reality of what's to come. Don't be a rebel without a cause.

Reflections on Life and Faith

Consider what a first-century Christian leader in the Roman Empire wrote: *"Live life then, with a due sense of responsibility, not as men who do not know the meaning of life, but as those who do. Make the best use of your time."* (Ephesians 5:15 Phillips Translation)

Intersections

An Unexpected Reminder of Resurrection

In the last few years, "Godwinks" has become a common part my vocabulary. It describes those serendipitous occurrences we often refer to as coincidences.

As my friend SQuire Rushnell likes to say, *"Godwinks are random events that serve as divine signposts helping us successfully navigate our career, relationships and interests."* Furthermore, SQuire, who coined the term some twenty years ago, goes on to say: *"By recognizing the 'Godwinks' our Creator has placed in our paths, we can understand — and embrace — the journey God has laid out for us."*

I had a Godwink a few weeks ago while walking through a nature preserve in our community. But before I explain, let me provide a backdrop to my "wink."

Pioneer Park, near to where I live, is a beautiful, forested expanse with several trails from which to choose. During COVID, I noticed plastic toys and miniature animals adorning random tree trunks and overgrown stumps on one of the trails.

Upon investigation, I discovered parents were helping their children in our neighborhood combat the boredom of lockdown by creating treasure hunts in the woods. Moms and dads would hide a menagerie of small superheroes, Disney characters and toy animals in unexpected places. Then kids would do their best to try and discover the hidden treasure. It was kind of like an Easter-egg hunt but without Easter eggs and not just in the spring.

For the two years of the pandemic, young families in our end of town have delighted in this new version of hide-and-seek. And now that restrictions are lifting, this two-step dance of discovery continues. Parents are still planting the booty and little ones keep searching for hidden treasure. I can't help but spot these tiny colorful objects adorning the branches and bushes as I exercise.

Now back to my recent Godwink. On an early morning walk in February, I admired a massive fir tree towering over the trail. Upon closer examination, I noticed a little head poking out of the hollow in the trunk a third of the way up the giant tree. It was a plastic lion. And the sight of that little beast warmed my heart. It spoke to me of God's presence. It was a picture of hope.

I'm fairly certain that most walkers in my nearby woods did not notice the miniature mane five feet in the air. I'm also pretty sure that of those who did see it, few made the connection that I did. Unless, of course, they were familiar with C.S. Lewis' classic children's story, *The Lion, the Witch and the Wardrobe*.

In that timeless tale, the hero of the adventure is a lion named Aslan. This Christ-like figure reigns over the peaceful kingdom of Narnia, befriending the children and animals who live there. They see him as their protector. While they know that Aslan is good, they also recognize that he is not necessarily safe. Sometimes his actions surprise them. But the lion always acts for the well-being of those who acknowledge his rule.

When an evil power attempts to invade Narnia, Aslan loses his life in an act of self-sacrifice. The children are grief-struck as they surround a stone table where Aslan breathed his last. They fear what will happen to them and Narnia now that the White Witch has defeated their friend. But then, without notice, Aslan appears to them in the forest. He assures them that he has defeated death and with it, his enemy.

As I stared at that little lion in the tree trunk, the hollow looked like the mouth of an open tomb. It was amazing. There, before my unexpecting eyes was a picture of what Christians around the world celebrate on Easter Sunday.

Seeing the tiny toy lion in an opening in that tree trunk reminded me that death does not have the final word in life. It also called to mind that the Living One is present everywhere and at all times throughout the year — that God can be found winking in our direction when we least expect it.

Seventy Things I've Learned in Seventy Years of Living

The day after Easter this year, I celebrated a milestone birthday. In addition to starting my tenth year as chaplain at Covenant Living at the Shores, this past Monday I began my eighth decade of life. In addition to blowing out candles and opening gifts, I've been reflecting on lessons I've learned in seventy years of living. Some are quite obvious. Others are deeply personal. Some are borrowed from people I respect. All of them provide a peek into what I value.

1. George Bailey isn't the only one who's had a wonderful life.
2. Years go by faster the older you live.
3. Parents know more than we give them credit for.
4. Everybody has a story worth sharing.
5. Asking questions is the key that unlocks a person's story.
6. The Creator desires a personal relationship with us.
7. Jesus is the means by which that relationship is made possible.
8. Change is hard.
9. Change is inevitable.
10. Beauty can be found everywhere.
11. Work that you love isn't work.
12. Worry empties today of its strength.
13. Today is a gift.
14. Gifts are meant to be unwrapped and enjoyed.
15. Memories are a lasting treasure no one can steal.
16. Debt is a heartless seducer.
17. Living life in twenty-four-hour capsules brings time-released joy.
18. Sunsets and ice cream make for cheap dates.
19. Stick trees silhouetted against a sunrise redeem winter blahs.
20. Working out helps our bodies work better.

21. Physically fit people die healthier.
22. Adversity makes us strong.
23. Love is a universal language.
24. Every memorial service we attend is one closer to our own.
25. Music is oxygen for the soul.
26. Children are a gift from the Lord.
27. Adult children keep you talking to God.
28. Grandchildren provide the joys of parenting without the responsibilities.
29. Poetry that rhymes is easier to understand.
30. Walking in the woods allows you to walk with God.
31. Pets provide a picture of God's unconditional love.
32. The death of a pet is equivalent to losing a member of your family.
33. Grief is the price you pay for really loving someone.
34. Christmas doesn't mean a thing without Easter.
35. Easter is not possible without Good Friday.
36. Eating humble pie requires swallowing pride.
37. It's more blessed to give than to receive.
38. Receiving is harder than giving.
39. Bad things happen to good people.
40. Good things happen to bad people.
41. You can never tell someone you love them too often.
42. A shared joy is a doubled joy.
43. A shared sorrow is half a sorrow.
44. Spending time with older relatives is a priceless gift to them (and you).
45. Memorizing Scripture pays dividends now and later.
46. Taking the initiative to restore relationships takes courage.
47. Handwritten letters and notes are more valuable than e-mails and texts.
48. Mementoes on a desk or a shelf recall moments we dare never forget.
49. Forgetting God's faithfulness is the most common kind of memory loss.
50. Those with the most money often have the most worries.
51. We begin our lives and end our lives wearing diapers and sleeping most the time.
52. Family traditions sustain values and perpetuate memories.

53. There is nothing more sad than watching alienated siblings at a parent's funeral.
54. Learning the love language of your mate does not require a degree in linguistics.
55. When you get married, you marry a family as well as your mate.
56. You tend to sleep better with a window cracked open.
57. Making small talk with strangers can lead to big opportunities.
58. Shopping at a thrift store is like going to a museum.
59. Furnishing your home or wardrobe at a thrift store saves you money and benefits others.
60. Beginning your day with coffee and prayer makes you alert to life and the Lord.
61. Taking time to visit a relative's grave gives cause to pause and reflect on the brevity of life.
62. Taking pictures with a smartphone is an inexpensive way to express one's creativity.
63. The church is a community of people, not a building or a certain denomination.
64. There's nothing like a pandemic to unmask what really matters in life.
65. When you lose your job unexpectedly, you discover flavors of grace you didn't know existed.
66. Unbelievable offers generally are.
67. Gratitude is the prelude to worship.
68. Mulligans aren't just for golf.
69. It's easier to ask forgiveness than to ask permission.
70. Birthdays are a necessary rest stop on the interstate of life.

Intersections

It's Time to Light the Holiday Candles

Alas, it's December when darkness prevails.
But also the wonder of biblical tales.
A miracle oil. A miracle birth.
A miracle visit of One sent to earth.

A season that's marked by tall tapers of wax
that light up our world with the truth they unmask.
This season of Christmas and Hanukkah too
means candles for Christians and candles for Jews.

Some grace a menorah and some grace a wreath.
The glow from these candles exposes cunning thieves
that lurk in the shadows and hide in the weeds.
One thief's name is Envy. The other is Greed.

These holiday bandits are hungry as sin.
They steal and devour contentment within.
Like vandals they lure us. They're really quite smart.
They pillage and plunder the peace in our hearts.

They kidnap our reason, insisting on new
while what we are using is fine and will do.
They hold our minds hostage to where we want more.
More money. More status. More stuff. So much more.

More big screens. More cell phones. More video games.
So much more technology. It is so lame.
These holiday villains just must be exposed.
Their criminal conduct's the cause of our woes.

We're weary. We're listless. We're often depressed.
We're angry. We're in debt. We're way overstressed.
And all the while famines and earthquakes and war
rob helpless young children of life like before.

No shelter. No supper. No sweet dreams at night.
No hope that injustices will be made right.
No parents. No siblings. No laughter. No time.
No chance for survival beyond eight or nine.

No lie. It's the truth. We are victims you see
of devious Greed and his partner Envy.
They're ruining Christmas and Hanukkah too.
But there's a solution. Three things we can do.

The first is to thank God for all that we own.
The second's to care for the needy we've known.
The third is to sponsor poor children abroad.
By sharing with orphans, we're honoring God.

Compassion, World Vision and, yes, World Concern
allow us to reach out to kids who've been burned
by random disasters that leveled their lives
reducing their childhood to hunger and sighs.

It's really amazing. By showing we care,
we'll lock up those bandits that cause our despair.
We'll find renewed freedom from unneeded stuff
and even the courage to shout out, "Enough!"

Enough of the shopping. Enough of the crowds.
Enough of more diddlies, for crying out loud.
Enough of just buying for family and friends.
Enough of this nonsense. It's time it all ends.

So as we light candles and ready our homes,
let's welcome the Presence that comes with shalom.
Let's listen for what in our hearts we might hear.
In candlelit silence, we find God. He's here.

Wanted Posters Needed in Church

The start of a new year is a time to reevaluate personal goals. For members of a faith community, it means determining what percentage the church or synagogue will receive in the way of regular contributions. For pastors and rabbis, the bottom line isn't always the bottom line. As important as one's financial gift may be, the contribution of time and involvement is a close second. It is the job of my colleagues and me to motivate members of our congregations to find meaningful ways to volunteer.

At our church staff meeting sometime back, the director of children's ministry lamented at how many volunteers were still needed to staff programs on the drawing board. Her voice wasn't the only one crying in the wilderness of congregational recruitment. The youth pastor chimed in and so did the coordinator of worship ministries. We all agreed that too many of our families involve their children (and themselves) in commitments that lack a spiritual payoff. I left the meeting contemplating the problem and determined to find an effective way to address it.

The following poem was the result of my creative brooding to be used in our church as a way of subtly calling attention to misplaced priorities in over committed lives. We ran it off on posters made to look like the "Wanted" signs in the old west and posted them around the church.

WANTED!

I saw a wanted poster at the church the other day.
It left me with a feeling that just wouldn't go away.
It listed opportunities for tithing of my time,
like helping toddlers learn to pray through finger plays and rhymes.
Like mentoring some teenagers or opening my home
or taking widows out to eat so they won't dine alone.

Like teaching in the Sunday school or singing in the choir,
or going on a missions trip with hammers, nails, and pliers.
The poster made me contemplate the ways I fill my week.
It caused me to review in prayer the schedule I keep.

Like driving kids to soccer, then to swim team or ballet,
to ball games every weekend and practice every day.
By working with the PTA and helping at the club,
I have no time to serve at church and that is... well... the rub.

Although I am quite busy now, I really must confess.
I'm not convinced that what I do is what God wants to bless.
I kind of think He wants me to reduce my frantic pace,
so I can volunteer at church and be a means of grace.

Although "wanted posters" are typically seen in post offices, churches would do well to tack them up in well-trafficked hallways. Not the kind that call attention to fugitives on the run, but those who are imprisoned by frantic lifestyles that lack fulfillment.

Intersections

The Circle of Life is More Than a Song

Those who know me well know I love to stand words on their heads. A perfect bumper sticker for my car would be "Puns are Fun!" My most recent play on words has to do with a soft drink and a hard place to live.

We all know that a cola is a beverage that refreshes. Akola, India, is a community in need of refreshment. In that impoverished industrialized city about the size of Seattle, severely handicapped individuals struggle to get around without the aid of a wheelchair.

Twenty-three local Rotarians traveled to Akola last month to offer the refreshment of friendship and to assemble and distribute lightweight wheelchairs provided by the Mercer Island Rotary Club. I smile just thinking about how the wheelchair mission to Akola came about.

Twenty-five years ago, Don Schoendorfer traveled with his wife in Morocco. This mechanical engineer from southern California saw people with gnarled limbs crawling on the ground. Returning to his comfortable life in Orange County, he couldn't forget what he had seen. Over the years, the images haunted him. In his spare time, he designed an experimental wheelchair in his garage.

Using resin patio chairs and mountain bike tires, he created a unique chair that could be assembled and shipped to third-world countries for less than fifty dollars per chair. Within a year, he quit his job, liquidated his savings and started a nonprofit organization with a goal to give away wheelchairs to twenty million handicapped people in developing nations. Today, Free Wheelchair Mission has served the needy in nearly one-hundred countries.

Reflections on Life and Faith

I met Don Schoendorfer three years ago when our family was preparing to move to the Seattle area from Chicago. Upon arriving, I challenged my new congregation to send chairs to the tsunami region of South Asia. Our church responded enthusiastically.

A year later, Schoendorfer visited Mercer Island. My colleagues in the Mercer Island Clergy Association had their interest piqued. More than a thousand wheelchairs were purchased to be distributed in war-ravaged Lebanon. The word spread. Members of Mercer Island Rotary who attend area congregations heard about it. Since this humanitarian effort resonated with Rotary's mission, they wanted to get involved. As a result, local Rotarians raised enough money (with matching grants) for an additional eleven hundred wheelchairs.

But that wasn't the end of it. Contacts with a Rotary club in Akola were made. The idea of a friendship trip was proposed. Twenty-three members offered to pay their own way and spend eighteen days in India to live in the homes of fellow Rotarians. In addition to viewing earth dams and visiting local schools, the highlight of the trip was to distribute wheelchairs.

I'm still smiling as I think of how one thing led to another. The wheels on lightweight inexpensive chairs that are now turning in India are the result of a wheel of creativity turning in the head of an engineer. He in turn got the wheels of mission moving among local churches on our Island. From there, Rotary got involved. And the interconnecting wheels continued to turn like gears.

If you know much about Rotary, you know that the logo of Rotary International is a wheel. Given the service club's name, you'd expect as much. But upon closer investigation, the Rotary logo is more than a circle or a wheel. It's a wheel with cogs all around the rim. Rotary's logo is a gear ready to engage another gear. That's very appropriate.

Rotary is at its best when it interacts with other humanitarian projects around the nation and the world. I like to think of it as the circle of life. A circle that turns in such a way that lame people find mobility.

Malnourished people are fed. Illiterate kids are educated. Unlike the memorable song in "The Lion King," the circle of life gears up to find

167

needs and fill them. It's a circle that rings our planet with tangible help and hope. When that circle of life turns, good things happen in people's lives across the street and around the world.

Reflections on Life and Faith

Pledging Allegiance Through Prayer

Three thousand years ago, a king of Israel recorded a promise from the God of Abraham, Isaac and Jacob. It was a welcomed word of hope to a nation with a checkered past when it came to honoring their Creator. Nonetheless, it was a promise that came with a specific condition.

The king must have had a quivering hand as he moved his quill across a scroll of parchment. After all, he was recording the words of the Almighty. Solomon wrote, *"If My people, who are called by My name, will humble themselves, and pray and seek My face, and turn from their wicked ways, then I will hear from heaven, and will forgive their sin and heal their land..."* (2 Chronicles 7:14)

According to this ancient text, the spiritual health of a nation is not without cause. It is the direct result of a sequence of events. Humility before God leads to prayer. A conscious reliance on God leads to repentance from wrong. The outcome is a sense of divine blessing.

Perhaps that's why Congress continues to begin its daily sessions with prayer. It is no doubt why concerned adults gather in places of worship on the National Day of Prayer on the first Thursday of May. Those dusty words from the Old Testament are no doubt why sanctuaries and synagogues were crowded in spontaneous prayer gatherings on September 11 seven years ago. It is why the Mercer Island Clergy Association came together for a service of remembrance and prayer when a gunman stole the lives of collegians at Virginia Tech eighteen months ago.

Eighteen years ago, another unique prayer gathering occurred that continues to be felt across the country and in our community. On

September 12, 1990, forty-five thousand high school students from a variety of church backgrounds in four different states met at their respective school flagpoles. The simple purpose of the gathering was to pray for the concerns of our country.

This student-run event that came to be known as "See You at the Pole" has become a cultural phenomenon. Its exponential growth is reflected in the number of communities where SYATP events take place and in the growing number of participants.

Last year, more than three million Christian students from every imaginable denominational stripe gathered at school flag poles before school in all fifty states. This unique expression of First Amendment rights is characterized by student-led prayer that focuses on the wellbeing of the nation.

This year, the "See You at the Pole" observance takes place around the country today, September 24. It is expected that students at both Mercer Island High School and Islander Middle School will participate. Following the protocol of other campuses, students will gather before the start of classes, circling the flagpole outside the front door.

Celebrating their religious freedom while welcoming diverse faith perspectives, the ecumenical group of Mercer Island teens will pledge their allegiance to the biblical truth preserved through Solomon's pen. They will simply call on God to guide our President, his cabinet and members of Congress, and for the protection of our troops overseas.

I applaud the courage of the students who will participate. It takes no small amount of courage to circle a flagpole and publicly pray (silently or aloud). As a member of the Mercer Island Clergy Association, I am thrilled that students from a variety of faith communities can put their theological differences aside in order to ask God to heal our land.

The poet is correct: *"In God We Trust's our only hope to have the confidence to cope. We stand most tall when on our knees we seek the Lord in prayer."*

Finding Common Ground

When my publisher approached me recently for endorsements toward my new book, *Rhymes and Reasons*, I had a challenge. I had to think of who I could ask to write a quote for the back cover. Since the book is a collection of poetic reflections on current events, name recognition was not enough. I wanted someone who breathed the atmosphere of popular culture.

I wanted someone who appreciated the artistic nature of the English language. Better yet, I wanted someone who valued the importance of faith while making sense of life. It didn't take me long to realize that the person who met those requirements was a friend living on Mercer Island. Gratefully, Michael Medved was most willing to write a testimonial for my book.

I'd known of Michael Medved's reputation as a film critic during the years when our family lived in the Midwest. What I didn't know was the place he called home. When a colleague in Chicago learned where our family was moving, he exclaimed, "Mercer Island? I think Michael Medved lives there!"

Never being labeled an introvert, I e-mailed Michael and asked if he would be willing to help me critique the religious landscape of greater Seattle. He invited me to sit in on one of his daily radio broadcasts once I'd moved to the Island. Following the three-hour show at the Lake Union Studio, we talked privately about the unique culture of the Pacific Northwest. Thus began an unlikely friendship between an Evangelical Christian and an Orthodox Jew.

Intersections

Over the past two-and-a-half years, that friendship has continued to grow. Wendy and I have been guests in the Medved home for dinner. Michael and I have enjoyed wine and cheese while discussing theology. He has attended worship services at Mercer Island Covenant Church, and I have attended Shabbat morning services at Congregation Shevet Achim. He has addressed one of our adult classes on the topic of redemptive themes and theological images in Hollywood films. I, in turn, have submitted original poetry to him that relates to some of the topics on his show.

Don't get me wrong. Michael and I don't see eye-to-eye on several theological points that each of us views as critical to our faith perspective. Neither do we agree on all things political. He is more conservative on some issues than I am and more liberal on others. But this year, when red states and blue states dominate the electoral spectrum, I find comfort in knowing that we both value the sacredness of God's green earth.

While most people are capable of color blindness in order to agree to disagree about candidates or policies, there are some issues that are just too black and white to bend on. Opposing litter is one of those issues for Michael and me. And for both of us, there is a theological basis to our bias. Both Judaism and Christianity celebrate the inexpressible beauty of creation and acknowledge the responsibility that the Creator has entrusted to us: caring for our world. As the psalmist declares, *"The earth is the Lord's and the fullness thereof." (Psalm 24:1)*

In all fairness to my friend, my passion for helping to rid our community of unwanted trash has been fueled by his example. Here is a man who practices what he preaches. I have lost count of how many times I have been driving down Island Crest Way and spotted Michael on an embankment of shrubs or a wooded path. gathering garbage that has been carelessly strewn by thoughtless passersby.

Seeing him at work with his "grabber" has motivated me to "go and do likewise." It's my hope that you will follow his example too.

Our Island is too beautiful a place to be blemished by Starbucks cups, Subway wrappers or Talking Rain bottles. Start carrying a plastic bag on your walk.

Who knows? You might meet a new friend in the process.

Intersections

Celebrating the Seniors Among Us

My eighty-one-year-old mother has a favorite expression as she contemplates growing older. *"Age is just a number ... and mine is unlisted."* While that may be a fun way to dodge admitting how old you are, I think there is merit in just eliminating the second half of the statement. Age is just a number. A person's length of life doesn't invite you to make broad-brushed assumptions.

Ken Lottis, my South-end Starbucks coffee mate, is seventy-two years old and has just signed a contract with a publisher for his first book. Nina Doornewerd, living independently at Covenant Shores, is in her late eighties and is still writing poetry. Retired construction executive Bill Dorsey is approaching his four-score anniversary running the human race. But he continues to lead two home-based Bible studies on the Island each week.

I continue to be inspired by a fellow Rotarian who answers to the name Ruth Brook. Ruth will celebrate her ninety-first birthday in a few weeks and continues to spend hours each day designing and creating custom greeting cards. Did I mention my aunt, Joyce Birkeland? This North Mercer resident is still teeing up her golf ball at Glendale Country Club even though she will soon celebrate her eighty-sixth birthday.

It would be one thing if the aforementioned folks were an exception. They are not. Mercer Island has a growing senior population and the vast majority of them continue to distinguish themselves as significant contributors to our community. Many have fascinating vocational pursuits and hobbies, not to mention stories that should be discovered and written. Fortunately, there is precedence for that sort of thing.

Reflections on Life and Faith

The Bible is replete with accounts of senior adults to whom the Almighty entrusted major assignments. Noah was conscripted to build the world's most famous boat long after his rowing years had passed. Sarah gave birth to a miracle baby when she was ninety. Jacob made a major move from Canaan to Goshen at an age when uprooting lox, stock and bagels was no easy task. Moses led the Israelites out of Egypt when he was eighty. Daniel survived his sleepover in the lions' den when he was about the same age.

In Psalm 90, Moses himself indicates the average age for the typical homosapien is between seventy and eighty. But there are numerous exceptions to that in Scripture and even more in our world, thanks to the advances of medical science. I recently heard that one insurance company consulting with Covenant Shores is looking (within the next couple of decades) to increase the projected life expectancy of future residents to one-hundred-ten years.

Unlisted or not, longevity appears in no hurry to pass away. In light of this reality, we would do well to celebrate what it represents and not pass it by.

A Heated Debate Over Tent City

"Have you heard the news coming out of Seattle? There's a Tent City on Poverty Rock? The haves and the have-nots have tied the knot." I can imagine Jay Leno or David Letterman having a field day with our town's most-talked-about topic on their late-night monologues.

But the issue of responding to the homeless is anything but laughable. It is a serious situation that calls for serious dialogue and sober reflection. If you canvass the community, you will no doubt be surprised by those who are willing to pound a stake into the ground in support of helping the homeless.

Nonetheless, this topic is one that has contributed to controversy and conversation. Pardon the pun, but the tensions surrounding Tent City are intense.

For members of faith communities rooted in a Judeo-Christian heritage, the intensity of responding to the homeless is compounded by what the Hebrew Scriptures have to say. We are not given a choice when it comes to assisting the poor. We are commanded to be compassionate no matter the cost. People of faith are consistently reminded that their ancestors were individuals deprived of a permanent home and forced to live a nomadic existence. Our spiritual grandfather, Abraham, was "a wandering Aramean."

Not long ago, I got a call from the head coach of the Seattle Seahawks. Mike Holmgren was preparing to speak at a prayer breakfast for governmental and business leaders in Seattle. Mike asked me to help him find an appropriate passage from the Bible that would illustrate the moral obligation that people of faith have to help the poor. I did some research and pointed the coach to Isaiah 58, in which the prophet Isaiah registers the Creator's heartbeat for the homeless and hungry.

"Is not this the kind of fasting I have chosen: to loose the chains of injustice and untie the cords of the yoke, to set the oppressed free and break every yoke? Is it not to share your food with the hungry and to provide the poor wanderer with shelter — when you see the naked, to clothe him and not to turn away from your own flesh and blood?" (Isaiah 58:6-7)

Subsequently, I have read and reread those verses. The context is this: God is challenging those who practice spiritual disciplines such as prayer and fasting to do more than do without. The ritual of fasting (foregoing a meal as a sacrificial offering) can become self-serving and lead to pride and arrogance.

Although there is a place for such observances, God suggests that a much more meaningful fast is to forego our normal routine of caring for ourselves in order to care for others. A God-honoring fast is not giving up but giving to. *"To provide the poor wanderer with shelter."*

"Not so fast," you might say. "That was then, but this is now." Exactly. That's my point. I believe Tent City is a tangible process whereby helpless yesterdays can be transformed into hopeful tomorrows.

Last month, I had a member of my congregation approach me and ask to be part of our church's Tent City task force. When I asked this well-to-do Island resident why she wanted to help, she told me her story.

When she was five her father died, leaving her mother with four little girls and a monthly income of less than one-hundred-fifty dollars. Her mother quickly remarried a man who frequently lost his job due to alcohol. They stayed in makeshift campgrounds, under bridges with other "campers," in decrepit motels, and slept in their station wagon for weeks at a time.

Today, Emily (not her real name) is a living example of one who survived homelessness and has become a contributing member of our community. She credits her faith, opportunities and people along the way who care for her. Her desire to flesh out the words of Isaiah 58 is rooted in memories of what it is like to be fearful, hungry and poor. It is also based in the knowledge that she can make a difference.

An Uncommon Friendship

It was quite a scene. A Greek-American pastor and a Russian Orthodox priest sitting in a Chinese restaurant on Mercer Island. The occasion was one last meal with The Reverend Doctor Samuel G. Sawitski, pastor of the Congregational Church on Mercer Island. After five years of ministry in our community, Sam has accepted a call to a congregation in suburban Phoenix, Arizona. Because my vacation would prevent me from attending his farewell celebration, I opted for a personal time to say goodbye.

As the eyes of the world turned toward the Summer Olympics in Beijing, my eyes studied the menu at our local Chinese restaurant. I finally decided on Mongolian Beef. So did Sam. Because there is so much about our lives that is different, I found no little joy knowing that we had ordered the same thing.

Over the past three years, I have grown to deeply appreciate my colleague with the flowing white beard who drives a dark green Jaguar and always dresses in black clerical apparel. Sam's unmistakable Russian accent requires that I listen carefully to what he communicates. But the effort in listening is well worth the effort. Hanging on his every word with the tenacity of an Olympic gymnast, I discovered just how different our life (and ministry) experiences have been.

While I grew up in a stable pastor's home, dabbled in public relations and broadcasting before going to seminary, have served four churches in three different states over the past thirty years and have written several books, Sam's vita is much more diverse and impressive.

Sam told me he was orphaned as a child in Russia. Before pursuing his undergraduate education and then attending seminary, he served in a special branch of the Russian military. After beginning his pastoral ministry in 1974, he did postgraduate work in psychiatry, earning licentiate in psycho-analysis, psycho-pathology, psycho-therapy and cognitive therapy.

While serving a Moscow congregation with a membership of five thousand, he also counseled drug addicts and social misfits. In addition, Sam moonlighted in the Kremlin as a master sculptor, stone carver and a restorer of icons, frescoes and murals. Amazing.

Sam informed me that he and his wife came to the United States in 1978 with their three children. Prior to coming to Mercer Island in 2003, he served a church in Nazareth, Pennsylvania that suffered a tragic fire. Concurrently, he also taught Ecclesiastical Art and Eastern Spirituality at Lehigh University near Philadelphia.

Whereas I combat stress by walking, playing golf, writing poetry or going to a movie, Sam's favorite ways of relaxing include yoga, becoming immersed in the contemplative prayers of the Church Fathers, practicing the martial arts and cooking gourmet meals.

As Sam and I manipulated our chopsticks and savored the beef and steamed rice, I realized what a special friend Sam has become despite our differences.

Whereas Sam and I do not see eye-to-eye on every nuance of Christian doctrine or ethics, we share more in common than a love of Mongolian Beef. We share a belief in a God who made the world and created humans with the need to have friends. My life is richer for having known Sam Sawitski.

Israel's most famous king once made an entry in his journal that reminds me of my friendship with Father Sam. It was King David who wrote in Psalm 119:63, *"I am a friend to all who fear you, to all who follow your precepts."* It is an entry that challenges me to reach out to those in my community who come at life differently than I do, yet who acknowledge the Creator.

In Praise of a Winter View

The past four months have been a meteorological phenomenon of astronomical proportions. In other words, this winter has been out of this world. And unlike the way we normally use that phrase, I'm not sure we'd all agree it was a good thing.

This year, contrary to what the calendar stated, winter started in November. That's when our state set a new record for the amount of rainfall in a single month. Then came the windstorm and blackout of December. In January and February, we dealt with snow and ice. Did I also mention the spell of frigid cold days when the family thermometer refused to climb up to the freezing mark? And what about those unprecedented numbers of snow days? Can we plan on combining an end-of-the-school-year party with a Fourth of July barbecue?

Viewing winter in the rearview mirror is bound to bring a smile to most of our faces. Whether we blame what we've been through on El Nino or Global Warming or an Old Man Winter that isn't as old and feeble as you might think, we are only too happy to welcome spring.

When we shopped for a home on Mercer Island, we noticed that several of the realtor descriptions boasted a "winter view of the lake" or a "winter view of the Seattle skyline." At the time, Wendy and I were clueless about what that meant. After our first winter, the meaning of that two-word phrase became obvious. Once the deciduous trees have disrobed until spring, you can see what otherwise is hidden. Our view of the world beyond our island is enhanced because of what happens to leaf-bearing trees during the winter.

This past season a "winter view" has come to mean something else to me. I'm thinking of how the challenges of the winter we endured have provided onlookers with a view of our island (and its residents) not normally seen. Winter tested our character and values big time. Those who observed what was going on had a view of who Mercer Islanders are when the chips are down. We are far more than upper middle-class suburbanites consumed with our private pursuits, affordable luxuries and personal stresses. We are people who bear the image of God as demonstrated by our genuine care and compassion for those in need.

During the week-long power outage, we helped each other by sharing portable generators with our neighbors. Those with gas-top stoves shared warm meals with those who could only barbecue on their outdoor grills. Extra bedrooms were made available to friends who couldn't escape to a hotel in Seattle. I can still see the line of down-coat-clad folks in the parking lot at the north-end grocery store. They were eating hotdogs and drinking hot cocoa, compliments of the store. But there was more than a spontaneous tailgate party going. There was authentic community — people sharing their stories of survival amid hearty laughs and empathetic nods.

I have a cousin in Norway who is known for his pithy sayings. One maxim attributed to him celebrates the advantages of maintaining a challenging exercise regimen. *"Plague your body or it will plague you."* Cousin Bjarne is also wont to say, *"Whether the weather is cold or whether the weather is hot, we'll weather the weather whatever the weather, whether we like it or not."*

And that's exactly what we did as a community of people from a myriad of faith backgrounds, various walks of life and an assorted array of professions. We weathered the weather together.

There is a proverb in the Old Testament that underscores what this past winter revealed in us. *"A friend loves at all times, And a brother is born for adversity." (Proverbs 17:17)*

Honoring Mother Earth

I remember when Earth Day was first established. It coincided with my eighteenth birthday. As my graduation from Wenatchee High School drew near, our senior class of 1970 was invited to contemplate the sacred nature of creation in an outdoor assembly. Crowded against the backdrop of the Vietnam War, the Kent State shootings and other anti-establishment protests, Earth Day mattered little to me. It was lost in the plethora of politically charged initiatives.

Now fast-forward thirty-seven years. Living on Mercer Island, I am keenly aware of the natural beauty Father God has birthed around us through Mother Nature. Spring is a season that heightens that beauty. The flowering rhododendrons and blossoming trees punctuate the theological doctrines of new birth and resurrection. Old things pass away. New things come. We are blessed to live in a virtual arboretum envied by the rest of the world.

Experiencing spring on our Island causes you to wonder if Elizabeth Barrett Browning wasn't walking through Pioneer Park when she was inspired to write *"Earth's crammed with heaven, and every common bush afire with God."*

My friend, Michael Medved, claims with a twinkle in his eye that Mercer Island is the Garden of Eden. Rabbi Daniel Lapin told me he views this corner of God's Kingdom as remarkably sacred.

Now, I know that not everybody sees the Creator's fingerprints in His handiwork that surrounds us. Did you happen to read that degrading description of our Island in "USA Today" a couple months back?

Describing the former home of Alan Mulally (new head of Ford Motor Company), the reporter called Mercer Island "a microcosm of millionaires, a verdant city littered with mansions, with Lake Washington serving as a moat on all sides."

Fortunately, such a jaded opinion is far from common. But for those of us who celebrate the incredible beauty of our community, we would do well to pause and consider our role in honoring the land that brackets our daily life with a sense of the Almighty.

Recognizing the mystery of the Creator's natural order does not automatically equate to taking responsibility to preserve it. Truly seeing the beauty of creation calls for an appropriate response. Browning's poem moves beyond simply acknowledging the glory of God in nature. She quickly adds, *"...only he who sees, takes off his shoes — the rest sit round it and pluck blackberries."*

No wonder Michael Medved isn't content to simply praise our Island as the crown jewel of God's creation. His knowledge calls him to action. Sincerely believing it is a pristine garden of sacred beauty, Michael can be seen picking up litter throughout Mercer Island. His determination to keep our Island clean is almost over-the-top. For Michael it is a spiritual mandate.

Recently, I was strolling down a trail near our home. Taking my cues from Michael, I was gathering all the garbage strewn alongside the path and in the bushes. Among the trash I accumulated was a crumpled and stained Starbucks cup. On the side of the cup was one of those "As I See It" quotes. This one was by former news anchor Tom Brokaw.

"It will do us little good to wire the world if we short-circuit our souls. There is no delete button for racism, poverty or sectarian violence. No keystroke can ever clean the air, save a river, preserve a forest. This transformational new technology must be an extension of our hearts as well as of our minds. The old rules still apply. Love your mother — Mother Earth."

I couldn't believe it. The disconnect was laughable. Brokaw's words obviously had fallen on deaf ears. The very thing he was calling for had become part of a growing dilemma.

Fortunately, we can make a difference. While the earth IS the Lord's and the glory thereof, he has entrusted us with privilege of being caretakers (and litter gatherers) of that which contains his glory.

Why not make this month's commemoration of Earth Day a holiday worth celebrating?

A Son's Tribute on Mother's Day

People of various faith traditions are tempted to celebrate their high holy days and then fail to embrace the meaning of those festivals the rest of the year. For example, we Christians typically don't contemplate the events of Good Friday once Easter has passed. When we fail to do that, we often don't see how the events of Holy Week speak to other lesser holidays.

Take Mothers' Day, for example. While reflecting on the death of Jesus, I made the following observations not long ago.

He'd been beaten and berated and then hung out to die. For six hours he'd endured searing pain while stretched on a cross beneath the blazing Middle Eastern sky. While his mother watched traumatized, Jesus bled profusely, losing vital body fluids. His tongue was noticeably swollen. His lips were parched.

And yet Jesus found the strength to speak to his close friend, John, who stood near his grieving mother. *"Here is your mother,"* Jesus sighed between his heaving breaths (John 19:27). His final words of instruction called John to care for his master's mother as if she were his.

On the cross we see not only a God who loved the world, but a son who loved his mother. His devotion for the one who gave him birth continued to beat in his breaking heart until he breathed his last. Amazingly, in front of skeptics, mockers and his executioners, Jesus used his ebbing strength to tell her so.

There is a bond between a son and his mom that defies simple explanation. Even though Jesus' relationship with Mary was a unique mother-son relationship, it is likely that his mother had nourished him in the ways of the heart. Mary would have faithfully nourished her son in the intangible qualities of love— tenderness, respect, courage, sensitivity and touch.

When I was an infant, my mother cradled me and sang the songs of faith as I drifted off to sleep. When I began to grow, she baked cakes for my birthdays. She sewed uniforms like the ones my sports heroes wore. She allowed me to dig backyard graves in which to bury birds, butterflies and squirrels.

As my values were being shaped, my mom helped me see treasures often hidden beneath the dust of discarded junk in a thrift store. Her probing questions would not allow me to live at odds with those with whom I did not get along.

My five-foot-two-inch mother taught me to never look down on those less fortunate than I and also to look up to those who had something to teach me (no matter their stature). Her love of music taught my soul to sing. Her sense of humor taught me how to laugh. My mother's intimate relationship with her heavenly father rubbed off on me. She taught me how to pray.

When my father suffered a near-fatal heart attack in 1990, I watched my little mother agonize over the possibility of widowhood. In the hospital waiting room I proudly observed the quiet dignity of the woman who had shaped my life and faith like none other.

As I witnessed her courage despite her fear, her hope fueled by her faith, and her undying devotion to my dad, I was overwhelmed with love. I shared her concern for my dad's survival, but my concern for her wellbeing was punctuated by my pounding heart.

It's no wonder that more long-distance calls are placed on Mother's Day than any other day of the year. There's a reason that when TV cameras pan professional football players on the sidelines, they are prone to wave to their mothers (read their lips!). Something deep within the heart of the most masculine man longs to pay tribute to the one who gave him birth and nurtured his life. So it stands to reason that Jesus would spend his depleted reserve of words to honor his mother.

When Faced with Other Faiths

Are you energized by those whose faith differs from yours? Or are you troubled by them? It's one thing to acknowledge religious diversity. It's quite another to embrace it and celebrate it. The reality of overlapping cultures within our community invites us to look beyond past differences and strive to understand those who live around us.

To that end, let me suggest a first-run film available at your local video distributor. "To End All Wars" is a low-budget movie that never hit the theaters on a national level because of financial constraints.

"To End All Wars" (starring Keifer Sutherland) is based on a true story set in Indo-China in the 1940s. It recalls the horrific experiences of a Scottish regiment in a Japanese-run prisoner-of-war camp during World War II. The graphic portrayal of war and POW abuse accounts for the film's R rating. It is about as gruesome as "Saving Private Ryan" or "Schindler's List." And although it is not a film for those easily disturbed by gut-wrenching realism, it is one that illustrates the universal tendency toward revenge and the untapped power of forgiveness.

The story centers on a soldier by the name of Ernest Gordon. Against the backdrop of the brutal confinement and forced labor at the hands of the Japanese, young Gordon helps to galvanize the hope of his beleaguered colleagues by instituting a jungle academy. Calling on the educational and life experience of his peers, this would-be teacher employs literature, philosophy, religion, poetry and music to create his unique curricula. In a truly unorthodox setting, Gordon proves how creatures easily motivated by hate can be humanized (even in the midst of war).

In real life Gordon becomes the Dean of the Chapel at Princeton University following his eventual release. It is a position he holds for the better part of three decades. His preparation for such a prestigious and influential calling was more than a seminary degree attained once he returned home to Scotland following the war. What he brought to his post was primarily the result of what he learned and modeled in the cauldron of injustice where he saw sacrificial love lived out before his eyes.

"To End All Wars" is a movie that challenges how we go about trying to convince others what fits our faith is worth trying on. In terms of what I've observed in my faith tradition, the principles of the Christian faith are often reduced to predictable words that have a religious-sounding ring to them.

Familiar phrases clothed in a Sunday-morning wardrobe are prejudged as unfashionable by a sermon-saturated culture. The mere fact that the preacher speaks the words (that might very well be life-changing), limits the degree to which those who hear him or her actually listen.

The themes of love, forgiveness and redemption are visually dramatized in "To End All Wars." The director (David Cunningham) has done such a brilliant job these core elements of Christianity cannot be easily dismissed or misunderstood. As I watched this poignant video recently, I found myself being pinned to the mat by the principles of Jesus. Although it is not a religious film, its challenge to understand and love those different from us (even those who have wronged us) is nonetheless deeply spiritual.

As an Evangelical pastor, I was at once inspired and humbled by "To End All Wars." Although the portrayal of undeserved mercy brought tears to my eyes, the film reminded me that religious truth is not always best conveyed by conventional means.

That's what celebrated poet Edgar Guest observed decades ago when he mused, *"I'd rather see a sermon than hear one any day."* In this remarkable film we are shown the way of love rather than being lectured about it. It's a persuasive device even Jesus endorsed. He's the one who said, *"Your love for one another will prove to the world that you are my disciples."* (John 13:35 NLT)

Reflections on Life and Faith

Listening to Freedom's Cry
Why Independence Day and Labor Day are the same

*The birth cry of Freedom heard so loudly at first
from a baby delivered in pain
can't be heard by deaf ears in a nation at risk
that ignores those first sounds to its shame.*

*What once moved us with passion in decades long past
doesn't grip us the way that it did.
Seems our hearts rarely race while saluting the flag
like when pledging allegiance as kids.*

*And the right to assemble, to worship and vote
has become commonplace in our minds.
To the fact that we're privileged to do what we do
we're clueless and too often blind.*

*We all take wealth for granted. We think we're still poor.
We forget that most all of the earth
tends to struggle with basics to just stay alive
while we minimize what we are worth.*

*It seems we have forgotten the Fourth of July
isn't just an excuse to have fun.
In addition to hot dogs and cold Mac and Jacks
on the lake in the warm summer sun,*

*We have good cause to gather with family and friends
and thank God for the land of the free,
for all veterans who served to assure us the right
to both practice and prize liberty.*

Intersections

*For the numberless options and chances to choose
where to live, what to eat and to wear,
for the laws that protect us from what is corrupt
and that shield us from what isn't fair.*

*For the peace on our home front and allies abroad
and for soldiers who willingly fight
against forces of terror with suicide bombs
who are dead-set against human rights.*

*Let us thank God for Freedom birthed so long ago
and the labor preceding her cry.
Let us ask Him to help us again hear her voice
amid fireworks in the night sky.*

Parenting Lessons

I forget who warned me not to blink. But I now realize it was someone who knew what he was talking about. How I wish I had heeded his caution. But, alas, I didn't.

In the millisecond it takes an eyelid to flutter shut and reopen, the unexpected occurred. A little life fresh from heaven became a college freshman.

It happened six years ago, but it seems like only yesterday. The emotions of that unforgettable day are deeply engraved in my heart. For four hours I drove home to Chicago from Holland, Michigan, and wiped tears from my eyes.

After depositing my firstborn daughter on the steps of her college dormitory, I began making withdrawal after withdrawal from a memory bank I'd opened eighteen years before. I could have sworn it was only the year before I was driving my bright-eyed, black-haired baby girl home from the hospital. I can still see her snuggled in her car seat next to my wife. Yep, my eyes were leaking that day, too. *Blink*.

Where did those six years go? Before I knew it, I was chauffeuring Kristin to her first day of first grade. *Blink*.

I'm absolutely positive that only a week passed before I was toting that little third-grader to Bible camp for her first taste of life away from home. *Blink*. And wasn't it only yesterday when I drove her to the DMV on her sixteenth birthday to get her long-awaited driver's license? *Blink*.

Memories flooded my mind as I blinked back tears that filled my eyes. Drives to the doctor. Drives to Nana's house. Drives to church, soccer games and the mall. And there I was, once again, on the road behind the wheel. But this time was different. A certain someone wasn't in her seat. I had left her in a strange room two states away.

Okay, I'll admit it. It wasn't the first time I got a lump in my throat and had to reach for the Kleenex box. That happened plenty of times when my "baby" began to exercise small steps of independence. Her first babysitting job. Her first date. Her first job at camp that took her away from home all summer.

But somehow that first year at college was the hardest by far. My goodness. That long drive home without Kristin in the car caused me to reflect on more than memories. I glanced in the rearview mirror and noticed more regrets than I wished. Why had I insisted on spending so much time at the office when I could have been home with her and her sisters? Why had I watched baseball on TV instead of playing catch in the backyard? Why hadn't I been more willing to spend time on the floor playing instead of sitting in my easy chair reading Time magazine?

Parenting is tough business. It calls for the balance and courage of a tightrope walker in a circus between blinks. In my opinion, it is the most difficult and rewarding occupation there is. It is the source of intense pain and incredible joy. And sadly, it seems we learn what it takes to be effective much too late in the process.

When opportunities are made available whereby parents can get a running start at doing it right, we should seize them with gratitude.

Becoming Soulmates

Ever since I started collecting baseball cards as a kid, I've been a saver. Stacks of journals and periodicals clutter my desk. In fact, every available flat surface in my home office holds some memorabilia: trophies, figurines, bookends. The walls are covered with photos, artwork and plaques. This museum of memories surrounds me with emotional warmth and security and fuels my creativity.

Wendy's idea of a perfect home is one that is utilitarian, easily cleaned and tidy. I do appreciate her penchant for keeping order; our home is always company-ready. But we clash over the definition of "neat and tidy." She grew up on the mission field, where her parents celebrated the twin virtues of simplicity and order. Because they didn't have money for nonessentials (and little space for what they did need), they made the most out of very little room. What couldn't fit on a bookshelf or in a cupboard was tossed out or given away.

When Wendy and I started to date in our late twenties, she was attracted to my creativity. She appreciated how I viewed people and things from a different perspective. But she didn't realize that my penchant for turning life on its side meant there would be other things I wouldn't store in their appropriate places. She hadn't bargained on all the baggage you claim when you marry a creative soul.

In addition to not wanting "stuff" on every horizontal surface, Wendy has a real problem with second-hand items. And those who know me well know how much I love garage sailing and thrift-store hopping. As a kid, Wendy had to dip into the missionary barrel for recycled clothes and toys more often than she'd like to recall. She detests recycled items.

After twenty-five years, we still don't always see eye-to-eye on the appropriate use of domestic space or where we buy what fills that space. But since we are committed to submitting to each other in love, we have agreed to define "orderliness" more loosely.

Wendy gives me the freedom to arrange my home office the way I want. She recognizes that I need to be surrounded by symbols of my eclectic world. But she still shakes her head when she attempts to dust all my stuff. In turn, I refrain from cluttering up other rooms of the house. (Well, I'm trying.)

Another way we have minimized our conflict over clutter is by decorating for holidays. We put up decorations on Valentine's Day, Presidents' Day, St. Patrick's Day, Easter, the Fourth of July, Columbus Day, Halloween, Thanksgiving and Christmas. We even use special events like birthdays, anniversaries, the Super Bowl and the World Series as occasions for creating a thematic display on the fireplace mantel. I am in heaven when I can invade Wendy's spartan space with what she defines as "acceptable short-term clutter."

Wendy and I are polar opposites when it comes to our personalities and our perspectives on many things. All the same, we are each other's best friend. Marriage guru Chuck Snyder titled one of his books *"Incompatibility; Grounds for a Great Marriage."* More than a clever title, it's the truth. The twenty-five years Wendy and I have invested as wife and husband are tangible proof. Our diversity has given way to a healthy reliance on each other. We complement each other. Wendy and I are soulmates.

But I'd be the first to confess we are still fine-tuning our relationship and learning how to serve one another, give in and compromise. It's a good thing marriage lasts till death do us part. We'll need that long to get it right.

By George, It's Lent!

I don't know about you, but I have a number of Georges in my life. There's George Bailey, George Toles, George Munzing, George Warren, George Harper, George Duff, George Haas, George Castle, George Storto, George Minerva, and George Chambers. I actually have three who are members of my church on the Island. Not bad for a name that isn't all that popular anymore. When's the last time you heard of a baby being named George?

This month one of our country's most famous Georges celebrated a memorable birthday. No, I'm not referring to either George Herbert Walker Bush or George Walker Bush. And while the father of our country qualifies (we just marked the 277th anniversary of his birth), I'm not referring to George Washington either.

On February 1 of this year, George Shea turned one hundred years old. "Who is he, for Heaven's sake?" you might ask. Well, that's a most appropriate question. If you were to ask this George what his purpose in life has been, he'd likely respond, *"Helping people I've never met prepare for Heaven when they reach the end of their life."* Actually, even though he has lived in the United States all but a few of his century of years, this George was born in Winchester, Ontario.

Still aren't sure who this famous George is? Perhaps it would help if I mentioned his middle name. BEVERLY. That's right. George Beverly Shea, the resonate baritone soloist of the Billy Graham Evangelistic Association, reached that historic milestone this month. He is ten years older than his more well-known colleague.

Intersections

I've never met George Beverly Shea, although I did work at the same Chicago radio station where he got his start in broadcasting. I have heard him sing in person on more than one occasion, however. Believe it or not, this remarkable man can still belt out a gospel song when most people his age can't blow out half the candles on their birthday cake.

Now, I'd be the first to admit that George Beverly Shea's style is not my favorite. I prefer something a bit more upbeat. But I am attracted to something about him I don't see much of anymore. Even though he doesn't own a violin, George's amazingly long career has found him content to play second fiddle.

For over sixty years, George has stood up in sports arenas and stadiums around the world to sing a song or two just before Billy Graham speaks. Although he has been very good at what he does, the purpose of his "doings" has never been to achieve a name for himself. This rather shy and introverted vocalist found fulfillment being a forerunner for a more famous communicator.

As with John the Baptist, who retreated into the shadows when Jesus came onto the scene, George's life has been similarly defined. He found fulfillment setting the stage for the one on whom the spotlight would be aimed to get the credit.

For Christians on Mercer Island and around the world, today is Ash Wednesday. It marks the beginning of a forty-day journey to Easter Sunday commonly called Lent. The Lenten adventure is an invitation to self-denial. Some give up meat. Some deny themselves caffeine or alcohol. Others go without television or sweets.

As I contemplate the life and legacy of George Beverly Shea, I'd throw out another way to embrace the concept of self-sacrifice. What about focusing on others and allowing them to get the credit instead of grabbing for the glory yourself?

Reflections on Life and Faith

Praying for Our New President

Last week, I watched Pastor Rick Warren and Rev. Joseph Lowery bookend the Inauguration ceremonies in prayer. As I contemplated from my living room what it would be like to be given such a unique opportunity, I realized I already knew. Well, sort of.

Several years ago my family lived in a Chicago suburb. A state senator friend invited me to give the invocation at the Illinois capital in Springfield. I was humbled and honored. Although the scenario paled in significance to what Pastor Warren or Rev. Lowery experienced, I felt honored. At the podium, I called on the Creator to guide the senators and to give them a sensitivity to His will as they served their constituencies.

Three months later, I walked with my senator-friend in an old-fashioned Fourth of July parade. At the conclusion of the parade, Peter said that he wanted to introduce me to one of his fellow senators. "Here's someone with as unusual a name as yours," Peter said to the tall, forty-something black man. "Barack Obama, meet Greg Asimakoupoulos."

The handsome young politician extended his hand. As I shook it, he inquired about the ethnic origin of my last name. I asked about his. After exchanging pleasantries, our brief meeting was over. A few years later when Obama won his race for the U.S. Senate, it dawned on me that he had likely been in the Senate chamber when I gave my prayer.

Even though Pastors Warren and Lowery's assignments last Tuesday remain the envy of most clergymen in America, I can claim to have prayed over Barack Obama in a much-less-publicized setting. But that is not the last time I prayed for him. I pray for him on a regular basis both in church and at home. In fact, I composed my own prayer for Mr. Obama as the events of the Inauguration played out last week. Sitting in front of both the television and my laptop, I typed:

God, bless America as You bless the new President America inaugurates today. As he pledges allegiance to Old Glory, be glorified through his admission that we are indeed one nation under You. As he listens to Your servants, Rick Warren and Joseph Lowery, pray over the proceedings of this day, help him hear Your heart beating with concern for righteousness, justice and compassion. As he lays his hand upon Your Word and takes an oath of faithfulness, lay Your hand upon his life and remind Him of Your promises to be faithful to all who dare to honor You.

As he stands to address those who look to him as Commander-in-Chief, stand beside him and remind him that he has been seated in this place of honor and responsibility by You alone. As You bless Barack Hussein Obama with a tangible sense of Your presence, God, bless America. Amen.

It is likely that you, too, prayed for our lanky Lincoln-esque leader that day (or in the days that followed). A Web site known as The Presidential Prayer Team (www.presidentialprayerteam.org) documents that hundreds of thousands of Americans regularly approach the Almighty on behalf of those who guide our nation.

No, Rick Warren and Joseph Lowery are not the only ones who have the privilege of praying for our new President. We all have that privilege. Having a seminary education or wearing a liturgical robe is not a prerequisite. Regardless of your background, religious preference or occupation, you have the right and privilege to approach Almighty God on behalf of President Obama.

Reflections on Life and Faith

My Favorite Holiday

Thanksgiving is a holiday for which I am truly thankful. For one thing, it is a holiday that isn't defined by commercialism. There is no expectation to buy presents. No decorations are required. Primetime television programs aren't preempted by holiday specials. And you don't have to endure nonstop seasonal music on radio stations for weeks beforehand.

I also appreciate the fact that this holiday primarily takes place at the family dinner table. It is family-based and food-focused. Kids come home from college for an extra-long weekend. Grandparents fly in for their annual grandchildren fix. Uncles, aunts and cousins drive from across town with video games and camcorders. All arrive with healthy appetites.

I love the way that Thanksgiving brings relatives together. In spite of the dysfunctions that characterize every family system, each home is furnished with an abundance of blessings. What unites people who share a common name, common ancestors and common memories is often under-appreciated. We fail to recognize the unique privilege of swinging from the same limb of an age-old family tree. Gratefully, the Thanksgiving table provides a priceless opportunity to reflect on gifts of shelter, employment, health and prized possessions.

In an increasing number of homes, there will be an empty chair at the family table tomorrow — a son away at war, an aunt in a recovery program, a brother having to work, a grandmother in an intensive-care unit, a daughter who is estranged.

Intersections

There will be an empty place at our table. It is the one ordinarily filled by my kids' Papou. After a fourteen-year battle with cancer, my dad died earlier this month. The chair normally positioned next to Nana will be replaced by the sofa-sized lump in my throat. My dad's absence will trigger tears. But there will also be laughter, knowing glances and smiles as remembrances are recalled of a man who can never be replaced.

Thanksgiving gives me a chance to toast my dad and his remarkable achievement in his role of patriarch. In addition to the box of Kleenex, there will also be a treasure chest of memories. Recognizing the empty chairs at your family table, Thanksgiving is a rare opportunity to say well-done for those of whom you are proud.

But there is yet another reason why I am particularly grateful for Thanksgiving. It is an equal-opportunity holiday. Whereas Jews lay claim to Yom Kipper and Hanukkah, and Christians own both Christmas and Easter, Thanksgiving is not a respecter of any one particular religion. Muslims celebrate it; Buddhists do, too. And while some Hindus may insist on a vegetarian feast, they don't have to ignore the fourth Thursday of November.

The major religions of the world verbalize a core value of gratitude. The need to say thanks to the Creator is at the heart of being human. It is more than a matter of good manners. Saying "thank you" is a matter of great importance. By giving thanks, we voice a declaration of dependence on the Almighty and embrace a proper estimation of ourselves. Thanksgiving motivates humility. When we express appreciation for what we undeservedly have or receive, we cut and serve ourselves a slice of humble pie.

Initial Ponderings of a New Pastor

Beginning a new ministry in a new community is a memorable experience. Believe me, I know. Take eleven years ago when we relocated from a church on the West Coast to the Midwest.

My family and I moved from the warm sun-drenched hills of Northern California to the drab flatlands of Illinois. As our moving van unloaded in the western suburbs of Chicago on Halloween, my wife and I wondered what we'd gotten ourselves into. We were ready to turn around and head back west.

No, it wasn't the miniature goblins and ghosts at the front door that scared us off. It was the weather: sleet and snow and frigid wind. Our three little girls traipsed out to go trick or treating in tears. Not only did they not know anyone from whom they would be soliciting candy, they had to cover their costumes with down jackets.

Our move to Mercer Island will prove just as memorable, but for different reasons. Having grown up in Washington State, Seattle weather is not that big of a deal. Quite honestly, after enduring stifling humidity, tornado warnings and thunderstorms of summer (not to mention the bone-chilling cold, colorless stick trees and snowstorms of winter), the moderate climate of the Pacific Northwest is a welcome relief. What makes my arrival at Mercer Island Covenant Church something I will long remember is my ability to predict the atmospheric conditions not reported by the local television meteorologists.

For one thing, there is the peaceful (and exciting) calm of a new day. Pastoral ministry is hardly new to me. Since 1979 I've served three congregations in three states. But for the past eight years I have channeled my skills as a pastor through the conduit of Christian publishing.

In addition to authoring books and writing magazine articles, I've traveled the country helping pastors discover ways to be more creative in their worship planning and more relevant in their preaching. But now I once again have the privilege of putting those principles into practice in a local church. The dawn of this new opportunity finds me energized while basking in the welcoming glow of a congregation happy to finally have a new shepherd.

Still there are the inevitable winds of change that accompany any pastoral transition. Ministers who blow in from the Windy City aren't the only ones who have a Chinook-like influence. Every new pastor brings new ideas. New pastors bring a new set of eyes with which to view what congregations have long since failed to view objectively. I've been in the ministry long enough to know that even a different person doing the same things can give the impression that something isn't quite right. All change, like the tornados in the Midwest, is frightening and unwelcome. My challenge is to be a change agent without causing the storm siren to go off.

Then there are the clouds that creep across the congregational sky. Some are harmless. They simply reflect legitimate questions and concerns that are blown in by the winds of change. At fifty-three years old, I welcome such feedback more than I did as rookie pastor on Queen Anne Hill. Back then I tended to be defensive and threatened. Today I'm less ambitious and more concerned about what those critical comments might represent.

All the same, I am prepared for the kind of clouds that are dark and angry — that overshadow the joys of connecting people to their Creator. My experience as a pastor alerts me to the fact that I don't need a weather forecast to know such clouds are coming. It's only a matter of time. Although I'm an experienced shepherd, I'd be the first to admit I'm not a perfect one. Neither am I one that everyone will relate to. As I enjoy the fair skies of what is often called the "honeymoon" period of a new ministry, I'm asking God to help me be loving and sensitive to those who are bound to inform me that my style just doesn't meet their needs.

Finally, there are the clouds I'd simply call congregational overcast. Few highs. Few lows. Just taking each day as it comes as a gift from God. It doesn't take long being back in the Emerald City to realize how many gray days it takes to give Seattle its colorful designation. Weather-wise, in our area, cloudy days are normal days.

As I begin my new ministry on the Island, I'm grateful that the same is true for churches. The intensity and emotional glow of being called and installed at a church feels great. All the same, I wouldn't want to live on that emotional high all the time. It's draining.

In all honesty, I look forward to three months from now when we're finally settled in our new residence, I've got a handle on names and faces and invitations aren't as frequent to have the new pastor and his family over for dinner. Come November I'll be wearing a pullover to cover the fifteen additional pounds around my middle, but also because Seattle weather will be typically overcast and a tad bit chilly.

You see, even for new pastors, getting to normal is a desired destination. Yes, there is something good about sweater weather.

Intersections

In Search of the Christmas Beast

You've heard of the Grinch, and the havoc he wraeaked;
No Christmas was safe from that furry green freak.
But are you aware of the beast that lives here?
He robs, steals and ruins our holiday cheer.

While Who-ville was home to that classic Seuss tome,
the-ville of this saga is where we call home.
The Christmastime villain that I have in mind
isn't furrish or greenish. And that's why we're blind.

He lives in a place where we aren't prone to look.
And because we're not looking, he's safe in his nook.
We don't see his fingers, but we feel him pryin'.
That sly impish villain's consistently lyin'.

He says what we have isn't nearly enough.
He says we're deservin' of more and more stuff.
He says we're entitled. We've earned it. It's ours.
More trinkets and baubles and jewelry and cars.

We always want better. We always want more.
And though we're quite wealthy, he makes us feel poor.
Unlike thieves who rob us and take what we own,
the villain who's stealin' adds more to our homes.

Reflections on Life and Faith

*He fills up our houses with more things to dust
and while we're distracted our joy bank goes bust.
We act like we love it. We smile through the pain.
Yet deep down we're crying. We know who's to blame.*

*This villain is vicious. He's heartless and cruel.
He knows how to fool us. He's got just the tool.
He tinkers and twiddles and wows us with new.
He weeds out what still works and claims it is through.*

*And after he's weeded he steals all our peace.
And though we have surplus, we feel we've been fleeced.
It's really quite awful, it's terribly bad.
Our hearts have been ransacked and that's why we're sad.*

*Our MERRY's been taken. Now Christmas is plain.
What once seemed like magic is now just a game.
What once made us happy and grateful is gone.
Instead we've a hunger that goes on and on.*

*It's true. We're in danger. It's time we took aim.
But what does he look like. And what is his name?
We'd best change our locks and install an alarm.
Perhaps ammunition will keep us from harm.*

*But lest you start looking for ways of protection,
Just look in the mirror. You'll see his reflection.
You see Christmas villains are inside us each
in spite of our actions, in spite of our speech.*

*Beneath our nice wardrobes and new SUVs,
these menaces hide so that nobody sees.
Like worms or a virus within our PC,
those villains within us just do as they please.*

Intersections

We're greedy and selfish and never content.
And based on the Bible, that's why we were sent
a Savior to save us from gangrenous greed.
To show us firsthand how to help those in need.

By giving, not getting, we'll find what we've lost.
And though it is costly, it's well worth the cost.
Our long-missing MERRY will soon reappear.
The villain will vanish at least till next year.

He'll flee from our overstuffed homes in a flash,
if he finds we're giving the needy our cash.
So let's count our blessings and put others first.
Our hearts will keep growing till they almost burst.

Reflections on Life and Faith

A Recipe for a Grateful Heart

My ability to write books is not matched by my ability to read a cookbook. My wife and three daughters will attest to that. Except for popping corn and blending chocolate milk shakes, most of my efforts in the kitchen taste like mistakes.

But don't be too quick to label me as a liability when it comes to preparing for the family Thanksgiving feast. In the five decades of life in which I've had the opportunity to digest my share of what the Lord has served up in my life, I've discovered a fail-proof recipe for a grateful heart.

First, crush a bunch of sour grapes for all the times you've felt someone else got credit for something you deserved. Drizzle in a drop of spilled milk for every remembrance you have of something you wish you could undo (no need to cry over it). Even though you may be tempted to, refrain from adding the "whine" you keep in the cellar for those pity parties you occasionally throw for yourself.

To this rather unattractive concoction, sift in some flavorful thoughts that come to mind of times when God was kind and bailed you out. You know the times I mean: when you were in real hot water and had real doubts whether or not you could stand up to the heat.

Then, while this mixture is sitting at room temperature, take some "thyme" alone and thoroughly measure out your blessings. Make sure you add in the plain vanilla ones (like health, shelter, employment, family, enough to eat and a good night's sleep).

Don't forget to spoon up some sweet remembrances of happy days gone by. With your honey at your side, go to a quiet part of the house and pour out what's on your mind. If necessary, ask for forgiveness.

While bringing the ingredients to a boil, combine a cup full of contentment, all the while skimming off any envy or greed that surface. Blend well.

Let the aforementioned batter rise until it occupies a place of prominence in your thinking. Preheat your heart to the point where it takes on a pliable consistency. While your will is warming to the idea of thanking God (instead of blaming him) for where you are at this time in your life, sprinkle the mixture in question with a dash of determination to do whatever it takes to honor God with your attitude.

Then bake the combined ingredients until they are well done. While it is still warm, serve yourself the "peace" you've anticipated, all the while chewing on God's goodness while swallowing your pride.

Well, there you have it. Even though you haven't seen this recipe demonstrated on the Food Network, it's a keeper. A grateful heart is guaranteed.

You don't need to be a Galloping Gourmet in order to serve up an aroma that will be pleasing to the Lord. All that is required is that you dismount from your high horse of self-centeredness and sit in the presence of the One from whom all blessings flow. As Israel's greatest king is credited with having said, *"Taste and see that the Lord is good."* (Psalm 34:8)

Death Reminds Us to Embrace Life

Consider the irony of the colorful fall leaves that are beginning to grace our Island. What fills us with wonder are actually dead leaves. Imagine that. There is actually beauty and amazement in death!

This past year, my life has been punctuated by death. Last November, my father died. A month later, my barber's wife passed away. Three months after that, my mom's only surviving sibling succumbed to Alzheimer's. In addition, I have lost several friends in Rotary to death this year.

This past Saturday, I attended the memorial service for Reverend Bill Clements of Redeemer Lutheran Church. As a member of MICA (Mercer Island Clergy Association), Bill enriched the lives of countless faith leaders in our community in remarkable ways. Because Bill was my age, his untimely death has been particularly sobering.

Thirty years as a minister has forced me to realize that death shows up unannounced quite often. We have no guarantee that we will wake up tomorrow. Whenever I am leading a liturgy for mourners gathered to pay their last respects, I remind them: *"Every memorial service we attend is one closer to our own."*

No matter how successful we become at buying, selling, trading and owning, our ultimate net worth is eventually reduced to a final figure. Death reveals that bottom line. Curiously, it is not a financial figure. It is a solitary figure that is incapable of movement, breathing or speaking. It is a human figure who has lost its ability to make peace with God or anyone else.

No matter how many hours we may spend at the gym each week, we cannot escape the fact that our days are numbered. Like the slogan I once saw on a bumper sticker: *"Physically fit people just die healthier."* There is no getting around it. The grim reaper eventually stops in front of our house, the hospital or the health club.

All the same, it has become my conviction that death loses its ability to derail us emotionally to the degree that we anticipate it and embrace it as an inevitable part of life. When we recognize our mortality and that of those whom we care about, we have the choice to make the most of the time we (or they) have left.

Similarly, we have the choice to tell those whom we love that we do. We have the choice to change behaviors or revise priorities that limit our ability to fully live "in the present." We have the choice to incorporate faith into life's equation so that the meaning of death is not limited to our understanding alone. In other words, how we embrace the inevitability of death is up to us. The buck stops here!

Three weeks ago, my wife and I were walking on Island Crest Way. As we passed Redeemer Lutheran Church, I looked up toward the sign on which Bill Clements routinely placed poignant and clever messages. To my amazement, there was a young buck with a small rack of antlers crowning his head. Knowing Pastor Bill was nearing the end of his earthly journey, the fact that the buck had stopped here invited reflection. Could it be the deer at the sign was in fact a sign?

As I thought of my friend and his faithful ministry, I celebrated the fact that life is filled with the unexpected. There is the unexpected nature of failure and joblessness and suffering and death as well as the unexpected nature of God's grace that allows us to deal with the unexpected setbacks and apparent defeats.

Yes, I believe God is attempting to speak to us through the predictability of fall colors and the unpredictability of a solitary deer standing near a sign. The question is: Are we listening?

Cheap Dates with Rich Rewards

Sadly, the cost associated with a growing marriage is not immune from inflation. Dinners out add up. So do tickets for a day on the slopes, a night at the movies or a weekend at the beach. When you are paying off your kids' college tuition, financing remodeling projects in an aging home and constantly quenching your car's thirst for gasoline, money for dates can be limited (especially in this economy). Fortunately, fun times with your mate need not require a small fortune.

Using One Car

Once home from work, there are always errands that need to be run. It's not uncommon to need milk and eggs from the supermarket, paint from the hardware store, prescriptions from the pharmacy and dry cleaning that's ready. Rather than dividing up the to-do list and taking our individual cars, it's kind of fun to run errands together while listening to our favorite radio station. Doing errands together saves gas. Besides, when we're done, we stop at McDonald's for a dollar cone.

Killing Two Birds

As Wendy and I entered our fifties, we recognized our tendency to gain weight while eating modest amounts. Our metabolisms had changed. Counting calories wasn't sufficient. We needed to add a regular exercise regimen to our daily routines. Membership at a health club wasn't necessary. We decided to start walking in our suburban neighborhood. Going at a brisk clip, we could cover almost three miles and burn quite a few calories in just forty-five minutes. Away from the demands of home and the office, we had time to simply focus on each other. Our bodies and our relationship were being toned up without spending a dime. Not only did we work up a sweat, but we brought up hopes and concerns that we had for our grown girls and aging parents. We held hands and prayed aloud while taking our route in stride.

Drinking Three Cups of Tea

"Three Cups of Tea" is more than a best-selling book about an American mountain climber in Nepal. It also describes a favorite thing that Wendy and I do on a lazy Saturday. We head to an older part of town where local growers and artisans market their fruit, flowers and crafts. We stroll by the stalls, chatting with the vendors and nibbling on the free samples.

It's a rare day that we buy anything, but without fail we find a little shop that sells loose tea and kitchen gadgets. Inside is a dispenser of hot spiced tea with an invitation to try a free cup. It's a tradition for each of us to enjoy a cup. Since I drink faster than my bride of twenty-seven years, I pour a second cup.

Splitting Four-Egg Omelets

Ever since we started courting, Wendy and I have enjoyed eating out. Early on, we discovered that breakfasts are the least expensive meals in a restaurant. What makes such occasions even more affordable is splitting meals. Four-egg omelets are large enough to share (since we are watching our weight). We love visiting a variety of early morning eateries, pretending to be restaurant reviewers. In addition to judging the entrees and the coffee (we're picky), we look back on the events of the past week and evaluate the way that we spent our time at work and at home.

Taking Five with the Father

Because faith is a huge part of our lives, Wendy and I include Someone else in our special times together. We take time to pray together while sipping our first cup of coffee in the morning. As we continue to launch our young-adult daughters while caring for our aging parents (not to mention the needs of a growing congregation), we realize that we can't do it alone. Life is too hard and complicated to attempt without spending a few minutes in prayer with the Creator.

On Unexpected Unemployment

How does it feel to be laid off? If you can't answer that question yourself, there's a good chance you know someone who can. Countless numbers of people in our community understand what it's like to be unexpectedly unemployed ... including me. After two decades of pastoral ministry, I went to work for a parachurch organization in 1997. I enjoyed the change of pace. What is more, I loved my work. But the financial downturn in the economy following September 11 took its toll. I was let go without any notice. I tried to process my anger and emotional pain in the pages of my journal.

When you lose your job, you feel like Job.
It seems that you've lost it all.
The world looks gray and colorless,
and tastes like bitter gall.

You seek the Lord, but He won't speak.
You lose your will to pray.
And when your "good" friends try to help,
you wish they'd go away.

Quite insecure, you doubt your worth.
You try in vain to hope.
You feel alone. You feel afraid
(without the means to cope).

It's so unfair to be laid off.
You gave your heart and soul.
While others loafed, you sacrificed
to reach your boss's goal.

Your sleep declines. Your bills add up.
Resentment stays the same.
You don't know what or who to call.
You don't know where to aim.
No business card. No payroll check.
You have no place to go.
Without a job in where you live,
you're just a big "zero."

What made my episode seem all the more frightening was the monster I felt breathing down my neck. His name was Midlife. I just had my fiftieth birthday. At fifty, a guy is supposed to be at the top of his game, but there I was, feeling like I was stuck in the penalty box.

I had one daughter in college and one about to be. I had a hefty mortgage payment and was suddenly responsible for my own health insurance. I was uptight and down in the dumps. Needless to say, my prayer life improved. So did my discipline of reading Scripture.

I reread the biblical account of Job. His pain far exceeded the trauma associated with losing a job. I was impressed by what I read. Having lost his business, his family and his health, this Old Testament prophet offered me a perspective worthy of being heeded.

"He [God] knows the way that I take; when he has tested me, I will come out like gold." (Job 23:10)

Those ancient words reminded me that God is capable of redeeming the hardships that come our way. I determined that God desired my unemployment to be a crucible in which my "mettle" would be tested and my ability to trust Him would be measured.

Although I'd known it before, my journey into joblessness caused me to remember that it's not until you lose something you've taken for granted that you fully appreciate how good you had it. At the same time, you realize that what seemed so important is not all that valuable when compared to what can't be replaced. In short, those for whom you bring home the bacon are far more important than the means by which you do it. As a result, I took on several part-time jobs.

Picking up my pen, I added a postscript to my journal entry:

Deep in my heart, I know I'm more than a zero.
The Lord thinks I'm a 'ten.'
My worth to him does not consist
in what I do (or when).

He's gifted me and knows my skills.
He loves me as I am.
And so, from Job, I'll take my cues
and trust God's unseen plan.

It took many months, but I did find another full-time position. And looking back on my adventure in being unemployed, I wouldn't trade it for anything.

A Little Piece of Quiet

'Start spreading the news...'

Did you know that New York's most famous island bears a remarkable resemblance to Mercer Island? That's right. Manhattan is about the same width as our Island and roughly twice as long. In terms of housing, those who rent and buy tend to pay top dollar. An appreciation for the arts is noteworthy on both islands. But there are some distinct differences, too.

While there are only five Starbucks in our community (compared with one hundred seventy-one in Manhattan), we edge out the big island on a per capita basis. Mercer Island has one Starbucks outlet for every four thousand four hundred people, while Manhattan has one for every eight thousand seven hundred.

Two years ago when my wife and I flew back to New York to watch our daughter perform in Carnegie Hall, we came under the enchantment of the city that never sleeps. Our bite out of the Big Apple only whetted our appetite. We could have munched all night and still have begged for more.

While Wendy and I loved walking the streets of Times Square, our daughter, Lauren, fell in love with a small section of Central Park known as Sheep Meadow. This fifteen-acre square of lawn was used as grazing land for livestock (especially sheep) until 1934. It is located adjacent to the famed Tavern on the Green.

Except in the cold of winter, Sheep Meadow is an ideal place for tourists and workers to enjoy a picnic lunch, a mid-afternoon nap, meditate in solitude or just catch some rays. Signs that surround this section of the park prohibit any kind of music. It is an outdoor sanctuary where silence provides the call to worship ... or study ... or sleep ... or tan.

Mercerdale Park, in the heart of our town, is about the same size as Sheep Meadow. Both our "meadow" and the more famous one provide a grassy island of refreshment in the midst of an expanding concrete aviary where multi-colored cranes have become almost as common as crows and robins. But our postage-stamp parcel of paradise (across from the post office) is more accessible.

Mercerdale Park is a little piece of quiet in our bustling community where office workers, shoppers and shopkeepers can take five on a bench or do ten laps on a lunch break. It's a calm and comforting place where grandma can walk her dog while a young dad wrestles with his preschoolers on the lawn. I often will walk to Mercerdale Park to enjoy the visual respite, sip a cup of coffee and write some poetry before engaging a couple in pre-marital conversations in my office.

I have become convinced that every one of us needs a "Sheep Meadow" in our lives. It might very well be Mercerdale Park. Maybe it's Luther Burbank Park or Groveland Beach. It may be a hammock in your backyard. It could be a bench overlooking the lake at one of our many street ends. Perhaps it's a lanai at a high-rise apartment overlooking downtown Mercer Island.

But your "Sheep Meadow" doesn't have to be an outside setting at all. It might be a closed office during lunch, when you can sit back in a chair behind your desk with your fingers interlocked behind your head while listening to the sounds of silence.

It was God who invited us to be still and quiet in His presence. He is the one whom King David called the divine shepherd. The timeless words of the twenty-third Psalm suggest that all of us are sheep in need of a calm and quiet meadow where we can be regularly reminded of our Creator's constant care. A place where we can lie down in green pastures, or be led by still waters in an attempt to have our souls restored. Yes, we all need a little piece of quiet.

Praying with Our Eyes Open

"And Abraham believed God and it was reckoned unto him for righteousness."
(Galatians 3:6)

Looking forward to the National Day of Prayer, I can't help but focus on the past. When I think of those defined by faith, I picture a man named Abraham.

In the family album of faith, his profile of courage is recognizable and frequently seen. The pages of history feature a man whose stature was head and shoulders above the others. His bearded face stood out in the crowd.

Abraham's call from God was a daunting one. He was led to leave his familiar past and lead his people into an unknown future. It was a lonely call — a trek toward a "land God would show him," marked by risk, rejection and the threat of death. And yet this man set his face like a flint toward his godly goals and refused to give up.

Of all the images of Abraham that I have encountered, I have a favorite. It captures a pensive countenance. No Kodak smile here. As I focus on that familiar face, I see his set jaw with closed-lips determination. I see those unblinking eyes staring to the east. In this particular snapshot, Abraham is seated on a throne-like chair. Legs uncrossed, arms extended.

No, the person I have in mind is not the "father of many nations" pictured in the Bible. It is one of the fathers of our nation. A man of faith who, like his ancient namesake, demonstrated that faith while following a divine call. This Abraham, like the wandering Aramean, looked to God as the source of his guidance, empowerment and courage.

Yes, Abraham Lincoln was a man of faith whose eyes were open to God's guidance even as they surveyed the ungodly character that punctuated America's soul.

As I picture that stone statue seated in the Washington, D.C., memorial that bears his name, I imagine our sixteenth President posed in prayer. He scans the Washington Mall and what that stretch of limestone, grass and water represents. A history marked by bloodshed and hope at home and abroad.

While memories of war are represented by the view to which Lincoln is privy, there is also Dr. King's "March on Washington" that verbalized a dream of racial reconciliation. There is Coach McCartney's gathering of a million Promise Keepers standing in the gap before a holy God on behalf of an unholy people.

On Thursday, May 7, I will join millions of Americans concerned for our nation's future. I, with them, will seek out a house of worship and assume a posture of prayer. As I sit in the back of the church sanctuary, silently praying with my eyes open, I will pray to Lincoln's God.

Gazing at the American flag at the front of the church, I will thank God for the freedom for which it stands. I will recall the blood that purchased our peace. Blinking back tears, I will thank my Heavenly Father for my earthly dad who died the very day our new President was elected. I will pray for others I know who have lost loved ones.

With eyes wide open to the current economic crises that challenge our sense of security, I will ask God to remind us as a nation where our hope in finding life, liberty and the pursuit of happiness is ultimately found. I will ask Him to protect our troops in Iraq and Afghanistan as they serve the cause of liberty in countries caged by terror.

Focusing on the open Bible on the communion table, I will ask Almighty God to guide our leaders and renew their ability to acknowledge His Word.

On the National Day of Prayer, I will pray with my eyes open to the frightening issues threatening to erode the spiritual foundations of our most blessed land. Won't you join me?

Intersections

Another Date That will Live in Infamy

There are just two days on the calendar whose mere date conveys their unique significance. One is July 4. The other is today, April 15. I find no little irony in this fact. The first date celebrates a hard-fought freedom from a tax-hungry king in England. The second signifies the undeniable reality that freedom is not free and that life, liberty and the pursuit of happiness still include taxation. According to Ben Franklin, the only certainties we have in life are death and taxes.

Speaking of death and taxes ... Long before April 15 became known as tax day in 1955, that midpoint mark in the fourth month of the year was a tragic milestone in our nation's history. It was in the early hours of Monday, April 15, 1912, that the Titanic sank.

The sad news, telegraphed around the world, was both devastating and surprising. The Titanic was three football fields long, eleven stories tall and ninety-two feet wide. Having taken three years to construct at a cost of $7.5 million, it weighed an astonishing forty-six thousand tons. The pride of the White Star British Lines was appropriately named.

With sixteen watertight compartments below sea level, the ship's captain had arrogantly claimed that not even God could sink the Titanic. The wealthy and influential passengers in first class didn't give a second thought to their safety. As the ship steamed toward New York City, those aboard the maiden voyage of the world's largest ship had no idea what they were about to encounter.

Late on Sunday night, April 14, the ship's crew disregarded a warning from a nearby vessel and the Titanic collided with a massive iceberg. In just a few short hours, one thousand five hundred twenty-two passengers and crew members perished in the open sea three hundred fifty miles southeast of Newfoundland. Only seven hundred six people survived.

For years to come, April 15 would signify the fragility of life for the families of those passengers who never reached their intended destination in spite of being assured that they had nothing to fear.

Curiously, a half century before the Titanic disaster, another unexpected tragedy occurred on that same date. It was the day before Easter, April 15, 1865, when our sixteenth President succumbed to a gunshot wound that he had received hours earlier on a not so Good Friday evening.

After a bloody civil war that had ended only days earlier, the bruised psyche of our nation was once again taxed. A fifty-six-year-old Abraham Lincoln had just been reelected and was enjoying unprecedented popularity. But dreams collided with an iceberg-like nightmare. For decades to come, April 15 would be a costly reminder that prosperity is only temporary and success is fleeting.

For the days following Easter that year, Americans grieved the death of their commander-in-chief. Many were comforted by the hymn lyrics they had sung in church the previous Sunday. Lyrics that affirmed how Christ's resurrection calibrates the way we look at loss.

More than a few Christians in our community (myself included) have just celebrated their first Easter since closing the casket lid on a loved one. While grateful for the hope such a holiday promises, they are painfully aware of the crosses we all must bear. They are reminded of how brief life is, how easily it can be interrupted and what constitutes true wealth.

Yes, April 15 remains a reminder that both death and taxes are unavoidable. There is no changing that fact. But we can change the way we compute our blessings, brace ourselves to be blindsided by setbacks and embrace the life we have left. Although my tax accountant can't help me with that calculation, I've filed for an extension recognizing I'm the same age that Lincoln was when he died.

Goodbye American! A Tribute to Paul Harvey

The last day of February found Americans in all fifty states grieving the death of a ninety-year-old man whose voice was most unique. On February 28, our nation lost a giant. Paul Harvey was our country's most popular newsman.

From the time he left Tulsa as a young reporter until he established himself as a household name broadcasting from the sixteenth-floor studio in downtown Chicago, Paul Harvey positioned himself as a man of conservative values and moral convictions with a distinctive perspective on current events. Through his twice-daily newscasts and his ever-popular "The Rest of the Story" segments, Mr. Harvey left his faith-based imprint on millions of Americans.

Amazingly, I had the privilege of spending time with Mr. Harvey twice. Twelve years ago, I was an in-studio guest during his midday newscast in Chicago. Two years ago, I enjoyed a thirty-minute stroll with him in Phoenix. I even remember when he visited my hometown of Wenatchee, Washington decades earlier and originated his nationwide broadcast from our local radio station. Though I was just a kid in junior high school, his visit seemed like the President had come to town.

Like the famous apostle whose name he bore, Paul Harvey's message has impacted millions. And as was true of Saint Paul, his words will continue to live on. Whether spoken or written, his daily epistles were missals of truth and life sprinkled with grace and peace. He reported on what others failed to see (or refused to). He would not simply give the headlines related to our sin-tinged world. To him, the top of the front page was rarely the bottom line of truth. There was always "the rest of the story."

At long last, what was typically limited to four imaginative pages of a fifteen-minute broadcast, there is finally a fifth and final page. The man we heard daily on stations across the country is himself experiencing the rest of the story. He has discovered the ultimate rest stop on the adventure of a lifetime. We clergymen call it eternal rest.

And while those who loved this legendary broadcaster struggle with feelings of loss this week, Paul Harvey has gained what no one can ever take from him: Life after death with the very One who conquered death through his post-crucifixion resurrection.

In a world dominated by tragic headlines, this is the ultimate in good news. And if he had the means, Paul Harvey would find the opportunity to broadcast from Heaven. Complete with his inimitable voice and pregnant pauses, Paul would likely quote from his namesake's letter to the Christ-followers in first-century Rome: *"And if the Spirit of him who raised Jesus from the dead is living in you, he who raised Christ from the dead will also give life to your mortal bodies through his Spirit, who lives in you." (Romans 8:11, NIV)*

Because of my hope in life beyond the grave, I anticipate seeing Paul Harvey again. In light of that, I do not simply bid him goodbye. Rather, I employ two little words that comprised his signature for seven decades and simply say, *"Good day!"*

Good Grief Is Not an Oxymoron

"Yea, though I walk through the valley of the shadow of death, I will fear no evil, for Thou art with me..." In Psalm 23, King David offers a metaphor for grief to those who have experienced the death of a loved one. He likens the landscape of loss to a valley of shadows. David's description is both poetic and comforting. I've proven that time and time again. In thirty years of pastoral ministry, I have waxed theological on the meaning of those timeless words at countless memorial services.

All the same, four months after my dad's death, I have come up with my own metaphor for grief. I see the struggle of lingering sorrow more like a hike up a mountain than a stroll through a shadowy valley. Both a vertical climb and bereavement sap your strength, suck your joy and weigh you down. Both breed exhaustion and aches that words can't describe. In preparation for a recent sermon on the life of Moses, I wanted to personally identify with his trek to the top of a mountain overlooking the Promised Land.

Since I had never hiked up Mount Si, I figured that this would be a good time to do it. I asked a friend, who had made that trek several times, if he would go with me. Andy agreed. The cloudless blue sky beckoned me upward. So did my naïve expectations. I began the hike with a brisk stride that soon slowed.

Andy encouraged me to pace myself. Within the first twenty minutes of the ascent, I was huffing and puffing. Grateful for the ski poles which Andy loaned me, I leaned on them. I also leaned on his advice to stop periodically to rest and drink water. When my legs began to burn, I felt like giving up. My vocalized sighs caused me to wonder if those who named Mount Si hadn't misspelled it. My friend encouraged me to keep on.

Two hours and forty minutes after leaving the parking lot, Andy and I reached the summit of Mount Si. Although I ached from shoulders to shins, the view of Mount Rainier and the snowcapped Olympics was indescribably beautiful. At the end of this exhausting climb, I enjoyed a breathtaking and insightful perspective. Coming to terms with where I had come from, to reach where I was, proved most instructive. But I wouldn't have made it without someone at my side.

Yes, the journey from an open grave into a future without a loved one does resemble a hike up a steep mountain trail. It is painfully difficult and unbelievably demanding, but unquestionably worthwhile. Four months into my own grief journey, I am more fully alive than I was before my dad's death.

Along the path leading from death, I have gained perspectives of life that I didn't know existed. I am especially grateful for my companions on "the trail" who have been there before. Family, friends and church members have been a godsend. Grief is a trail that is definitely too difficult to be traveled alone. Did you know that there are a variety of grief support opportunities in our area from which to choose?

Youth and Family Services offers a monthly course at the Community Center at Mercer View, the second Thursday of each month. Overlake Hospital has grief-support groups that meet regularly. Covenant Shores offers periodic classes for those who have experienced loss. Individual congregations on Mercer Island have their own classes to aid those who have experienced death, divorce or unemployment. I am grateful that the church I serve has just started such a course.

An old Swedish proverb says it well, *"A shared joy is a doubled joy. A shared sorrow is half a sorrow."* Having someone with whom to share your heartache doesn't remove grief from your life entirely, but it helps you to reach a height far beyond what you thought possible. I would call that good grief.

Tent City: A Personal Reflection

Birk was only twenty years old when he found himself at a crossroads in life. Separated by a significant distance from his parents, he was homesick. But times on the family farm were tough and couldn't support him. With only a few bucks in his tattered trousers, he braved an uncertain future.

Birk's hunched back and prominent limp were visible reminders of his bout with infantile polio. But there was something else about his five-foot-six-inch frame that was just as observable. His young face boasted a determination impossible to ignore. He would do whatever it took to make it.

Birk lived in a tent city (of sorts) on the Olympic Peninsula. It was a logging camp. The near-constant rain and damp surroundings resulted in cold, miserable nights. Birk complained about bed bugs and lice. The red rash on his limbs proved that his bark was not inconsistent with the bites he endured.

On those cold, wet and lonely nights, Birk took comfort in the fact that there were other homeless loggers who shared his plight. He was also warmed by the motto he had seen as he made his way to Washington State. As his ship steamed into New York's harbor, Birk had seen the Statue of Liberty and the core values of the country now welcoming him. This teenage immigrant couldn't ignore what was engraved on the base of the copper lady.

"Give me your tired, your poor, your huddled masses yearning to breathe free. The wretched refuse of your teeming shore. Send these, the homeless, tempest-tossed to me..."

Birk made his way west. He had no idea how he would survive, but he was convinced that he would. Determined to prove that he had what it took to succeed, he dreamed with his eyes open and prayed with them shut. If the process included makeshift living situations, Birk was not opposed to them. He welcomed help along the way and celebrated the companionship of fellow travelers. Community was a core value of his faith that he'd carried with him since leaving the fjord country of Norway.

I know Birk's story well. You see, Gunder "Birk" Birkeland was my maternal grandfather. He died in 1976, but I can still picture Papa recalling his "survival" stories in broken English.

Fortunately, my grandfather's temporary housing tenure was short-lived. Living in a transient community provided him with the necessary lifeline to save money in a safe environment until he could land a full-time job and a permanent address. Birk was involved in the construction of the first multi-storied building in Bremerton. He later became a successful general contractor in Seattle and built several homes on Queen Anne Hill. Would you believe a former mayor of Seattle currently lives in one of my grandfather's showplaces overlooking downtown?

The young immigrant who battled a crippling disease, homesickness and transient employment and housing never forgot the path that led to prosperity. He was a generous supporter of charities that benefitted the homeless and jobless.

As I contemplate the ongoing debate between those who are in favor of Tent City 4 returning to our community and those who are opposed to the idea, I can't help but think of Papa Birkeland. I'm forced to wonder how many "Birks" can be found in the traveling community of sleeping bags and tarps. What if such encampments were not permitted to exist? What if the unexpected loss of job and home also resulted in the loss of dreams of starting over?

Perhaps you are reminded of a relative, neighbor or classmate whose journey to economic stability or job security led through the wilderness of temporary housing. Does their experience impact how you feel about those whose names you don't know and whose faces you wouldn't recognize? Shouldn't it?

How the Church Stole Christmas!

Today is January 5. It's the twelfth day of Christmas.

I didn't need twelve drummers drumming to remind me of that fact. There is a cadence in my clergyman's heart that helped me long ago learn to mark time in such a way to extend the yuletide season as long as possible.

For as long as I can remember, Christmas has been my favorite holiday. I love the music. My poetic soul resonates to the lights, color and nonstop rituals associated with the season. My children haven't always shared my enthusiasm. Having a pastor for a father meant that Dad had to be away from home more than other dads. And, though I really enjoyed all the commitments of Christmas, they were not as impressed.

While other families took exotic vacations or visited relatives, we stayed behind for Christmas Eve services. Since our families lived at a distance, we occasionally caught red-eye flights or drove for hours after the midnight service to open presents with grandparents on Christmas morning.

Our girls always knew who Santa Claus was — Daddy. But it took much longer to convince them that I was not the Grinch who stole Christmas. That I bore little resemblance to the green guy in their Dr. Seuss book was beside the point. They just knew that church was taking their father from them and robbing them of a full-fledged festival.

Wendy and I took our girls' feelings to heart. We decided to create holiday traditions unique to our family that would compensate for what my occupation tended to steal from them.

Intersections

On December 1, three little ceramic kings begin a five-week journey from the far end of our home to the nativity scene atop our piano. They move a little each day.

Our church has Swedish roots, so we decided to celebrate Santa Lucia Day (December 13). This angelic girl martyred in the third century is heralded for giving up her dowry to care for the poor. Wendy, wearing a crown of candles, wakes the family by carrying a tray of warm bread and hot cocoa room to room. She sings words I've written to the old Italian melody "Santa Lucia."

We give new meaning to the phrase *"peace on earth, goodwill to men"* by giving one present purchased from a Goodwill thrift store. Recycled gifts are a hoot. In addition, what we spend goes to help needy people.

Because much of Christmas Eve is spent getting ready for services that night, we go out for breakfast at an especially nice restaurant. We even ask the waitress to take our picture, which we include in a special book that has twenty-six years of snapshots.

Our favorite tradition is a Day of the Kings celebration. Tomorrow is Epiphany, which commemorates the day when the magi arrived in Bethlehem to worship the Christ child. Tonight our dinner table will be graced with individual quilted crowns containing three small gifts. After a Chinese meal, we'll read the biblical story of the magi and "The Story of the Other Wise Man." We'll sing "We Three Kings" and "The Twelve Days of Christmas," celebrating the fact that the little Asian wise men have finally joined the nativity scene on the piano.

My family still bristles at times when they realize my Christmas responsibilities will prevent us from having the same freedom as other families enjoy. But with the traditions we've established, they look forward to Christmastime as much as I do. You might consider creating some unique customs of your own. At least keep celebrating until "the twelfth night."

An Antidote to Whine Flu

Not a day goes by that we don't read about the swine flu in the media. Everyone is talking about it. Even denominational leaders are looking to minimize the risk of contagion at the Communion table. They are suggesting new ways for pastors to administer the sacrament of the Lord's Supper.

As we commune as families at the dinner table for turkey and all the traditional trimmings, it's likely that we'll be having 'pork' as well this year. Swine flu will certainly factor into our conversations as we pass the mashed potatoes or dish up the pumpkin pie. And for good reason.

But, may I be honest? While we have just cause to be concerned about swine flu, I am also alarmed about another virus to which our community is vulnerable. I call it "the whine flu."

In spite of the fact that we live in one of the most desirable ZIP codes in America, have you noticed our tendency to grumble and gripe? Although our creature comforts are nothing to sneeze at, we can't seem to stop complaining about our lot in life. We have a chronic case of whining.

We've all been infected by this bug. We whine about what we don't have as well as about what we do have. We whine about where we work as well as where we don't. We whine about the stock market, health care and property taxes. We whine about where we're not going to be able to vacation next summer. We whine about our kids' teachers. We whine about decisions made at church or synagogue. We whine about salary cuts (even though we still have a job).

Intersections

The whine flu is a contagious viral malady. The frequency with which we grumble, grouse and regurgitate questions like "How come?" "Why not?" "Why me?" must make God sick.

But, whine flu has a direct impact on us as well. It dehydrates our joy. It leaves a bitter taste in our mouths. It sours us on life. Our whining ways cause others to keep their distance from us. And then we find ourselves whining about feeling lonely.

But don't despair. Did you know that the cause of whine flu has been determined? We don't get it from forgetting to wash our hands. We get it from forgetting to count our blessings. When we uncork our gratitude, we bottle up our tendency to whine.

Taking stock of God's many blessings (like family, friends, job, home and health) can be as therapeutic as a steaming bowl of chicken stock and noodles. When we compare our net worth to the majority of the world, "knowledge of our bottom line undermines our right to whine." Being thankful is the key to recovering from this pandemic. It's impossible to be grateful and gripe at the same time.

So, how about it? Aren't you sick and tired of complaining? Aren't you weary of whining? Why not determine to make Thanksgiving more than just a day. Giving thanks can be a way of life. Simply put, gratitude is an attitude. It's an attitude that looks for the good in our lives every day and then looks to thank the One responsible.

No wonder the ancient psalmist wrote, *"Praise the LORD, O my soul, and forget not all his benefits — who forgives all your sins and heals all your diseases." (Psalm 103:2-3 NIV)*

Although we have a tendency to forget the good things in our lives (much of which we don't deserve), Thanksgiving can be a memory-jogger. It can point us to the Great Physician and the road to recovery. Whine flu is a treatable disease. Gratitude is the time-tested antidote.

Yes, Virginia, There Is a God

Yes, Virginia, there is a God! You and the other forty-nine states that make up our union don't need to doubt that. In the words of a journalist who lived in the late nineteenth century, *"He exists as certainly as love and generosity and devotion exist."* In fact, God's existence is the reason such attributes punctuate our lives this time of year.

If there were no God, would we find breathless wonder as we attempt to analyze the science of a snowflake? Each delicate flake is unique and cannot be reproduced. Without God would we marvel at the beauty of a poinsettia? How would we explain our innate appreciation for justice, redemption, forgiveness, beauty and creativity?

If there were no eternal Light, would we bother to string lights, decorate our homes, trim trees, light candles and ritualistically tell the same old stories and sing the same old songs? It is the urge to celebrate that points to a spiritual dynamic in each of us. And if that is true, does that spiritual reality not point to a spiritual source?

If each member of the human family were not created in the image of Almighty God, could we possibly have the ability to imagine a benevolent being who sees us when we're sleeping and knows when we're awake? A being who knows if we've been bad or good and is bound by a moral code of absolute truth to render appropriate consequences?

Does not the imaginative existence of a jolly and generous, gift-giving person point to a belief that somewhere there is actually someone who epitomizes our dreams of the perfect provider and ethical judge?

Yet, Virginia, you and other states have many within your borders who balk at any mention of the Almighty. At this time of year, atheists in Washington State and Washington, D.C. are especially vocal in challenging His existence. While browsing at an area bookstore, I skimmed the contents to "The Atheist's Guide to Christmas." I was appalled at what I read.

Francis P. Church, an editor for a major New York newspaper one hundred thirteen years ago, could well have been describing those who make it their mission in life to belittle we who light candles on menorahs or Advent wreaths in celebration of Hanukkah or Christmas.

"They have been affected by the skepticism of a skeptical age. They do not believe except what they see. They think that nothing can be which is not comprehensible by their little minds. All minds, Virginia, whether they be men's or children's, are little. In this great universe of ours man is a mere insect, an ant, in his intellect, as compared with the boundless world about him, as measured by the intelligence capable of grasping the whole of truth and knowledge."

Virginia, I am grateful that I live in a community like Mercer Island where God is honored and faith is valued. Thanksgiving is embraced as an interfaith opportunity for praise of God. High school commencements include student-led baccalaureate ceremonies in which God's blessing is on our graduates. I know such opportunities do not exist elsewhere.

No God? God forbid! What would we engrave on our money? In Us We Trust? It doesn't have the right ring to it. And believe me, it would have the wrong result.

Yes, Virginia, there is a God! And according to a first-century rabbi, the evidence for a Higher Power is universal. *"For since the creation of the world God's invisible qualities — his eternal power and divine nature — have been clearly seen, being understood from what has been made, so that people are without excuse."* (Romans 1:20 NIV)

Remember to Stay Alert to the World Around Us

Thursday marks the sixty-fifth anniversary of the surrender ceremony that ended World War II. On September 2, 1945, the eyes of the world focused on history's stage and a performance that would not soon be forgotten.

That was the day when General Douglas MacArthur (with his Parker fountain pen in hand) conducted a symphony of peace aboard the USS Missouri in Tokyo Bay. This version of "victory at sea" would be repeatedly captured on film and newsreel.

As MacArthur cued the various performers to play their part on this historic day, a nineteen-year-old farm boy from Lapwai, Idaho, looked on. He is seen in the bottom right-hand corner of a familiar photograph. That Marine corporal looking back at the camera was my father, Edwin Asimakoupoulos.

Before he died twenty months ago, my dad took great pride describing his memories of V-J Day. As part of the Marine Corps detachment aboard the "Mighty Mo," he was selected to be one of the honor guards that day. My dad was chosen as an escort for Lieutenant General Kuzma Derevyanko, who signed the treaty on behalf of Russia. By virtue of his privileged assignment, my dad stood about fifteen feet behind MacArthur and the other dignitaries.

Although my father is visible in several historic photographs documenting the end of the war, I like this one best of all. The fact that he is not facing the ceremony sets it apart and raises questions. Apparently, one of the Russian newsmen covering the event dropped his camera from an elevated perch. My dad turned around to see where the noise was coming from.

That picture of my curious father is a reminder to me to be interested in people, places and things. After all, our ability to reflect on the meaning of life is rooted in what we take time to observe. Blindly going about our routines keeps us from seeing the unexpected and being sensitive to the serendipities around us.

At an ecumenical clergy conference that I recently attended, I heard a facilitator challenge we who speak for a living to seek to "be more interested than interesting" as we hone our craft as communicators.

What he suggested is good advice for more than just rabbis, priests and ministers. We all would do well to exercise the curiosity muscle between our ears as well as opening our eyes to the wonder of daily life. Our norm is not to.

Leonardo Da Vinci recognized our tendency not to turn around to see where "the noise" is coming from. Five centuries ago, this noted scientist and artist waxed theologically eloquent. He described the average person as one who *"looks without seeing, listens without hearing, touches without feeling, eats without tasting, moves without physical awareness, inhales without awareness of odor or fragrance, and talks without thinking."*

Why not open your eyes to your surroundings? Sunrises. Sunsets. Turning leaves. Aging parents. Disappearing veterans. And speaking of those vets, why not take some time this week to hear their stories of the war? Remember, they won't always be with us.

Reflections on Life and Faith

Looking Back and Looking Forward

While most people in our community have been looking forward to summer weather, I have been spending this season looking back.

This summer marks some noteworthy anniversaries in my life. Five years ago, our family moved to Mercer Island. Twenty-five years ago, I was ordained as a minister of the Gospel. Forty years ago, I graduated from Wenatchee High School. With each observance, I've found myself sorting through mental photographs while paging through family albums. With each commemoration, I've been reminded how quickly life passes and how the past has influenced the present.

For our community, this is a season for looking back as well. Last weekend, our annual Summer Celebration! invited us to focus on decades gone by and recall "the good old days." This coming weekend, we will gather in Mercerdale Park for a celebration cleverly dubbed "Mercerversary." It will provide us with numerous opportunities to reflect on a half-century of memories since our city was incorporated as a municipality.

But public occasions that call us to ponder the past give us more than just an excuse to throw a party. Memories of yesteryear provide us with the context to be grateful for "the good old days." They also offer a perspective by which we can better understand how far we've come. While giving us a chance to catch our communal breath, retrospective glances over our shoulders enable us to better face the future.

In both the Jewish and Christian faith, reflection on past events is not merely encouraged; it is demanded. Followers of Judaism are instructed to remember how the Lord rested on the seventh day after creating the universe and all forms of life in six. Looking back, they are to observe the Sabbath day as a memory jogger. Similarly, my Jewish neighbors and friends are called to recount God's deliverance from the ancient Egyptians some three thousand years ago by celebrating the Passover each spring. By doing so, they remember the historical evidence of supernatural redemption.

Christians, meanwhile, are instructed to commemorate Holy Communion on a regular basis. Through this simple (but sacred) meal of bread and wine, they remember the death of Jesus and His power to forgive sin. Similarly, His followers practice the ancient rite of baptism. In this symbolic act of being immersed in water, they are forced to remember God's power to raise up what was dead and buried and bring it back to life.

What is true for religious groups is also true for families (and communities). Recalling historic events that marked our ancestors' life journeys provides us with a sense of identity. What defines who we are today can be understood only as we take an honest look at circumstances that have influenced us directly (and indirectly). Looking back enables us to look within. That inward focus reminds us that we are not alone, but part of something that is bigger than we are.

Because we are uniquely shaped by events and people that preceded us, pondering our past is productive. As we contemplate the experiences of previous generations, we have opportunity to acknowledge their mistakes and wisdom. Those insights, in turn, motivate us to act on what we've learned.

Memories are the key that enable us to unlock the doors which lead to understanding, gratitude and change. In this nostalgic season of reminiscing, I invite you to look back that you might look forward with confidence and hope at what is still to come.

Walk, Pray, Love

For six decades our country has called us to a National Day of Prayer, indisputably a great notion. But how do we make the most of such a day?

With that dilemma in mind, what follows is a simple suggestion for making the most of the National Day of Prayer on May 6. I call it a progressive adventure. And much like a progressive dinner, it will require driving to different locations on the Island to savor the flavor of the day.

A logical place to start is at Mercerdale Park. While standing beneath the Veterans Memorial, spend some time in silent reflection and prayer thanking the Almighty for those who were willing to pay the ultimate sacrifice to provide us with a democracy in which our personal freedoms are both protected and practiced.

Then to Luther Burbank Park. A park named for one of our nation's foremost botanists is a perfect place to express gratitude to our Creator for the beauty of creation. Walk along the lakeside path and admire the splendor of the flowering bushes and trees.

A pause at City Hall would be a great next stop. While there, pray for our local government officials. Ask the God of justice, mercy and order to give wisdom to our city manager, mayor, members of the City Council as well as our police chief and fire chief.

From City Hall make your way to one of the several schools on the Island. Express gratitude that our school district is one of the most envied in the entire nation. Ask God to help our students make wise choices when faced with tempting opportunities related to drugs, alcohol and premature sexual intimacy. Remember their teachers and administrators who help shape the moral development of our kids.

Where do you practice your faith? If that house of worship is on Mercer Island, drive to that location. If the sanctuary is open, why not go inside and spend ten minutes in silent contemplation. Pray for your spiritual shepherds. Ask God to encourage them when their task is overwhelming and they are underappreciated. Pray for our state lawmakers. Pray for our President, his cabinet, members of Congress and the Supreme Court. Ask the Divine Judge to be their moral compass.

But your progressive prayer adventure is not quite done. As you drive to your residence, talk to your Heavenly Father about your children, your siblings and your aging parents. While the residents of the White House need our prayers, those who reside in your house need them, too. Your family (and mine) has unique challenges and opportunities requiring Divine intervention.

Finally, if your church or synagogue has planned a community-wide National Day of Prayer service, why not attend with your family? It could become an annual tradition.

Caffeinated Faith

I have friends who feel less-than-holy until they've had their first cup of coffee in the morning. Others I know faithfully commune with their friends at St. Arbucks. Ken Lottis is one such acquaintance. For this seventy-five-year-old Islander, drinking coffee is a spiritual experience.

While Ken is quick to express gratitude to the Creator for a flavorful cup of joe, the spiritual component to his coffee-drinking fixation isn't limited to a blessing for good beans. It has more to do with the meaningful conversations he has with those who enjoy his habit. Several times during the week, Ken can be found at a Noah's, Tully's or Starbucks conversing with friends about how faith intersects with daily life. His circle of cappuccino compadres includes Roman Catholics, Jews, Protestants and agnostics. Ken has been chewing on philosophical ideas while sipping an espresso in coffeehouses for a long time. (Would you believe half a century?) He first realized the value of such a venue while working with university students in Brazil.

From the early '60s to the late '80s, Ken and his wife, Carol (and their three sons), worked with a parachurch organization called The Navigators in Rio, São Paulo and Curitiba. Soon after arriving in South America, Ken discovered that the traditional style of religious dialogue to which he'd been exposed growing up in North America was of no interest to Brazilians. By observing the culture around him, he saw how a cup of coffee and a newspaper promoted the free exchange of ideas far easier than a chalice of communion wine and a sermon.

For Ken, unlearning the vocabulary of American Christianity was almost as difficult as learning Portuguese. But he was willing to barbecue sacred cows in order to win friends with whom he could eventually feast on the big philosophical questions. Such a roasting of religious rituals included abandoning Sunday morning church services for informal gatherings with students of various faith backgrounds in their home.

Seeing coffee through the eyes of faith enabled the young American to focus on more than just caffeinated beverages as an important social function. Ken became a student of Brazilian culture and lifestyle, even becoming a fanatical soccer fan. In little and big ways, Ken attempted to translate the essence of his God-centered worldview into a dialect that Brazilian students would understand. The results were remarkable. In response to the encouragement of colleagues and family members, Ken has chronicled his Brazilian coffeehouse (and pub) conversations in a book.

This first-time author has titled his adventures, *Will This Rock in Rio?* The title is nearly self-explanatory. It suggests the kind of question that Ken and his colleagues asked as they attempted to structure experiences that would promote deep and meaningful conversations. The subtitle of the volume (available at Island Books) conveys the relevance of Ken's insights in twenty-first century Seattle: *Finding God in an Urban Culture*.

As I read *Will This Rock in Rio?*, I could easily see why Ken and his wife, Carol, walked in the 5k event last month in the half-marathon Rotary Run rather than choosing to show up at church. His brand of faith is best expressed where people are engaged in living and enjoying life. Traditional religiosity is not this coffee drinker's cup of tea. What steeps in Ken's heart is a passion to express his faith in creative and relevant ways. And that includes good food, a satisfying beverage and a community of friends. It's really no wonder that drinking coffee is a spiritual experience for Ken. More often than not, sipping the "drip of the day" calls to mind meaningful conversations with lifelong friends on two continents. And as he reflects on these relationships, he can't help but thank God.

And the Rest is History!

One of the highlights of this summer was playing tour guide to two sets of cousins visiting Seattle from Norway. Both groups were making the most of their time off to explore the United States. When I asked how much vacation time they were given each year, I was envious of the response. Five weeks!

It appears that European employers are more generous when it comes to "R and R" than American employers. As one European admits, "*We work so that we can go on vacation. You Americans go on vacation so that you can go back and work.*"

For Europeans, vacations are the end that provides them meaning. For us, time off is the means to a much more important end. We vacation in order to go back to work. Dr. Gordon Dahl concurs. This sociology professor at UC San Diego claims that we Americans tend to "worship our work, work at our play and play at our worship."

A damning indictment to be sure! Worshiping our work? Working at our play? No wonder we are a sleep-deprived culture and exhausted most the time. No wonder we return pooped out from summer getaways. It's no wonder we play at our worship. Our over-inflated view of our professions and productivity has diminished our understanding of God's provision and blessings.

It's time we reconsidered the reason for our summer vacations and our need to relax. After all, rest restores our view of reality.

Taking time to rest is nothing new. It's as old as the "Ancient of Days." That's right! Even the Lord Himself, the All-Knowing One, knew it was best to rest from the routines of life. On the first page of the Hebrew

Bible, we read that God took a break after creating the cosmos in six days.

By the seventh day, God had finished the work He had been doing; so on the seventh day He rested from all His work: *"Then God blessed the seventh day and made it holy, because on it he rested from all the work of creating that he had done." (Genesis 2:2-3 NIV)*

The Lord rested from His labor that He might reflect on and celebrate what He had made. Creation led to recreation. Our weekends and vacations are rooted in the Creator's example. Doing nothing is the most important something we can do. Our recreation recreates!

The Blessing

Father's Day 2006 was the most memorable one I've ever experienced. I had asked my retired pastor-dad to preach at Mercer Island Covenant Church. Because my dad was battling terminal cancer, I knew it would likely be the last time he'd give a sermon. It was a poignant morning. Dad preached like there was no tomorrow (perhaps because he wasn't sure how many tomorrows he had left).

Before getting up to deliver one of his favorite messages, he called my brother and me forward. In front of the entire congregation, our dying father reached out and placed a hand on each of our heads and gave us his blessing. Although my dad had frequently told me he loved me, this time was different. With carefully chosen words he verbalized his unconditional acceptance and called on our Heavenly Father to fill our lives with a sense of His presence and holy purpose. I fought to hold back tears.

Have you been the recipient of your father's blessing? If you're a father, have you found a meaningful way to communicate to your children the pride and pleasure they bring you? A formal ceremony isn't necessary, but a creative expression might make such a declaration more memorable.

Both Jewish and Christian traditions celebrate the significance of "the blessing." In the Old Testament, Abraham blessed Isaac. Isaac blessed Jacob. On Jacob's deathbed, a feeble patriarch strained to sit up to speak a blessing over each of his twelve sons. The New Testament makes clear that even Jesus needed (and received) His Father's blessing. At the beginning of His public ministry when He was baptized in the Jordan River, Jesus heard a voice from above saying,

"You are My much-loved Son in whom I am well-pleased." (Mark 1:11) Much-loved. Well-pleased. There is something about those words falling from a father's lips that cause you to stand a little taller and try a little harder. Every person who has ever lived longs to hear their dad say there is nothing they could ever do (no matter how good or bad) that would cause him to love them any less than he already does.

Father's Day is obviously a perfect time for kids to honor their dads. It is also a great occasion for fathers to be reminded of how critical their affirmation is to the long-term well-being of those who call them Dad.

The Hallmark of Valentine's Day

What Valentine's Day represents (like Thanksgiving or Christmas) is applicable every day of the year.

Do you know where the tradition of giving and receiving valentines comes from? It can be traced back to a Catholic priest who was martyred in the third century and later granted sainthood.

According to legend, St. Valentine secretly performed marriage ceremonies for young lovers when the emperor outlawed weddings. When the priest was imprisoned, he received letters and tokens of love from young people throughout the Roman Empire. Hand-scribbled notes were slid under the door of his cell.

Curiously, the original "valentines" were not romantic love notes at all. They were expressions of friendship. They were a tangible way to let a lonely pastor know he was being thought about. They were a way to offer encouragement.

I've received such "valentines" throughout my life. I keep them in a special place. One is from my father. In his beautiful penmanship, he scrawled on a piece of hotel stationery how much he loved me and how proud he was of my achievements.

Another is from an elderly woman in my first congregation. In her not-so-legible handwriting, she thanked me for my creative approach to worship. In a setting where some were criticizing me for my innovative approach, Elsa's note provided much-needed encouragement.

I also keep a homemade card one of my daughters made for me. In addition to the stick figures representing her and me, there are tall nervous-looking letters that spell out how much she loves me.

The power of a timely word has been attested to for millennia. A famous Jewish proverb celebrates the power of communication:

"The right word at the right time is like a custom-made piece of jewelry, And a wise friend's timely reprimand is like a gold ring slipped on your finger." (Proverbs 25:11 MSG)

There's nothing like a card, letter or note you can hold in your hand (and refer to again) to personify friendship. Like a valentine greeting, they convey encouragement, commitment, gratitude and love. Sadly, in this age of texting, Facebook messaging and emailing, the handwritten note is an endangered species.

What has been the hallmark of personal communication forever is becoming a thing of the past. Don't let it. Pick up a pen and write!

A Prayer for More Than Lawmakers

I received an unexpected gift over the holidays. State Representative Judy Clibborn's office contacted me with an invitation to give the opening prayer at an upcoming day-of-business at the House of Representatives in Olympia.

As it turned out, I was assigned to the opening day of the current session. Mindful of the politicized issues and the financial woes that will define this controversial session, I scripted my prayer carefully. I wanted to speak to the Almighty on behalf of those on both sides of the aisle as well as for those from a variety of faith backgrounds.

The result was a prayer that I hope will be voiced by more than state lawmakers. If leaders in our local government, churches, synagogues and school district prayed these words, the challenges that face us all this year will be minimized.

O God, our help in ages past, our hope for years to come, we call on You for guidance as this new legislative session commences. Forgetting those things that are behind and straining forward toward those things that are to come, help these men and women press on to serve those who look to them for leadership.

In this month when we as a nation celebrate the sanctity of every life and pay homage to a King whose reign was all too brief, may their efforts be crowned with compassion, justice and mercy.

In this challenging economy, as the deposit slips of state revenue reflect less income than they hoped they could bank on, compound their interest in finding creative solutions. Give them the ability to resist the temptation to pass the buck. Allow the currency of the time they spend to be consistent with those four familiar words engraved upon our history and our dollars… "In God we trust."

And when they are called upon to make change, may they be tellers of truth as well as cashiers of compromise. May the bottom line of decisions made in this House make sense to those who make them and to those who will be impacted by them.

And though taxing at times, may this session be marked by an adequate reserve of respect and humility as well as a windfall of gratitude for the privilege You have allowed them in their calling as public servants. In Your Holy Name I pray. Amen.

Reflections on Life and Faith

The Year Thanksgiving Came Early

October 31, 1994. It's a day our family will never forget.

It was a cold, windy and rainy Halloween. Our young family of five had just arrived in the western suburbs of Chicago having relocated from warm and sunny Concord, California. I had been called to be the new pastor of Naperville Evangelical Covenant Church. But given the extreme contrast in weather, I'd wondered if I'd misheard God's call conveyed through the voice of the congregation.

Because the front door remained open for hours as the movers unloaded and unpacked our belongings from the moving van, our home was chilly and dank. As the day progressed, the weather became more miserable. The rain turned to sleet and by late afternoon it had started to snow. Our three young daughters were not only homesick for California friends, they were also distraught. The Halloween costumes (that my wife had not packed to allow for easy access once we arrived) would be covered up by their newly purchased winter coats. The new neighborhood in which they attempted to trick-or-treat was unfamiliar and strange. They couldn't mask their disappointment.

And then the unexpected. A woman from the church I'd soon be serving arrived at our open front door. Her friendly greeting and contagious smile immediately warmed the entry way. Donna Svensen presented us with a cardboard box. Inside was a steaming homemade casserole of chicken tetrazzini, a mandarin orange salad, freshly baked biscuits and raspberry jam. It would be our first supper in our new home. And like the Last Supper in the Upper Room so long ago, it would prove to hold sacramental significance. Sitting down to that sacred meal we thanked God for Donna's hospitality.

I don't remember a meal ever tasting so satisfying. It was as if we were having Thanksgiving dinner a month early. Against the backdrop of inclement weather and missing people and things what we'd left behind, we celebrated God's goodness and His tangible provision for our family. With grateful hearts we paused and thanked God for a warm meal on a cold and stormy night.

Looking back that unexpected meal was a picture of how the Lord would provide for us over the next eleven years. Storm clouds would gather from time to time on the horizon of our lives. There would be job loss, financial worries, health scares and fears for our future. But amid the unpredictable forecast, we had a point of reference. We remembered His gracious faithfulness expressed through a delicious dinner on an unforgettable Halloween. And God continued to bring unexpected people and circumstances across our path at just the right time.

That first night in our new home on the last day of October resulted in a family tradition that we have observed every year since. Each Halloween my wife recreates Donna's meal. Along with chicken tetrazzini and mandarin orange salad, she bakes homemade biscuits. For the past twenty-eight years without fail we've greeted the pint-size masked bandits at our door while feasting on tetrazzini. And that isn't all. Our married daughter has taken up the baton as well. She, too, recreates the memorable pasta dinner for her pastor husband and two young daughters. It's a pasta dinner Allison first ate when she was only eight. I guess you could say that Halloween is the unofficial start of the Thanksgiving season for our family. And for good reason.

On Giving and Receiving

This coming Sunday I'll walk my middle daughter down the center aisle of a Chicago church. In over thirty years as a clergyman, I have performed countless weddings. But this will be the first one as father of the bride. I have it all rehearsed in my head.

I am guessing that I'll feel something like a sliver in my heart as my feet progress slowly in our forward direction. Though I'll be thrilled beyond description that my baby's now a bride, I'm anticipating there will be a bittersweetish splinter that can't be tweezed out. You know what I mean? A shard that's caused by memories of all those precious years planting seeds of faith and wisdom as her mentor and her dad. I fully expect that sliver in my heart will fester the rest of my life. But that's not a bad thing. I'd classify that under the category of "good grief."

Upon reaching the front, I'll kiss Allison on the cheek before placing her hand in the hand of the tux-clad man who will be patiently waiting. When asked, *"Who gives this woman to be married to this man?"* I will respond with a catch in my throat, *"Her mother and I!"* I'm also fairly certain there will be a knot in my stomach as I continue up the steps to the chancel of the church to take over officiating the rest of the knot-tying ceremony.

Giving another man the daughter you've spent a quarter of a century investing in and nurturing is not easy. Someone has likened this transaction to handing over a priceless Stradivarius violin to a gorilla. Hyperbolic? Perhaps. Accurate? Absolutely! As capable and trustworthy as sons-in-law may be, they never are deserving of

Daddy's little girl. The offering dads are called to contribute at the front of a church is a painful sacrifice.

But I must admit the anticipated pain of that impending sacrifice was minimized while spending a few days on vacation. At Lake Chelan I had an insight about "giving away my daughter" that was reassuring. As I worshiped at St. Andrew's Episcopal Church, the congregation was invited to verbalize the prayer of St. Francis. *"Lord, make me an instrument of Thy peace..."* When we got to the part of the prayer where it says, *"For it is in giving that we receive..."* I felt a check in my spirit. God was speaking to me. I realized there was more to the upcoming wedding than giving away my daughter. I would also be gaining a son.

Living in a home with one wife, three daughters and two female Shih Tzu dogs, I have been outnumbered for years. That said, Tim will be a welcomed addition. At last, someone with whom to do manly things. And since my son-in-law was raised without a dad, I will have the privilege of being a father figure in his life. Yes, in giving I will receive.

The fabric of the Christian faith is replete with that pattern. For example, Jesus said, *"Give and you shall be given to you." (Luke 6:38)* St. Paul observed, *"A man reaps what he sows." (Galatians 6:7)* But it's not just a Christian principle. A Jewish proverb claims, *"One person gives freely, yet gains even more." (Proverbs 11:24)* I would contend that the principle of "receiving through giving" is a universal axiom.

And a wedding is just one opportunity to validate the truth of that axiom. In everyday life, we are invited to give up something we prize. It could be our money, our time, our rights or having the last word. Ultimately, we all have a choice of holding on or letting go.

Reflections on Life and Faith

Sharing a Common Cup with the World

This month I begin my tenth year as a regular columnist for the Mercer Island Reporter.

Over the past decade, I have shared personal observations about faith and culture against the backdrop of current events and everyday life. My goal has been to find common ground with a diverse readership that reflects various faith expressions.

Since my first column appeared in July 2005, Mercer Island has continued to become a culturally diverse community. Even as the nations of our planet descended on Brazil this past month, our school district is increasingly multiethnic. With that in mind, finding shared religious and cultural values is at once a challenge and an opportunity.

While watching several World Cup matches over the past four weeks, I have pondered the iconic image of Christ the Redeemer overlooking Rio de Janeiro. With arms extended in a gesture of acceptance, the gigantic statue of Jesus silently welcomes all peoples. It is a beautiful picture: a God who understands the beautiful mosaic of a diverse world defined by distinct colors, languages and cultures. That symbolism invites you and me to strike a similar pose of hospitality and openness.

Taking the time to get to know people who are different than I am is the first step in being able to understand them. Making friends with those outside of my circle of friendship not only increases the size of that circle, it reduces the number of strangers in my life.

Whereas there will always be beliefs and values that I hold that others do not share, there is a deep joy that fills my heart when I am celebrating those things I do have in common with another. The degree to which we got caught up in the euphoria surrounding the USA World Cup team is an illustration of that.

Although people in our country are bitterly divided about issues like gun control, immigration, same-sex marriage and the legalization of marijuana, when it came to cheering on our soccer team, we were delightfully united. For a couple weeks, we found ways to put our differences aside and focus on a goal about which we agreed. The World Cup found us sharing a common cup.

And while the world's month-long "focus on feet" is over, we still have the opportunity to join hands and put into practice what we learned this past month. It all begins with picturing the statue with the open arms.

Reflections on Oso

Since the sixth century, the six weeks prior to Easter have been known as Lent. During this season, Christians contemplate the cost of their salvation. It is a time for self-examination, reflection, fasting and repentance. On a voluntary basis, Christ-followers identify with the temptations of Jesus and personalize his suffering. It is a slow-motion journey that culminates in Holy Week and Easter Sunday.

In the midst of the Lenten season, the massive mudslide in the community of Oso precipitated involuntary suffering that ground "life as it was" to a halt and saw attempts to experience a new normal move ahead at less than normal speed.

The aerial photographs contrasting the hillside prior to the slide with the debris field following it are mind-boggling. I called a friend who has been a parish pastor in Darrington for over thirty years. The Reverend Les Hagen described for me the aftermath of a tragedy whose cost may never be fully calculated. He related that what he saw was worse than a war zone.

Buried bodies and leveled homes explain the community-wide sorrow that still hangs over Oso like a low-lying emotional fog. The continual motorcade of hearses from local churches to area cemeteries provided a visible reminder of the perpetual pain that remains. Death hangs in the air. Fractured dreams lay in the dust. Heartache hovers over homes (and homeowners) that are no longer.

As I watched the ongoing media coverage of the recovery zone, I pictured the Skagit Valley some thirty miles to the west of Oso. While film crews captured the chaos of a collapsed hillside, thousands of digital cameras were clicking at the fields of tulips that draw tourists from around the world each spring.

I found the contrast in scenes deeply moving. It was, in fact, a dramatization of the Easter message churches will be articulating this weekend. What is buried and seemingly gone needs not result in hopeless despair.

Buried tulip bulbs are not visible. They are as good as dead. But come this time of the year, tulips rise from their earthen graves in a brilliant display of color and design. Like a miniature trumpet, each flower bugles an Easter tune announcing the cycle of the seasons. Winter has surrendered to spring. It is Mother Nature's symphony that affirms the biblical message: *Death is swallowed up by life.*

That message offers comfort to those in Oso who are, oh, so sad. As Saint Paul wrote long ago, *"We do not grieve as those who have no hope."*

Christ is risen! He is risen, indeed!

Reflections on Life and Faith

A Christmas Prayer

Almighty One, we call You Emmanuel (God-with-us) because of this day. On this magical morning (and every Christmas morning) we attempt to wrap our minds around a mystery that exceeds our ability to fully understand. You, who created the world, visited our world as One-with-us.

You, who made the Milky Way, suckled human milk from a virgin's breast. You, who called the seven seas into existence, cried salty tears in need of being comforted. You, who rested on the seventh day of creation, slept within a feeding trough filled with hay.

On this Christmas Day, we recall the extraordinary strides You took stepping across time and space in order to experience life-with-us. Laying aside Your glory, You clothed Yourself in our skin exposing Yourself to the sin of our making. And after two thousand years, the sin of our making continues to manifest itself all around us. Having endured our human condition, You ache with us, God.

But on those silent nights when Your presence seems absent, remind us that You personally relate to our plight as we suffer in silence. Admittedly, while we sing "Joy to the World," there is not much joy in our world. Homelessness and hunger, injustice and poverty, abuse at home and war abroad undermine our joy. These chronic realities prevent us from experiencing the life, liberty and pursuit of happiness our founding fathers pictured.

We deck the halls with boughs of holly, but our hearts are draped in despair. Unemployment is rampant. Gun violence is unprecedented. The political process is demoralizing. Our personal and national debt is on the increase while church attendance is in steady decline.

Intersections

As much of our nation dreams of a White Christmas, many of us are dreaming of a day when the moral courage of a beloved black leader would increasingly mark our lives. Thank You for Nelson Mandela's example of forgiveness, his pursuit of justice and his championing of human rights.

Yes, today we mark the birthday of the Prince of Peace even as the death of a peace-loving president continues to occupy our attention. The global grief surrounding Mandela's passing reminds us how a single life can alter the course of history. Jesus did. So did Moses, Esther, Mohamed, Copernicus, Luther, Lincoln, Gandhi, Graham, King and Teresa. And we can.

May we honor this day with more than carol-singing, over-eating or gift-giving. May our presence in this world be the gift that keeps on giving. Amen.

The Lord's Day vs. Game Day

While church attendance in North America has been in decline for the past few decades, it would be ill-advised to suggest that worship is no longer a part of our culture. In light of the devotion that marks professional football fans this time of year, it would be safe to suggest our inbred worship instincts have simply been redirected.

We still worship on Sundays, just not the way we used to. The Sunday-go-to-meeting garb of years gone by has been replaced by team logo sweatshirts and replica jerseys.

Every Sunday football's faithful, robed in sacred color schemes, chant their praises to the pigskin god on high. In both domed and dome-less cathedrals throughout the country, devoted fans converge at the appropriate hour to confess their belief in something bigger than themselves. With unguarded emotional responses they raise their arms heavenward. Their week-in and week-out rituals verge on superstition.

It's religion pure and simple. But the liturgy observed is not limited to those in the "pews." I'd call attention to the priests who officiate the three-hour service. (Can you believe we used to complain about mass lasting sixty minutes?) In their black-and-white vestments, the pastoral team directs the sacred drama and prompts the congregation's responses with their amplified announcements.

On the field, some ancient sacrifice is reenacted. The obvious pain and suffering call to mind the brute and gore of gladiator days when the faithful hid in catacombs as opposed to sipping beer and eating brats comfortably seated in outdoor stadiums. With rapt attention, the worshipers vicariously feel the pain of those who suffer on their behalf.

In both joy and in sorrow they pray to the pigskin god, pleading that this deity above will fix the score.

Yes, it appears that football's faithful comprise the fastest-growing religion in our nation. The conversion rate is stunning. Sadly, the longing for belonging and community many failed to find in their local church has been met in sports bars and stadiums. Equally sad, what was once a source of benign amusement has become idolatry. For too many, the Lord's Day has given way to Game Day!

When the Parent Becomes the Child

November 4, 2008, was a red-letter day for our nation as well as our family. The same day we elected our first black President, my dad lost his lengthy battle with cancer. Within a few months my brother and I moved our mom, Star Asimakoupoulos, into a retirement community near her home. At first she seemed to thrive.

Soon an uninvited companion known as dementia came to live with Mom. The demands it made were heartless. Dementia dictated she repeat herself over and over. It robbed her of her ability to track with television programs or read a book. Further, dementia insisted she play hide-and-seek while it proceeded to conceal her purse, her camera, her reading glasses, her door key and her cane.

When it became clear that Mom's fuzzy mind was sabotaging her safety, my brother and I attempted to convince her she needed assisted living. She would hear nothing of it.

Observing that Mom was not eating healthily or bathing regularly or remembering to take her meds, we had to act. I knew that I was now the parent and my little mother was the child.

The night before moving day, my mother threw a tantrum. She yelled at me and through a veil of tears tried to pull rank on me. *"You can't do this. I'm your mother! I'm not moving!"*

By morning I'd awaken with a knot in my gut. How could I hurt my mom by forcing something on her that she vehemently opposed? I was acting in love, but she was convinced I was robbing her of what little independence she had left.

It was then that I recalled words my mother had spoken decades before when she felt obliged to take away some of my freedoms. *"This hurts me more than it hurts you!"*

Yes, it hurt me more than it hurt her. But I had a sense deep inside that we had done the right thing. My prayer is that her advancing dementia will in time cause her to forget the place from which she'd been moved.

Almost four years to the day after I promised my dad on his death bed that I would take care of Mom, we moved her to assisted living. And as difficult as it was to take that step, I believe I kept my promise.

Finding Buried Treasure

Did you hear about the family in Florida that recently found buried treasure at the bottom of the ocean? The value of their unexpected find was estimated to be in excess of a million dollars.

I have never gone searching after pirates' plunder, but while sorting through my parents' garage recently, I came across meaningful mementos I had no idea existed.

Imagine my surprise when I opened a box of old books and came upon a world civilization textbook from the 1930s. As I opened the cover, I discovered who the young student was who had once toted it home from Wenatchee Junior High School. None other than the publisher of my hometown newspaper.

Speaking of newspapers, I also came upon a yellowed front page of the Seattle Post-Intelligencer from August 15, 1945. The giant blue and white headlines announced PEACE. The war that had defined my father's young life was over. The war that had resulted in sixty million deaths had finally ended. No wonder he kept it.

But the most significant find was a letter my maternal grandfather had written to my mom's sister in 1949. It was a brief typed letter in which Papa Birkeland asked his daughter to pray about a decision her brother needed to make about a job offer in Lewiston, Idaho.

As I read the carbon-copy letter on onionskin paper, a lump formed in my throat. For the first time in my life, I realized how significant that letter was. Had my uncle decided not to take the Lewiston position, I'd never have been born.

It was because my mom's brother decided to opt for the job that he moved with his family to Idaho. It was while working in Lewiston that my Uncle Benny met a young unmarried minister. As my uncle spent time with Pastor Eddie, he realized that this handsome cleric would be a great catch for his unmarried baby sister. Four dates and seven months later, the two were married. Fifteen months later I was born.

Happening upon that letter was like finding a small fortune. Being faced with the stark reality that I might never have been born has allowed me to look back on the past sixty-three years with a deeper sense of gratitude.

So what about those boxes in the attic you've successfully managed to ignore? Perhaps it's time to start a treasure expedition. There's no telling what you might unearth. But based on my experience, whatever you find is bound to be worth the effort.

What I've Learned Since High School

Forty-five years ago I graduated from Wenatchee High School. This month I will attend our class reunion. Anticipating that event, I've been reflecting on lessons I've learned since graduation.

The year we reached for our diploma, Richard Nixon was President. The draft was populating our military presence in Vietnam. Earth Day was established. In 1970, Clearasil was the drug of choice. Image was everything. What we wore mattered almost as much as whom we hung out with. Jocks. Greasers. Band geeks. Drama nerds. Smokers. Students.

Actually we were all students. Many were average. Some were good students. A handful were really good. Those below average were smarter than their grades indicated.

And then we graduated. (Well, most of us did.)

Attending Friday night football games gave way to focusing on the game of life. Concerns over lost homework would give way to attempts to lose weight or finding ways to deal with the loss of moms, dads and mates. Some are even attempting to cope with a diagnosis of memory loss.

Preoccupation with pimples on our faces gave way to fixation with pictures on Facebook. Wearing our hair the right way has given way to feeling grateful for the hair we have.

What mattered forty-five years ago doesn't seem to matter so much. What does matter is time with children and grandchildren or caring for the needs of aging parents.

Students who mocked those who were quick to verbalize their faith in high school are more apt to embrace the need of God as their own health declines or as family issues find them on their knees. Those who tended to be a bit Pharisaical about their faith are more inclined to be less legalistic.

I'm grateful for one more opportunity to interact in-person with those who are more than a young face in an old yearbook. Those with whom I will gather are far more than a clever post on a Facebook page. They are people with whom I share a common past and an unpredictable future. They are people who realize every memorial service we attend is one closer to our own and that each day is a gift.

A Godwink While Hunting for a House

Ten years ago as Wendy and I prepared to move to Mercer Island from Chicago, we faced the challenge of finding a place to live. Our equity from a home in Illinois wouldn't go far. Quite discouraged, we happened on a home for-sale-by-owner that showed promise.

As Emil Riccardi and his wife, Roberta, escorted us through their home, he told us how much they loved the residence they'd owned for thirty-five years. They went on to explain how they'd raised their five children in the Catholic faith in a home that radiated God's peace.

At that moment I looked up and saw a framed picture of Jesus. The face on the hallway wall that greeted my wife and me was no ordinary religious art. It was Sallman's "Head of Christ" that had graced my boyhood bedroom. It was the famous brown-tone profile that also hung in my grandparents' house on Queen Anne Hill. At once I could sense the countenance of God smiling on our home-hunting expedition.

The picture on the wall provided me an immediate connection with a man I'd barely met. It was mutual. Mr. Riccardi proceeded to acknowledge a doctor's diagnosis about which he was quite apprehensive. I suggested we pray about it.

To my delight he was willing to let me. As the Jesus on the wall looked on, the four of us joined hands as I prayed for healing and grace for the journey ahead.

Needless to say, we bought the home. Looking back, it was the familiar face in the frame in the hallway that gave us the "Godwink" we needed to proceed.

Remarkably, the tenth anniversary of our purchasing our home is the seventy-fifth anniversary of the Sallman's "Head of Christ." Since 1940 that representation of Jesus has been reprinted over one billion times. It is thought to be the most reproduced image in history.

Ironically, my married daughter and son-in-law are moving to suburban Seattle from Chicago next month to join the staff of a church. A couple weeks ago I visited them. God winked again! I learned that the bungalow where Warner Sallman once lived and where he'd painted his masterpiece was just five doors from my kids. I introduced myself explaining my interest in their historic residence. When they showed me around his upstairs studio, I sensed God's smile again!

Thankful for Normal Days!

This Thanksgiving I'm thanking God for the beauty of an average kind of day. I've come to see that normal isn't boring. It's an underrated blessing in our lives.

The recent contamination of our community's water supply with E. coli requiring us to boil our water for a week helped me to see normal through new eyes. So did that major wind storm a few weeks later that left our neighborhood without power for four days.

As I contemplate God's goodness this year, my list of things for which I am grateful is dominated by the little things that enrich my life. Little things like...

Drinking water from the tap without boiling it. Flipping on the wall switch and lighting up the bedroom without need of a flashlight. Turning up the thermostat and feeling warm without having to don a down jacket.

Brewing a cup of French roast from our electric coffeemaker instead of driving to the local Starbucks for a Grande drip. Watching the Seahawks on TV instead of driving around town in my car listening to the game while charging my iPhone.

A couple years ago while writing a book about Frank Capra's classic movie "It's a Wonderful Life," I was reminded of the beauty of everyday blessings. After George Bailey is granted "the greatest gift" of being able to see a world in which he was never born, he resumes his normal life. As he does, he discovers just how wonderful normal is. The little things of life that once irritated him have become sources of joy.

George's bleeding lip, the result of being punched in the mouth in a bar scuffle, becomes a cut for which he is thankful. The loose banister knob on the stairs that had been a source of frustration to George for years he now views with gratitude.

He is also elated to find his little girl's flower petals in his watch pocket. Although not a fragrant dozen roses, Zuzu's petals are a bouquet of blessings nonetheless. George Bailey's temporary deprivation of "the little things" gave him the ability to see normal as the essence of a wonderful life.

Being thankful for normal days is rooted in the soil of contented hearts. A first-century rabbi by the name of Paul invited his disciples to discover the joy that is rooted in contentment. He wrote *"I know what it is to be in need, and I know what it is to have plenty. I have learned the secret of being content in any and every situation..."*

This Thanksgiving season I have discovered the same secret. Being grateful for normal days and being contented with the small things of life definitely isn't normal. It's a learning process. And, ironically, it takes going without the things we take for granted to appreciate what really matters.

The Boiling Point

During our recent "water days" I was reminded of that famous line from Coleridge's Rime of the Ancient Mariner. *"Water, water, everywhere but not a drop to drink..."*

Since our boil-water alert coincided with Yom Kippur, I also found myself reflecting on the triumphs and trials of God's people in the Old Testament. The exodus of the ancient Jews from Egypt caught my attention.

After four hundred years of captivity, they celebrated new-found freedom. But after only a few days into their joyful journey towards the Promised Land, they were hostages once again.

This time they were victims of their own thirst. No drinkable water was in sight. Dreams of exploring "a land of milk and honey" gave way to longings for a simple sip of water.

As residents of a fairly affluent community, we relate. Freed from the captivity of hourly wage occupations and no longer enslaved by financial worries, we eye our own "promised land" of comfortable lifestyles and early retirements.

Living in one of the most desirable ZIP codes in America finds us self-sufficient, self-focused and often insulated from the suffering of people a continent or two away. That is until our drinking water is contaminated and what we mindlessly take for granted is denied.

Like the ancient Jews, when we found ourselves without drinking water, we had a choice. We could gripe and complain or we could choose to let the problem refocus our perspective. Most likely we responded both ways.

So did our spiritual ancestors. Initially, the freed slaves of Pharaoh read Moses the riot act. But then they saw in their dilemma an opportunity to alter their perspective, trust Yahweh and mature in their faith.

When the water issues of our community reached the boiling point for the second time in a week, School Superintendent Gary Plano chose not to cancel classes.

While providing alternative water sources and assuring parents of their students' safety, Dr. Plano saw an opportunity to help kids understand the plight of two thirds of the world.

What we assume is normal life is merely a dream for millions. What a great teachable moment!

But E. coli contamination scares aren't the only times we find ourselves in hot water. Our comfortable lives are often blindsided by unexpected unemployment, an unanticipated doctor's diagnosis and unthinkable heartache related to our aging parents and adult children.

It's at times like these where we'd do well to remember heat has a purifying effect in our lives… if we let it!

The Slippery Slope of Common Ground

I recently traveled to Greece to research my roots. A highlight of the trip was spending a day in Athens walking among the temple ruins atop the Acropolis. In addition to the incredible view that vista provides of modern-day Athens, the ancient pillars provide a historical perspective of the architectural genius that punctuated the civilization that gave the world democracy.

I began my descent down the steep trail toward the bustling Agora with one further desire. I wanted to stand on Mars Hill that is located at the base of the Acropolis. As a student of the Bible, I was aware that the Apostle Paul stood on this marble perch to make his case for Christ before a pagan crowd.

I began my ascent up the marble steps without thinking how slippery the well-trafficked stones might be. As a result, I lost my footing and fell. Feeling more embarrassment than pain, I picked myself up and proceeded to the top. From the summit I looked around and could see the remains of countless altars and temples. I recalled Paul's words from Mars Hill (see Acts 17:22-31).

Based on what he observed from his vantage point, Paul attested to the fact that the Athenians were a very religious people. I love the way Paul engaged those whose spiritual and cultural backgrounds were distinct from his. Instead of putting them down, he affirmed their faith journey (albeit pagan) proceeding to offer his own personal perspective. In other words, he looked for common ground in which to till the soil of understanding and mutual respect with hopes for eventually sowing seeds of truth.

Finding common ground can be a slippery slope. It requires exposing yourself to attitudes and ideas that may feel foreign to you. Nonetheless, finding common ground is worth the risks that are part of the process. In the end, it provides a perspective that enables each of us to view diversity and find points of connection.

As the world's athletes compete in Brazil, we are provided a picture of just how diverse the people who populate our planet are. The opening ceremonies of the Summer Olympics were a beautiful reminder of how we approach a common purpose differently. Each nation brings something of value from which others can learn.

Similarly, each person in our sphere of influence has something with which to inform our view of life, faith and truth. And we have something to contribute to their understanding.

But first we must understand where others are coming from by taking time to listen to them.

Reflections on Life and Faith

Confessions of a Streetwalker

In the six decades I've driven along life's highway, I've passed numerous mileposts. College graduation. Marriage. Becoming a dad. Becoming ordained. Buying my first home. Publishing my first book. Burying my father. Walking a daughter down the aisle. Landing my dream job at Covenant Shores.

Blurring mileposts have brought a timeless truth into focus. Time seems to pass more quickly the older we get. But I've come to see that growing older is nothing to fear. The vitality that defines the eighty-somethings and ninety-somethings in my life has reframed my perspective of the aging process.

Take my friend Ted Katsanis. Even though he is ninety, he leads a hiking club that finds him and his friends in some of the most scenic vistas of the foothills each Tuesday.

And then there's ninety-three-year-old John Lindberg, who thinks nothing of a train trip to Glacier National Park on a long weekend. Jon Parkinson lives for his weekly golf game even though he's eighty-six.

But I am most impressed by my friend Dave McKenna. At eighty-seven, this retired seminary president has just published his fortieth book. His most recent offering bears a most curious title: *Confessions of a Street Walker*.

What I love about *Confessions of a Street Walker* (in addition to the very compelling title) is Dave's take on what really matters in life. Resumes, accolades and titles fade when contrasted to first-name friendships. The book chronicles the people Dave has met while walking his dog, Molly, on the streets of Kirkland.

Intersections

By his own admission, Dave is an old dog who is capable of learning new tricks. It took this learned academician decades to understand the value of forgoing labels like Ph.D, institutional president or church pastor. Quite contentedly, my longtime friend is happy to be known simply as Molly's master or just plain Dave.

The insights shared in this great little read reflect big lessons accumulated over a long and productive life. As I walked through the pages of the book with Dave and his little dog, Molly, I vicariously walked the streets of Kirkland and met new friends. I discovered that even though life tends to speed by more quickly as you approach your ultimate destination, what can be learned later in life makes up for how quickly the years pass.

The ABCs for Graduates

Accept responsibility for your own actions. Trying to pass the buck will get you sacked.

Believe you have what it takes to make the world a better place.

Cast your cares on your creator. Anxieties that hold you hostage rob your peace of mind.

Do unto others as you would have others do unto you.

Exercise regularly. Cardiovascular activity clears the mind and contributes to restful sleep.

Fuel your body with healthy food. If you want to live a long time, eat more fruits and vegetables.

Give to charitable causes. You'll feel good about yourself when you share with others.

Hang on when you feel like letting go. Perseverance is the price tag for realizing the dreams God has planted in your heart.

Invest your money. Deferring gratification compounds your interest at the bank and in what really matters.

Just do it! Doing today what shouldn't be left for tomorrow produces yesterdays devoid of regret.

Keep short accounts with others. Taking the initiative to resolve disagreements reduces stress.

Lick an ice cream cone instead of eating it. Savoring life's little pleasures makes them last longer.

Mind your own business. Be grateful you're not everyone's judge.

Never say never. When tempted to hold airtight convictions, leave space for breathing room.

Open your eyes to the wonders around you. It was Browning who said, "Earth is crammed with heaven and every common bush afire with God. But only he who sees takes off his shoes. The rest sit round and pluck blackberries."

Preach what you practice. Don't keep your passions to yourself.

Question easy answers. The world is filled with bumper-sticker platitudes that stick only to the chrome of a car.

Read for fun. There's more to life than technical books that prepare you for degrees or deadlines. Lose yourself in the pages of poetry or fiction.

Seek the ultimate meaning of life. The great thinkers of history invite you to think with your soul.

Talk to strangers. Some things you learned in kindergarten need to be unlearned. People you haven't yet met hold keys to doors of opportunity currently locked.

Unleash your imagination. Let your creative mind run free. Daydreaming isn't just for kids.

Value each day. The present is a gift. "Today is the first day of the rest of your life."

Waste time. Wasting time isn't the unpardonable sin. If you play hard, you'll work better.

X-amine your motives. Ask yourself what Rotarians do: Is it the truth? Is it fair and beneficial to all concerned? Will it build goodwill?

Yearn for a kingdom that's out of this world. Jesus said it best: "Seek the kingdom of God above all else ... He will give you everything you need."

Zip it! When a friend shares something in confidence, keep your mouth shut. Trustworthiness is a priceless virtue.

Grateful for a Mother's Legacy

This Mother's Day, I'll be mindful of four life lessons my mom modeled for me.

Look for value in what others deem worthless. For as long as I can remember, my mom loved to shop at thrift stores. Someone's discarded junk became "a find" that found its way into our home.

As I accompanied her to the Goodwill, my mom did more than teach me how to seek hidden treasure. I learned to look beneath the surface in people to discover the value that lies within. I'm so grateful.

Keep a song in your heart. I love to sing. At Covenant Shores, I'm known as the singing chaplain. Singing has defined my life. I even taught our three daughters how to spell our "big fat Greek name" with an original song. My love for song came from a mom who was always singing. At eighty-nine, she still is. Although she is battling dementia, our phone visits conclude singing a duet. Mom can't recall what she had for lunch, but she has no problem remembering lyrics to old hymns.

What I inherited from my mom was more than the ability to carry a tune. She bequeathed me the importance of making music no matter the circumstances of life. I can't thank her enough.

Make others laugh. Anyone who's met my mother knows she always has a joke. Sadly, her dementia has reduced her repertoire of funny stories to the same few she repeats over and over.

But Mom's joy in bringing enjoyment to others has rubbed off on me. I look for ways to lighten a serious staff meeting or insert laughter in a worship service. I'm grateful for a mom who personified the biblical proverb: *"A merry heart is good medicine."*

Seek God for guidance. From the time she was a little girl, faith has been Mom's compass. It continues to be on a journey marked by unexpected twists and confusing turns. I often overhear her calling out to God for help while trying to find her keys. She talks to the Lord as if He was her best friend. And for good reason. He is.

As we end our phone visits, Mom insists we pray. To hear her, you'd never know she has Alzheimer's. With uncanny eloquence, she asks God to help me serve my flock and family effectively. How very thankful I am for a mother who has modeled for me how to call upon the Father.

Now That I'm Sixty-Four!

"When I get older losing my hair, many years from now ..." I first heard the lyrics to that Beatles song "When I'm Sixty-Four," when I was fifteen.

As I sang the words, I couldn't imagine what it would be like to be that age. For a freshman in high school, it seemed like light years away.

Well, this week I turned sixty-four. Curiously, I have lost most of my hair. And for the record, what's left of my hair has lost its curl and original color.

As I reflect on what it's like to be on the threshold of retirement age, I realize that other lyrics of the "Fab Four" provide me a meaningful perspective.

Take the words to "Yesterday." At this age, I am tempted to put too much stock in yesterday. While life was simpler back then, the older I get, the more I tend to romanticize the past.

As someone once said, "What makes the good old days the good old days is a bad memory." There is nothing quite as wonderful as today. Even when it appears that troubles are here to stay, my three-score-and-four years have taught me *"I can do all things through Christ who gives me strength."*

While I long for yesterday on occasion, I'm grateful to God for the gift of today. In terms of tenses, there is a reason why we call it "the present."

Now that I am sixty-four, I also find myself meditating on the refrain of McCartney's masterpiece "Let it Be." While Paul was thinking of his mother (Mary) who died when he was only fourteen, I'm inclined to think of the Virgin Mother.

Remember how Mary responded to the angelic messenger who informed her she had been chosen for the overwhelming task of birthing and raising the Son of God? She humbly acquiesced and replied *"Let it be to me as you have said!"*

When I find myself in times of trouble (and who doesn't as they enter the autumn of life), I find great comfort in voicing Mother Mary's words. *"Let it be!"*

I tend to believe that verse in the Bible I learned as a boy that says, *"All things work together for good to those who love God ..."* Accepting what God allows in my life and not fighting it is the first step in trusting Him for how things will all work out for good. And so I am increasingly learning how to pray, "Let it be, Lord! Let it be!"

First Impressions Can Be Misleading

Good Friday at first blush appears misnamed. What could possibly be good about a day that recalls the public execution of a peace-loving prophet falsely charged and wrongly convicted? But first impressions can be misleading.

Take that opening scene in the movie, "The Martian." While caught in an unexpected storm on the surface of the red planet, actor Matt Damon's character is impaled by metal fragments from a flying antenna and left for dead. Mark Watney's friends abandon his lifeless body and blast off from Mars. They grieve their loss and reluctantly go on with their lives.

Subsequently, Mark regains consciousness and discovers that the metal that punctured his space suit has sealed in enough oxygen to allow him to get back to the space station. Reality sets in. He can't survive on a three-month supply of food. This botanist's scientific mind contemplates how he can survive.

He creates a greenhouse, fertilizes the soil and plants pieces of potato from the space-station galley. But to irrigate the soil, he needs to create a flame to generate heat to create water from hydrogen. Mark discovers a fellow astronaut's small wooden crucifix. With his pocketknife he scrapes wood fragments from the cross into a pile of kindling and ignites the shavings.

As a minister, I find delight in the fact that it was a cross that became the means of hope that kept the astronaut alive. The cross was a source of life.

Good Friday is a day in which I contemplate a solitary figure impaled by pieces on a wooden cross and left for dead by his friends. There appeared to be no cause for hope.

But then came Sunday. What had seemed hopeless resulted in an unexpected ending. First impressions had been misleading. The One left for dead surprised His friends. He was very much alive.

Easter weekend invites us to contemplate possibilities not initially evident. Unanticipated unemployment may be the "cross" that allows for the dream job you couldn't imagine becoming a reality. A dead marriage may be the means that finds you seeking help that can revive a relationship that seems beyond hope.

A doctor's diagnosis might be the very thing that awakens your hibernating faith and motivates you to begin to redefine what it means to really live.

From my perspective, the cross and the empty tomb are what kindle our faith and fuel our hope against the backdrop of certain peril.

Lessons I Learned from Bert and Ernie

Last month I officiated the memorial service for a friend who recently celebrated his one-hundredth birthday. Bert Pound moved into Covenant Shores about the time I began working there as chaplain. As I became acquainted with Bert, I also began to spend time with a retired college professor by the name of Ernie Dawn who was two years younger.

Both Bert and Ernie were remarkable men. In spite of their advanced age, they had a childlike enthusiasm and an ability to unwrap each day as if it were a gift. The more time I spent with them, the more I discovered aspects of their lives I wanted to incorporate into my own.

While my three daughters watched Sesame Street religiously as preschoolers, they are not the only ones who owe a debt of gratitude to characters by the names of Bert and Ernie. I can honestly say my life is richer from the lessons the Bert and Ernie on Fortuna Drive modeled for me. Let me identify a few.

1) Celebrate past achievements.

Bert never tired of talking about being part of the University of Washington marching band. Bert took pride in knowing he was part of the UW during an exciting time in school history. As "The Boys in the Boat" were taking gold in the 1936 Berlin Olympics, the boys in Bert's percussion section were providing a cadence that found the football team headed to Pasadena. Bert proudly displayed his Husky letterman's jacket that included a patch commemorating his participation in the 1937 Rose Bowl.

Bert's look back at his accomplishments motivated me to follow his lead.

2) Invest in present opportunities.

Although crippled by a spinal injury and forced to use a walker, Ernie was no couch potato. The professor was an active member of the Covenant Shores investment club and a political think tank. Reading the New York Times and watching cable news programs were essential ingredients in Ernie's daily diet. He found joy in a good debate on current events with other residents.

Watching Dr. Dawn greet each day with curiosity taught me the importance of remaining engaged with the world around me.

3) Let faith guide your future.

By his own admission, faith had not played a key role in Bert's life. His wife had been the devoted churchgoer. But when she died, my friend expressed a desire to explore the spiritual dimension of his life and became a regular participant in my Sunday services. Offering unsolicited critiques of my sermons, Bert often noted I spent too much time challenging my flock to love the Lord and not enough time encouraging them to love their neighbor.

Bert taught me the importance of balance. After all, both "loves" were part of the Great Commandment. Perhaps it was his many years at Boeing that found him focusing on the fact that it takes two wings of a plane to fly.

A Letter to the Christ Child

Dear Jesus,
This week, as over two billion of your followers prepare to celebrate your birthday, I find myself attempting to manage a myriad of emotions.

I love this time of year. The twinkling lights, festive traditions and familiar music bring out the child in me. But this Christmas season, it's not just my inner child that cannot be contained. My married daughter is in the ninth month of her pregnancy. Within a few weeks, my wife and I will become first-time grandparents.

Jesus, as I look at my adult child, I can't help but picture your precious mother on the threshold of giving birth. Her face, like my daughter's, must have glowed with the radiant beauty unique to expectant moms. I can hardly wait to hold that little one.

Still, this Christmas finds me perplexed with the problems of the world into which my grandchild will be born. The spirit of giving has been replaced by a spirit of taking. Countless individuals are taking to Facebook to demean those who disagree with their political perspective. Too often Facebook "friends" are anything but.

The season surrounding your birthday has often been called "the most wonderful time of the year." But this year, it's less than wonderful. Although we sing about a joyful world filled with silent nights and recite verses that speak of "peace on earth goodwill to men," we know better.

Homelessness is on the rise both at home and abroad. So are the growing numbers of refugees seeking a safe place to raise their children. Add to that the terrorists and delusional dictators who hold our hope for peace hostage. Yes, the thirst for power and the appetite for domination resemble the Roman Empire into which you were born.

Jesus, you certainly must relate to the world in which I live. Contrary to the lyrics of that popular carol, I'm guessing you didn't really sleep in heavenly peace as your mother struggled to comfort you in that cold and wet barn smelling of cow dung. How could you not identify with the homeless population in my city where make-shift shelters dominate the underpasses of the interstate?

You understand only too well the fear and hate associated with terrorism and political exile. Shortly after you were born, a blood-thirsty tyrant blindsided young parents in Bethlehem murdering their helpless children. Your parents fled with you from a terrorist plot as they sought asylum in Egypt. They had no idea where they were going or what awaited them when they got there.

No wonder you identify with the plight of refugees around the world who have left their home countries in search of a life free from war and prejudice. Being homeless and fleeing from terrorism, it's no wonder you have a heart for the dispossessed and the marginalized among us. Having been welcomed by strangers in a strange land, your experience inspires us to be willing to do the same.

Pondering the world of fear and hate into which my grandchild will soon be born, the child within me begins to kick and scream in protest. I refuse to believe that we can't do better as travel companions on spaceship Earth. After all, the place where I first came across your birth announcement clued me into the fact that every man, woman and child has been created in the image of our Creator. There is something in us worthy of redemption.

Come to think of it, Jesus, isn't that why you were born in the first place?

Signed,
An Honest Christian

A Veteran of Gratitude

For ninety-seven years, my friend Victor Bergquist modeled gratitude. Long before Hollywood Film Director Frank Capra introduced us to a thankful George Bailey, Vic was celebrating his own wonderful life.

Vic began running the marathon of life on November 11, 1918, the day the Allied Forces declared victory in World War I. His parents, grateful the conflict had ended, named their firstborn Victor in honor of the armistice.

When I met this Mercer Island resident eleven years ago, it dawned on me just how perfect Vic's name was. Early on he'd learned how to claim victory in the midst of defeat. When he was only nine, his mother died unexpectedly. The grief-stricken lad proceeded to lean on a Heavenly Father who would not let him go.

As he grew up, Vic never found himself unemployed. His regular paycheck was a source of gratitude. As a young husband and father of a two-year-old son, Vic was drafted in 1944. In spite of the fact that his wife was pregnant with their second child, he was grateful for the privilege to serve his Uncle Sam. When his baby girl was born the following year, Vic rejoiced that he would be granted an early discharge. Vic kept finding blessings to count when he settled into a career as a successful salesman.

Born the same week as Evangelist Billy Graham, Vic's life was punctuated by a similar passion. He was consistently inviting others to experience what he believed to be the source of his happiness.

Intersections

As I got to know Vic at Covenant Shores, I discovered every day was Thanksgiving Day for this positive pilgrim. Three little words dominated Vic's vocabulary. *"Thank you, Lord!"*

He was grateful his oldest son and his oldest grandson had followed calls on their lives into pastoral ministry. He gave God thanks that his contagious faith had been successfully passed to future generations.

A year ago, Vic was diagnosed with inoperable cancer. Still, the thankful heart of this veteran of gratitude didn't skip a beat. He looked forward to Heaven. He was excited to be reunited with loved ones (including his wife) who waited for him on the other side.

On more than one occasion, Vic had confided how much he longed to see his mother. With tears in his eyes, my friend confessed that he had pined for her since her death some nine decades before. One of the tangible reasons he was so grateful for Heaven was the fact that he'd be able to wrap his arms around a woman who left him too soon. It was a reunion that took place exactly a week after Thanksgiving Day.

What's Faith Got to Do with It?

For nearly ten years I've been the fulltime chaplain at Covenant Shores. It's my dream job. Going to the office is like being on vacation.

But that's not why I wear Hawaiian shirts to work. Rather, I enjoy saying as I encounter residents on campus, "I bring you God's aloha!" I love that South Pacific expression. If you've spent time in the Islands, you know it means hello, goodbye, peace and love.

The ancient Hebrews had a word similar to "aloha." Shalom not only means peace, it also suggests wholeness, balance and integrity. Some refer to this desired state of being as "wellness." And among the aging population where I am privileged to minister, wellness is consistently personified.

William Danforth, who founded the Ralston Purina Company in the late 1800s, saw a correspondence between faith and wellness. Danforth was struck by the description of Jesus' holistic development as recorded in Luke 2:52. *"And Jesus increased in wisdom and stature, and in favor with God and with people."*

The business executive called the four elements of a faith-based life "four square living." He created a checkerboard logo for his product line to symbolize what he believed to be the key to a healthy life.

On the campus where I serve, I see these four elements of wellness lived out in spades.

Intellectual curiosity cultivates a desire to live. In a setting where ninetieth birthday parties are no big deal, mind-stretching opportunities are. I am impressed by those who are actively involved in book clubs and film-discussion groups.

Physical exercise mitigates against the consequences of aging. Stretching one's mind isn't enough to maintain a balanced life.

Physical stretching, weight training and balance exercises are also important. Scripture teaches that the body is the temple of the Holy Spirit. Such a sacred edifice deserves upkeep and refurbishment.

Spiritual expression expands the windshield of one's worldview. The essence of a healthy balanced life is rooted in the soil of the soul.

On a campus like ours, residents attend twenty different congregations in greater Seattle. Faith is foundational to a meaningful life (and death). A personal relationship with their Creator equates to an assurance of eternal life.

Relational involvement reduces the alienation of loneliness. Statistics indicate that people who conclude their lives in a retirement community live some ten years longer than those who live alone.

In Genesis we read, *"It is not good for man to live alone!"* The rest of the Bible illustrates the importance of community.

The Day Mr. Potter Went to Church

When it comes to the classic Christmas film "It's a Wonderful Life," am I the only one who wonders what eventually happened to Mr. Potter? Is it too much to think that the villainous banker of Bedford Falls might one day sit with the Bailey family at the Christmas Eve service at church?

As much as I love Frank Capra's timeless holiday movie, I would have preferred a different ending. I wish there had been some kind of reconciliation between the two foes. A storybook ending to my favorite movie seems as unlikely, however, as a happily-ever-after script in Washington, D.C.

But it's not just in politics where we see the fabric of our union being pulled apart by polarizing perspectives. It's evident in religious preferences, lifestyle choices, health care options and views on gun control.

Even though "It's a Wonderful Life" ends with unresolved conflict between the two lead characters, the people of Bedford Falls exhibit the kind of lifestyle I long for. It's uncomplicated. There is a culture of acceptance, self-sacrifice, cooperation and contentment. It's my kind of town.

Last December I visited Seneca Falls, the small town in upstate New York that many people think inspired Frank Capra's fictional Bedford Falls. I was invited to preach at the local Presbyterian church, do a workshop on the movie and sign copies of my book (*Finding God in It's a Wonderful Life*). In addition to appearing with the aging actors who played the Bailey kids seventy years earlier, I met Donna Reed's daughter and Frank Capra's granddaughter.

As I strolled through the town, snow began falling on the quaint storefront buildings of Fall Street. I pictured myself encountering Violet Bick, Sam (Hee Haw) Wainwright and Uncle Billy while walking by Gower's Drugstore, the Bijou Theatre and the Building and Loan.

In Seneca Falls, where the Republican Party was born and the Women's Rights Movement came of age, townsfolk and business leaders have joined hands to sponsor the IAWL Festival each year. In so doing they are perpetuating the popularity of a movie that celebrates the payoff of working together. In Seneca Falls (like Bedford Falls) I glimpsed what I hoped might be a prototype for cooperation in our divided culture.

The Sunday I preached at "the real Bedford Falls," something occurred that gave me reason to hope that a positive ending to my favorite movie and our polarized nation might just be possible.

Quite by chance two couples who had never met were seated next to each other on the front pew of the church. Both couples had traveled a great distance to attend the festival. Following the service they introduced themselves to me as the Baileys and the Potters. What? Really? I looked at the visitor registry in the narthex to make sure. I could hardly believe what I saw.

And get this. Mr. Bailey's first name actually was George. That "Godwink" gave me cause to think that those who approach life from different perspectives can actually sit down together and find a common purpose. And at this time of year we are reminded that such a common purpose is ours to embrace. He is called Emmanuel ... "God with us!"

A Bittersweet Holiday

This Christmas season marks the tenth anniversary of the last one I would enjoy with my dad. My father had been combating prostate cancer for thirteen years. This proud Marine who had stood behind General Douglas Mac Arthur at the surrender ceremony ending World War II had fought many battles in uniform, but his personal war with cancer had demanded his greatest courage.

Our last holiday meal together was not all that out of the ordinary. Turkey and trimmings, pumpkin pie and a table grace from my retired-pastor father. After the plates were cleared, we took turns going around the table expressing something we were especially grateful for that year.

Only eleven months later I held my dad's hand as he took his final breath. Looking back, if I'd known that would be our last holiday meal, I would have expressed my gratitude with the following words:

1. Thanks for modeling a daily walk with your Heavenly Father. Dad, I will never forget how you began each day sitting in your favorite chair with an open Bible in your lap. Your knowledge of God's Word guided your life and inspired my desire to follow your lead. Your disciplined life of prayer encouraged me to pour out my heart to the Lord.

2. Thanks for showing me how to nurture romance with your wife. Your relationship with Mom was one-of-a-kind, Pop. It was truly a marriage made in Heaven but lived out on earth. My friends said the two of you looked like movie stars, but your marriage was anything but the kind defined by Hollywood. You wrote love notes to each other. You expressed your affection in front of my brother and me. You

resolved disagreements before they could evolve into resentments. I am motivated to invest in my relationship with my wife by what I saw in your marriage.

3. Thanks for regularly telling me you loved me. When I hear people tell me they can't recall a time their dad told them he loved them, I recoil in disbelief. I can't imagine what that must feel like. Dad, you made sure I always knew I was loved. In words, embraces and letters, you tangibly expressed how you felt. And that example accounts for why my three grown daughters know (without doubt) that I love them.

4. Thanks for generously helping me get a leg up. You bought my first car for me. You helped me with a down payment on our first house. You willingly loaned us money when we were in a pinch. While some fathers are inclined to invest in personal hobbies, you invested in your family, Pop. You never turned a deaf ear to a request for help even when you didn't share my enthusiasm for what I needed help to purchase. As a result, I am becoming a generous man.

5. Thanks for the freedom you gave me to express my independence. Although there were times I chose to ignore your advice and counsel, you didn't try to control my choices. Like other adolescents and young adults attempting to find their way, you allowed me to learn by my mistakes. Dad, just like our Heavenly Father, you gave me the space to embrace the truths one can discover only on their own.

6. Thanks for your service to our country. Dad, I didn't tell you often enough how proud I was of the fact that you enlisted in the Marine Corps as an eighteen-year-old. Even though you knew you were headed to the frontlines of a bloody war, you wanted to do your part to protect the freedoms we too often take for granted as a nation. I know you were proud of what you did. I hope you knew how proud I was of you, too.

My Favorite Martin

This month finds me thinking about individuals by the name of Martin who have impacted life.

The first was a fictional one. Uncle Martin (played by Ray Ralston) was a character on "My Favorite Martian." It was one of my favorite television shows when I was in elementary school.

Another Martin was Dr. Albert Martin who was our family dentist. From my first visit, it was obvious his interest in my life was not limited to my teeth.

Then there was Martin Koll. Shortly after he began attending our church, I discovered he loved playing golf as much as I did. When his faith began to blossom, he asked me to baptize him — on the ninth hole of the local country club. It's the only time I've officiated a baptism in a water hazard.

Martin Hampton, another congregant, inspired me with his faith and courage in the midst of adversity. When his daughter was born with spina bifida, Martin modeled a "can do" attitude that inspired our congregation. This young dad's trust in his Heavenly Father motivated his little girl to become an overcomer.

But in all honesty, my most favorite Martin was a Catholic priest to whom I was introduced forty years ago when I entered seminary. Although he came from a different faith tradition than the one in which I was raised, I found myself attracted to his free-spirited perspective.

Father Martin (as he was known) enjoyed discussing theology while drinking beer in a pub. Having been reared in a teetotaler home, I initially found his routine off-putting. But as I gave myself permission to sip a pint while plodding through a passage of Scripture with classmates, I discovered why Martin found it meaningful.

The more I got to know Martin's perspectives, the more I liked him. He objected to the way singing in church on Sundays was limited to a few folks up front. He felt the entire congregation should be engaged in worship and not just the performers. To that end, he wrote original hymns for Sunday mass.

Martin was also an advocate for utilizing a contemporary translation of the Bible so that average churchgoers could understand it. He was known to translate the Hebrew and Greek texts himself. As you might guess, Martin was a popular preacher. His homilies were both inspiring and earthy.

But what really inspired me about Martin was his propensity to protest ecclesiastical activity that he viewed as unbiblical. He wasn't afraid to express his opinion even though his was a minority voice.

I remember hearing about a time when the church leaders downplayed a central doctrine of the church in order to raise funds for a building project in Rome. Father Martin disputed the initiative from his pulpit. Although he was rebuffed by church officials, Martin refused to be silent. He published his opinions through social media. And they went viral.

Yes, my favorite Martin is none other than Martin Luther, the father of the Protestant Reformation. This week is the five-hundredth anniversary of Luther's posting of his ninety-five theses calling for renewal in the Church. This protesting priest has made both Protestants and Catholics more thoughtful in the practice of their faith. And I for one am grateful.

God, Bless America (Revisited)

GOD, BLESS AMERICA. Not because we deserve Your blessings. We don't. However, You'd never know it by the way we sing those familiar words. It almost sounds like we are demanding something from You. Forgive us, Father, for the cavalier way we attempt to order You around.

LAND THAT I LOVE. It's true. In spite of the fact that she is far from perfect, we love this country of contrasting contours. Its amber fields of grain that wave in the wind. Its majestic purple mountains that steal our breath. Its dry desert valleys and orchard-filled plains. Its Great Lakes and Badlands. From the brownstones of inner cities to the White House in the city named for our first President, we love this land where the seeds of freedom continue to grow two hundred forty-one years after they were first sown.

STAND BESIDE HER. Since that tragic September morning sixteen years ago, our country has come to realize how vulnerable she really is. As she continues to fight terrorism and export justice, the continual cost in dollars and human lives leaves her dizzy and in need of support. Deep within her fractured soul she knows she needs You. Without Your overshadowing Presence, freedom's fruit will no longer grow for future generations to enjoy.

AND GUIDE HER. Yes, Lord, please guide her. Our beloved nation has never needed a compass like she does today. She is disoriented, divided and too often double-minded. Unsure of what she stands for, she is prone to fall for anything that is halfway believable. Time was when she looked to Your dictates for direction. The Bible was once her road map. The Ten Commandments were her milepost. But, by bending over backwards in an attempt to become tolerant, she has become a victim of moral vertigo.

Intersections

THROUGH THE NIGHT. *Even though the nightmare of September 11 has passed, the twilight zone of war continues to eclipse the promise of a new day we all long for. The crescent moon in the dark sky overhead reminds us of the religious diversity that is foundational to our democracy. But it also finds us fearing Islamic extremism as we nervously long for the dawn.*

WITH THE LIGHT. *There are glimpses of light all around us, Father. Candles in churches. Spotlights on flags. A kaleidoscope of colored fireworks exploding overhead. They remind us of the hope that we have in You (and our fellow citizens) when we are engulfed by black storm clouds of political debate or are forced to walk through the valley of death's dark shadows.*

FROM ABOVE. *But candles burn out and fireworks are temporary. Even spotlights eventually need to be replaced. Only Your light can dispel the darkness that we most fear. With laser-like precision, please penetrate the membrane of apathy and anxiety that blankets our nation and suffocates our joy.*

FROM THE MOUNTAINS. *From Mt. McKinley to Pike's Peak, from the Rockies to the Smokies. From the green timbers of Mt. Rainier to the Blue Ridge Mountains of Virginia. From Mt. St. Helens in Washington to Mt. Washington in New Hampshire. Lord, may the glory of Your creation in this breathtaking land continue to cause us to lift up our eyes to the hills as we celebrate our freedom.*

TO THE PRAIRIES. *Windswept, yet fertile. The heartland of our nation, where hardworking people prove that determination irrigated by sweat and tears, is essential to growing the American dream. Although the mountain peaks may seem more exotic, we are grateful for those who tame the earth by farming level ground. Reward their efforts, Lord.*

TO THE OCEANS WHITE WITH FOAM. *A nonstop surf that dances effortlessly on a stage of undisturbed beaches. A dance in which every move is choreographed by the moon You hung in the sky. East coast, west coast, left coast, right coast. The Atlantic and the Pacific define the borders of the land called brave and free. But our white-foamed oceans are more than water boundaries. They are also the waterways immigrants have traveled in search of a better life. Lord, may You continue to bring to our land those who will enrich us by their varied experiences. Won't You also bring those whose poverty we can eliminate by our bounty and Your grace?*

GOD, BLESS AMERICA. It is a prayer we offer with fervent hope. Knowing what we know, we cannot imagine life in this land apart from Your blessing. Our enemies are few, but deadly. Our vulnerability is unmistakable. Our destiny is solely in Your hands. And so, we confess that, unless You bless us, we will topple from the pedestal to which we have become accustomed for a quarter of a millennia. God, won't You bless our country once again?

MY HOME SWEET HOME. While it is not home to all who populate our planet, America is our home. She has sheltered us from threat of war and given us a place of belonging. It is the home in which we have grown up nursed by moral values, coached in taking our first steps along the open paths of opportunity, coaxed to claim our right to freely speak and encouraged to find our calling in a land where everyone's voice deserves to be heard. Yes, America is our home. And thanks to You, Almighty God, it is very sweet indeed.

There's No Place Like Nome

Never underestimate the uncanny consequences of an unanticipated opportunity.

It was thirty years ago this month. A thirty-five-year-old pastor of a growing church in northern California responded to a radio station's emergency call for help. The church-owned station on the Bering Sea was facing a financial and staff crisis.

KICY's signal was a critical source of news, information, and entertainment to a dozen native-Alaskan villages. Its overnight Russian programming had also become a valuable link to Siberia.

Because the pastor had worked at a radio station in high school and college, he approached his congregation with the opportunity. They enthusiastically commissioned him, his wife and two young daughters to spend seven weeks in the old gold-rush town. What took place would have a profound impact on this pastor's ministry for years to come. I know this story very well. I was that young minister.

The seventeen hours of traveling from Oakland to Nome were quite harrowing. But they were nothing compared to the challenges we faced once we arrived. The learning curve was steep, but the pay-off was rewarding. Those who have lived in a remote location know how quickly friendships form. They know that a sense of community more than compensates for the lack of conveniences.

Because of those seven weeks spinning records, anchoring news broadcasts and getting to know the people of Nome, I came to appreciate the impact KICY radio has on its listeners. Fifteen years later, I was commissioned to write the history of KICY. The book contract was all because of that unanticipated opportunity the summer of 1987.

My research for writing *The Ptarmigan Telegraph* revealed more than the story of a bush radio station. It exposed me to yet another example of how unplanned opportunities pay big dividends. I learned about a pastor in Sweden who was imprisoned by Russian authorities in the 1880s for attempting to establish Evangelical churches in the Orthodox nation. While Alfred Nobel, the Swedish industrialist, was eventually able to get Axel Karlsson out of prison, Karlsson could not get the thought of planting churches in Russia out of his heart.

Giving up on the idea of going into Russia through the front door, Karlsson decided to attempt entry through the back door. He sailed to New York, traveled by train to San Francisco and secured passage by ship to Alaska. From there he would sail to the Russian Far East. That was his plan. But as Karlsson was in the process of preparing to cross the Bering Sea, he found success in sharing his faith with the Alaska natives. He planted a series of churches on the Seward Peninsula. By the time he died in 1910, the Swedish missionary was a celebrated hero. But his dream of reaching Russia was buried with him. Or so he thought.

Fifty years later, on Easter Sunday 1960, KICY radio went on the air. And today its directional signal blankets the Russian Far East with more than just music and headlines. KICY is the source of good news to countless listeners. Karlsson's dream was realized at last. Just another example of my premise: Never underestimate the uncanny consequences of an unanticipated opportunity.

Intersections

Reflections on a White House Visit

I will never forget my first visit to Washington, D.C. I was seventeen years old and traveling with a choir of high-school-aged kids from various churches in our state. We visited Arlington Cemetery, the Washington Monument, the Lincoln Memorial and the Smithsonian.

The highlight of the visit, however, was singing in the rotunda of the U.S. Capitol for one of our senators. As Henry "Scoop" Jackson looked on, we belted out the words to "This is My Country."

Now forty-nine years later, I had the opportunity to tour our nation's Capitol again. Mr. Lincoln, seated on his throne, is just as imposing as I remembered him. The Marine Corps Memorial at Arlington Cemetery recalling the flag planting at Iwo Jima remains a must-see.

But much has changed since the summer of 1969. There are several memorials that have been added: The Vietnam Wall, the World War II and Korean War Memorials and the MLK statue. The Newseum was an exceptional repository chronicling the way news has been reported through the centuries. As a news junkie, I was fascinated by the history of American media including newspapers, radio and television.

But the highlight of this summer's visit was touring the White House. Although we had driven by it in 1969, I had never set foot in it until this trip. A Congressman friend helped my wife and me secure tickets to see the historic home of our nation's First Family. It was a dream come true.

As we stood in the first-floor rooms of the President's residence, I imagined the Presidents of my lifetime who have walked these same halls. Beginning with Truman all the way to Trump, I pictured leaders of the free world entertaining their counterparts. The portraits on the walls called to mind chief executives who challenged the status quo and effected positive change, as well as those who stumbled ethically and morally.

Our hour-long, self-guided tour of the White House reminded me that Presidents come and go and yet this elegant home symbolizes a lasting democracy. Our visit was a memory jogger that all Presidents have their strengths and their weaknesses. Each one stands in need of God's wisdom and blessing. Each one is vulnerable to his own ego and our prejudice. No wonder St. Paul entreats the Christians of the first century to intercede for those in authority.

But then a thought occurred to me. While the Scriptures entreat us to pray for governmental leaders, the inhabitants of the White House aren't the only ones on God's radar. The Creator is just as concerned about those who occupy your house and mine. In fact, the long-term health of our nation will most likely be determined by the moral condition of those governed as much as by the integrity (or lack thereof) of those who govern.

Reflecting on my visit to the White House, I have a renewed commitment to seek Divine guidance on behalf of our President. But that is not the only action step I can take. I can also decide on a daily basis to follow the advice of the Hebrew prophet, Micah. *"To do justly, love mercy and walk humbly with our God."*

Intersections

At the Heart of It All

At the heart of February is Valentine's Day. It's a day for expressing love to that special someone in our lives. Often we do that with cards, candy or flowers. But for those whose valentine is no longer living, February 14 can be a melancholy day. That's especially true for someone I met a few months ago.

Merle Phillips is the oldest person I've ever known. She will celebrate her one-hundred-eleventh birthday in April. I made her acquaintance while attending church with my oldest daughter in Chicago. As we turned to pass the peace, this little lady who loves her Lord stole my heart with her signature smile. I sought her out when the worship service was over to find out more about her.

Here was a four-foot-ten-inch giant whose life perspective towers over most everyone living. She was born six months before the Chicago Cubs won their first World Series in 1907 and eighteen months before Henry Ford rolled out his first Model T. She was five years old when the Titanic sank. Her first President was Teddy Roosevelt.

With a winsome glance she told me about the only love of her life, someone who left her through death too soon. Merle met Leonard in graduate school at the University of Iowa in 1937. Within a month of meeting at a party, Leonard proposed to her on Valentine's Day, presenting her with an original poem.

But then I discovered how February 14 became a tangible means of celebrating the heart of their romance. Every Valentine's Day throughout their marriage Leonard created a homemade card. It was something Merle looked forward to every Valentine's.

Tragically, after only thirty years of marriage, Leonard was diagnosed with leukemia. Dreams of spending their retirement years together were dashed. After months of being cared for by his adoring wife, Leonard died on February 13, 1968.

Losing her sweetheart the day before their special day was heartbreaking enough. Then came the realization she would not be getting his personalized expression of his love. It was almost more than Merle could take.

But the next day as she shuffled through papers at home, she discovered the unexpected. Leonard had anticipated he might not be around on Valentine's Day and had created a card in advance of the actual day. It was in an envelope with her name on it.

Half a century after Leonard's death, Merle's eyes well up with tears recalling that final valentine. To hear her tell it, her heart was so full of one man's love she didn't see a need for getting married again. Rather, she gave herself to her work as a chemistry-lab worker and later as a child-care professional.

When I asked if I could have my picture taken with her, she agreed but promptly tossed her walker aside and stood as tall as her four-foot-ten-inch frame would allow. My smile grew even wider.

Let There be Peace on Earth

Fifty years ago next Monday, Martin Luther King, Jr. blew out thirty-nine candles on his birthday cake. He had no way of knowing it would be the last time he'd hear "Happy Birthday to You" sung to him. Less than three months later, the King of the non-violent civil-rights movement would be dead.

The young civil-rights leader had packed a lot of life into less than four decades of living. Though Dr. King stood only five-feet-seven-inches tall, he was a giant of a man. Like the One whose Gospel he proclaimed from the pulpit at Ebenezer Baptist Church in Atlanta, MLK practiced what he preached. And as was true with Jesus, his enemies robbed him of his life, but they could not silence his call for liberty and justice for all.

I was only fifteen year old when Dr. King was gunned down on the balcony of the Lorraine Motel in Memphis. As such, I was too young to fully appreciate the impact of his life or his death.

Growing up in a mostly white community, far from the Mason-Dixon Line, I was insulated from the gravity of the civil-rights movement. Not until I did my own research years later was I able to appreciate the larger-than-life influence of this diminutive prophet. In addition to looking beneath the headlines, I also discovered a rather unusual fact.

Did you know that the name on Dr. King's birth certificate was Michael King, Jr.? It's true! On January 15, 1929, when the Reverend Michael King's wife gave birth to a boy, he informed his congregation that his son would carry his name. The baby would be called Michael King, Jr.

But, in the summer of 1934 something happened that would change both their names and the course of history.

The elder King traveled with some of his pastor colleagues to the Holy Land. After *"walking where Jesus walked"* in Palestine, the group stopped in Germany to attend the Baptist World Alliance. King took advantage of the opportunity to explore the region where the Protestant Reformation had been birthed in 1517. He was particularly impressed by the courageous faith of a young Catholic monk who had stood up to the injustices of his day. The more the elder King learned of Martin Luther, the more he liked.

Upon returning to Atlanta, the Baptist pastor felt compelled to initiate lasting change in his life and in his world. To that end, he petitioned the courts for a change of name for both himself and his son. Michael King, Sr. and Jr. would be henceforth known as Martin Luther King.

King's five-year-old son entered first grade with a historic name into which he would grow. It would prove to be a name reminding the "preacher's kid" of a destiny bigger than he could imagine. When tempted to give up, Martin would need only to recall where his new name came from and what it stood for.

And for Martin Luther King, Sr. it meant much the same. A change of name signified a commitment to challenge injustice that continues to fly in the face of the Christian faith. It was a commitment his namesake maintained to his death.

And isn't it interesting that the fiftieth anniversary of MLK's death coincides with the five-hundredth anniversary of Martin Luther's courageous protest of unjust Church? It is interesting, indeed!

...and Let It Begin with Me!

Nineteen twenty-nine was a milestone year for our nation. Ninety years ago the cost of living (without fear) took off astronomically. In the year the market crashed, a King had a son who would be known as a prince of peace in a world of continual conflict. In 1968, hate stilled his voice but not his song.

The haunting melody the Rev. Martin Luther King, Jr. taught us still echoes in our hearts long after his death. The lyrics of love continue to leap from our lips as we remember his message of tolerance, acceptance and nonviolence. As we pack up our Christmas decorations, the unfulfilled prophecy of "peace on earth goodwill to men" still rings in our ears.

Every MLK Day at Covenant Shores, people blend their voices to sing "Let There Be Peace on Earth." The harmony of the notes pictures the harmony that is possible among nations. Can you imagine a world of diverse cultures, languages and beliefs in which each person contributes their part according to a score that has been carefully orchestrated to include all performers?

A few months ago a group of at-risk youth from a Brazilian barrio toured our town. Included in the variety of songs performed in their native Portuguese, they sang "Let There Be Peace on Earth" in English. It was beautiful. It was harmonious. It was choreographed. It was a glimpse of what can happen when we learn the steps to communicate love to those who are different from us.

Dr. King's "song" is more than just sing-able. It is danceable. It's a two-step that requires "give and take." When we give ourselves to the cause of peaceful cooperation with those with whom we differ, we take the first step. When we take a stand for peace-at-any-price in the war against prejudice, we give our children a chance to see our commitment to being part of a global family.

"Give Peace a Chance" was a bumper sticker slogan of the 1960s. Half a century later, it remains more than a slogan. It's an indicator of our desire to make Dr. King's dream a reality. So we must continue to give peace a chance and take issue with injustice. That, too, is a sign that we will not let intolerance and privilege easily coexist with liberty and justice for all.

We simply have to give up on our felt need to defend our feelings of entitlement. Meanwhile, we need to take the needs of others into consideration while navigating the challenges and opportunities we're dealt. The two-step dance of "give and take" is a natural starting point for demonstrating the peace our world is dying to see.

Remember how the *"Let There Be Peace on Earth"* song ends? If you do, you know the key to finding global harmony. *"And let it begin with me."* The end for which we long begins with us. The dream Dr. King bequeathed us will come true only when we take personal responsibility for it coming to pass.

Intersections

My Father Was a Failure

As this Father's Day approaches, I find myself in reflective mood thinking about the things my dad did and didn't do. The more I reflect, the more I find myself focusing on his failings.

My dad failed when it came to not influencing me to believe in God. While some dads believe they should leave the choice of faith up to their kids, my father was convinced it was his responsibility to pass on to his children their need of a Savior. As Dad and I watched the 2008 Summer Olympics, we groaned in unison as the US men's 4×100 meter relay team dropped the baton and failed to qualify for the finals. My father contrasted the dropped baton to what happens in a family when parents fail to pass on spiritual faith to their progeny.

My dad failed to put time with my brother and me ahead of time with our mom. His relationship with his wife always came first. But, I didn't mind. I loved seeing my parents' love grow. It gave me a sense of security. In the process of prioritizing his marriage, my dad showed me by personal example how to remain true to one's wedding vows.

My dad failed at keeping his promises. On more than one occasion when I was misbehaving, he promised that he would renege on taking me to a special event on which I had my young heart set. But, when I showed a repentant heart, he failed at following through on his declared discipline. His willingness to give me grace provided me a picture of my Heavenly Father's love.

My dad failed to brag about what he did in World War II. As part of the "Greatest Generation," he kept quiet about his life as a Marine. The sacrifices he made and the horrors he witnessed were not to be trivialized by casual conversation. His service to his Uncle Sam was not viewed as heroic. He saw it as his grateful duty. Only near the end of his life did he share aspects of his experiences he wanted his family to know.

My dad failed to model the popular notion that claims grown men don't cry. I saw my dad shed a tear on multiple occasions. A tender heart beat within his Semper Fi physique. His willingness to show his emotions gave me permission to acknowledge my feelings without fear for what others would think.

My dad failed getting me to join him and my brother in the family business. Fortunately, my father was aware of my call to pastoral ministry. He could tell that my gifts would not be best utilized in property management and maintenance. Affirming my skill set, he released me to follow my heart even though it meant I would live at a distance from my folks. It meant a great deal to me that he celebrated my calling.

My dad failed to make me wait until his death to benefit from my inheritance. He knew I would one day benefit from his hard work and successful investments. But, he also knew the resources he'd eventually leave behind would make the biggest difference when my wife and I wanted to buy a house or put our kids through college. His failure to follow what many fathers do proved a gift to both him and me.

As you can clearly see, I had a failure for a father. But I'm hardly sorry. I hope that my kids will come to the same conclusion about me one day when I am gone.

Intersections

Hope Is Restored by the Dawn's Early Light

The day my dad died was actually night. The grandfather clock in the hallway had just chimed midnight. When the hearse arrived two hours later, a steady rain was falling in the darkness.

I stood on the front porch of my childhood home and watched the funeral director wheel the shroud-covered body of my pastor-father to the waiting car. Through a veil of tears, I watched the black minivan drive away.

That night I also watched for the dawn. More than ever before, I wanted the darkness of night to dissolve into day. Whereas, a new day technically begins at midnight, it is dawn that provides the tangible evidence that morning has broken. My broken heart looked for a new day to arrive in hopes it would distance my grieving heart from its grief.

I remembered the words of the psalmist who chronicled his own confessed longing for dawn. *"Weeping may linger for the night, but joy comes with the morning ...."* (Psalm 30:5 NRSV) I resonated with his anticipation.

That overnight vigil eleven years ago was a turning point for me. I have never been a morning person. Late nights were more in sync with my circadian rhythm. But that all began to change. I became much more drawn to dawn.

There's just something about daybreak that I have come to embrace. I have come to see that dawn is a mysterious moment when my perspective is calibrated. The regrets of yesterday succumb to the expectations of a new day. It's like flipping a light switch.

The dawn's early light was obviously meaningful to the poet who penned the lyrics to our national anthem. Francis Scott Key celebrated a victorious defense of Fort McHenry as he welcomed a new day. First light also proved holy to the women who found Jesus' grave empty on the first day of the week. Dawn revealed a reason for hope.

As I contemplated my dad's death that cold and rainy November night, the approaching dawn was more than a predictable reality. The coming light represented the means by which I could see to navigate a new norm. Life without my dad would be difficult, but I realized the separation would be only temporary. The first light of that first Easter guaranteed that.

I remember a children's book my girls enjoyed when they were small. The beautiful illustrations pictured the start of day in a busy city. As the city awoke, birds began to chirp. Garbage collectors picked up refuse. Shopkeepers swept sidewalks in front of their stores. Bridge operators raised the moveable spans to allow waiting boats to pass beneath. Commuters in cars began their daily drive to office buildings.

Every time I turned the pages of that board book for my girls, something in me responded with anticipation. I couldn't quite explain it at the time. But through the years, it dawned on me. I finally understood my fascination with my girls' bedtime story. Dawn had become a symbol of hope. And hope is something that magnetically draws us no matter how many candles adorn our birthday cakes.

Just as Jesus' disciples associated dawn with death's defeat, I, too, have come to see how grief gives way to hope. Each day life begins anew. With each new sunrise, I have the chance to dance with new possibilities and refocus my gaze on what faith promises.

And in light of the current coronavirus pandemic, focusing on faith's promises is more critical than ever. Although Holy Week and Passover finds us living in the shadows of an invisible enemy, the dawn's early light provides us an opportunity to celebrate God's penetrating presence that dispels the fog of fear.

The Rest of the Story

From the time I was a boy of twelve, I listened to Paul Harvey every morning before heading off to school. My dad had our radio tuned to our local station as America's newsman would greet me and millions of others with *"Hello, Americans! Stand by for news!"*

His warm engaging voice drew me in as if I were listening to a favorite uncle. And his "The Rest of the Story" segments introduced me to Godwinks before I knew anything about dusting for Divine fingerprints.

When Mr. Harvey came to our small town as keynote speaker for a convention, it was as if the President himself had arrived. Because I was only in junior high school, I was too young to attend. But I was old enough to feel the excitement of this radio celebrity's visit.

Fast forward forty-five years. I was the pastor of a growing congregation in suburban Seattle. The head coach of the Seattle Seahawks was a member of the church. As a kind gesture, the coach and his wife offered a week at their vacation home in Phoenix as a gift to my wife, our daughter and me.

As I picked up the key and instructions for use of the vacation home, the coach's wife told me, *"You'll enjoy our neighborhood. It's right near the luxurious Biltmore Hotel. And, oh, by the way, do you know who Paul Harvey is? He winters in our gated community. You just might see him while you're there."*

"Did I know who Paul Harvey was?!" If only she'd known he has been a hero of mine since I was a kid, she'd never have asked the question. If there was ever anyone I would enjoy seeing, it would be Paul Harvey. I secretly began to hope that possibility would become a reality. But I wondered, what would be the odds?

When the taxi dropped us off at our destination in Arizona, I couldn't believe my eyes. There he was. Eighty-eight-year-old Paul Harvey was out for a stroll on the sidewalk in front of the home we'd be staying in for a week. What were the odds?

Not knowing if I'd have another Paul Harvey sighting, I unloaded all the suitcases in the house and told my wife I'd be back before too long. Walking as fast as I could (without appearing in a hurry) I caught up with the object of my fascination.

Without batting an eye I greeted Mr. Harvey with "Hello, American!" He smiled. I proceeded to introduce myself. He invited me to join him on the remainder of his mile-long stroll. For thirty minutes I savored a dream come true. Making the most of the fleeting moments, I asked my favorite newsman questions about his most fascinating life. I asked him about famous people he'd met.

As we reached his driveway, he thanked me for my company. I asked him if I could have the privilege of praying for him. He agreed. I thanked the Lord for his life and asked God to watch over my new friend in the waning years of his life and work. I sensed it would be the last time I would have the opportunity to be with him. Two years later, he passed away. And now you know the rest of the story!

Making Peace with the Past

As a chaplain in a retirement community, I deal with death on a regular basis. The most meaningful part of my job description is helping residents "pack their bags for heaven."

Recently the hospice nurse, attending one of our residents, indicated that Tom didn't have much time left. I approached his adult children and asked if their dad had any "unfinished business." They knew what I meant.

They told me Tom had spent the previous day saying goodbye to family members and giving each of his grandchildren a blessing. As I handed my friend a little wooden cross and prayed my own blessing over him, I could tell he was at peace. Tom died the next day.

The reason I asked about "unfinished business" relates to what I witnessed in my own father's final days. From the time he was a Marine in the South Pacific during World War II, my dad battled prejudice toward Japanese people. Even though he was called into the ministry and was a beloved and successful pastor, what he witnessed in the war left a bias he couldn't seem to shake.

My dad readily admitted he knew his attitude was wrong and wanted to find peace. This one who, as a nineteen-year-old, had stood behind General MacArthur on the Battleship Missouri witnessing the Japanese surrender could not seem to surrender his prejudice.

As my brother and I sat with our father near the end, he admitted to another wound. It was one that preceded the injuries he endured in the war. Dad wept like a baby as he told my brother and me how his father beat him as a boy. Although our grandfather had a life-altering experience with Christ and became a Christian later in life, he died before Dad could process his emotional pain with him.

I watched a man I loved, who loved Jesus, courageously acknowledge unfinished business. The issues on which he looked back were a source of pain. All the same, my father's ability to admit to and talk about his prejudice and the abuse he'd experienced in his youth provided him a sense of relief. Aware of God's amazing grace, he was able to make peace with a past he couldn't undo.

Baptism on the Ninth Hole

After pastoring a church in California for eleven years, my wife and I sensed God's call to a congregation near Chicago. As our family prepared to move, we were showered with wonderful gifts: a painting by Thomas Kinkaide, a crystal vase, and a French Psalter from the 1600s to add to my prized collection of hymnbooks.

But the most meaningful gift arrived just a few days before we moved – an invitation to play golf with my friend, Marty. Seven years earlier, after much family coercion, Marty reluctantly agreed to accompany his wife and two daughters to church. Marty had been turned off by institutional religion long before – Sunday mornings were best spent on the golf course.

I met the Koll family in the parking lot after worship had begun. They arrived late, and there I was: hiding among the cars in my Middle Eastern robe. I didn't want to spoil the effect of my first-person sermon by being seen by the congregation prematurely.

Marty's face said it all: *Is that the pastor without shoes and in a bathrobe? What kind of church is this? I'd rather be golfing.*

The morning's worship folder promoted an upcoming annual men's golf tournament. Golf was a language Marty spoke. He signed up for the outing and arrived the following Saturday with his clubs slung over his shoulder and with a sparkle in his eye. I had no idea he was a ringer.

After Marty won, the organizer of the tournament asked him if he could be in church the next day to receive the trophy. Marty complied. Whether it was the fact I wore a coat and tie and shoes that Sunday, or that Marty and his wife were warmly received by the young-adult class, I'll never know. What matters is they decided to stay.

Within a few months, Marty's two elementary-school-aged daughters prayed with their Sunday school teachers to make Jesus their Lord. They began to ask their parents questions about their new faith. Mom and Dad realized they needed to make the same commitment as their daughters. At the end of a sermon, I asked those willing to entrust their lives to the Lord to lift their heads and look me in the eye. Marty and Cindy returned my gaze.

Marty responded with child-like enthusiasm to the father-like love of God (his father had died before he was born). Within months his tender faith was tested: He watched his mother wither from cancer and die. About that time, I was coming to grips with my father's nearly fatal heart attack. We found consolation together, followed little white balls around the golf course, and prayed for each other. Our friendship grew.

Marty threw himself into church life; he became our church custodian; he and Cindy led the Sunday school class that welcomed them. But for some reason, known only to Marty, he was never baptized. The years sped by.

Then came the invitation to play golf one last time. The day seemed perfect: the weather was warm, and my game was on. Two friends from church joined us. There was laughter and honest conversation. I swallowed hard, realizing I'd soon be two thousand miles removed from these men I'd grown to love as brothers.

As we approached the ninth tee, with a meandering brook and a cascading waterfall, Marty surprised me with a question: *"Pastor Greg, would you baptize me?"*

I thought he was joking and reached for my driver. Marty reached in his golf bag and retrieved the Bible I'd given him the day he became a Christian.

"I'm serious," he said. He handed me the Bible. *"You know I've never been baptized. And, well, here's water. What's standing in the way?"*

My open mouth widened into a smile; my eyes teared up. I remembered the Ethiopian's request of Philip in Acts 8 and decided there was a precedent for unorthodox baptisms. We removed our shoes and socks, rolled up our slacks, and stepped into the flowing brook. While our friends looked on, I read aloud the twenty-third Psalm (somehow "green pastures" and "still waters" seemed appropriate). I quizzed Marty about his faith in Christ. I applauded his boldness. I asked God to transform the gurgling stream into a means of grace. Then I baptized him in the name of the Father, Son, and Holy Spirit. I welcomed my dear friend with a bear hug as he stepped out of the water.

A circle of four men holding hands and praying God's blessing on Marty could be seen by the twosome on the green behind us. They smiled their approval, although I'm not sure what they thought was going on. A water hazard on the ninth hole had become holy ground.

Reflections on Life and Faith

Remembering a Life Well-Lived

Sports legend John Wooden was an amazing man who touched our culture in remarkable ways. You can't think of March Madness, the Final Four or the National NCAA Men's Basketball Championship without thinking about King John. Although he reached many milestones in his life, he failed to achieve one that was on the near horizon. He fell just short of reaching his one-hundredth birthday when he died on June 4, 2010.

The one who became known as "the wizard of Westwood" was born in Martinsville, Indiana in 1910. That was only nineteen years after the game of basketball was invented. Early on he discovered how much he loved the game. As an eight-year-old, he stuffed rags in his mother's hose and took shots with it aiming at a tomato basket his father had nailed to a wall in their barn. As a teenager he led his high school basketball team to a state championship. Then it was off to college where John distinguished himself at Purdue University. Thanks to his accurate shot and disciplined play, the Boilermakers won the national championship and John was named College Player of the Year.

Wooden's love affair with basketball became a full-blown romance as a coach. From 1948 to 1975 he courted success as the head coach of the UCLA Bruins. His impressive (and unmatched) success underscores why roundball was a source of ongoing infatuation. During those years the Bruins set all-time records with four perfect 30-0 seasons, eighty-eight consecutive victories, thirty-eight straight NCAA tournament victories, twenty PAC 10 championships, and ten national championships, including seven in a row.

Before moving to Mercer Island in 2005, I had the privilege of interviewing Coach Wooden. For an hour we talked about basketball, marriage and Jesus Christ. In those moments that seemed to go by too quickly, I discovered how much John loved his wife.

John married his high school sweetheart in 1932 after graduating from Purdue. It was a marriage marked by storybook commitment and romance that lasted fifty-three years.

"In my marriage to Nellie," John recalled, *"I learned how important it is to find peace in yourself so that you can overlook the flaws in others. My marriage also taught me how to work through misunderstandings. The devotion I had for my wife had a tremendous impact on me. It allowed me to overcome all kinds of obstacles."*

Even though Nellie Wooden died on March 21, 1985 after a lengthy battle with cancer, the dedication that marked the coach's devotion to basketball was evidenced in the way he continued to honor his wife's memory.

"Every year since Nellie died I have written a letter to her on the twenty-first day of each month," the coach told me. *"In each letter I express my love and confess how much I miss her. I also chronicle the activities in the lives of our children, grandchildren and great-grandchildren."*

That stack of 252 letters was tied in a ribbon and sat atop her side of the bed that has remained undisturbed since the day of her death. During their marriage John slept on the left side of the bed. He continued to after she died. In spite of such amazing devotion, there was something that outdistanced John Wooden's affection for his wife. Without apology John voiced his love for his Savior to me. He compared his walk with the Lord to his marathon marriage.

"Both require hard work," he admitted, *"but the benefits are worth it. There's no way I can fully describe how my faith in Christ has influenced the way I coached,"* John said without hesitation. *"It gave me an inner serenity in the face of stressful situations. It also motivated me to treat my players and colleagues with a degree of understanding that was beyond my natural ability. By learning to accept people and circumstances I didn't fully agree with, I was able to act in ways I would not later regret."*

"Coach" (as his former teammates called him) continued to speak to a limited number of corporate groups and business conventions each year. He attributes his ability to remain physically fit by watching what he eats and maintaining an exercise program. All the same the coach also prioritized a spiritual workout daily. In addition to spending time with the Lord in prayer, he read the Scriptures every day and reflected on sacred poetry he'd memorized in his nine decades of life. Although he hadn't coached collegiate ball for thirty years, John Wooden never forgot how to differentiate between winning on the court and winning in life.

"There is only one kind of a life that truly wins and that is the one that places faith in the hands of the Savior," John told me. *"Until that is done, we are on an aimless course that runs in circles and goes nowhere. Material possessions, winning scores, and great reputations are meaningless in the eyes of the Lord, because He knows what we really are and that is all that matters."*

He Was Everything to Me

The father of contemporary Christian music was born in May 1927. Although Ralph Carmichael passed away in October 2021, his legacy lives on. I will never forget the day I met this gifted musician.

In June 1968 my mom and dad took my brother and me on a road trip from our home near Seattle to Southern California. It proved to be a most memorable vacation for this sixteen-year-old.

We stopped at the Ambassador Hotel in Los Angeles where Robert Kennedy had been assassinated a couple weeks earlier. We met the actor, Fess Parker, at a restaurant. To our amazement, he invited us to the soundstage to watch an episode of Daniel Boone being filmed with costars Jimmy Dean and Ed Ames. One evening my brother and I encountered television personalities Regis Philbin and Joey Bishop on the street outside our motel.

But the highlight of our vacation was sitting in on a recording session with the legendary Ralph Carmichael at Capitol Records in Hollywood. My mom had gone to Bible college with one of Ralph's best friends. When Bud Tutmarc learned that we would be in the LA area, he contacted Ralph and arranged for us to meet.

Those black horned-rimmed glasses and long flowing white hair framed a smiling face that greeted us in a recording studio. For a pastor's kid who'd been introduced to Ralph's contemporary take on Christian music in Billy Graham films like "The Restless Ones" and "For Pete's Sake," I felt like I was in the presence of royalty.

"He's Everything to Me" – a sing-able tune from the soundtrack of "The Restless Ones" – had become the theme song for our weekly

Christian club at the public high school I attended. Every Tuesday as we sat in the choir room to eat our sack lunches and hear a local pastor speak, we sang *"In the stars his handiwork I see..."* before focusing our thoughts on the Creator.

I had no way of knowing that warm June day just how much Ralph Carmichael would continue to impact my life as a young Christian. A few months after meeting Ralph, I was invited to preach my first sermon at my home church. I was feeling a call to the ministry, but I also wondered if the church of my youth would provide me the freedom to explore the gifts God had given me. Listening to my Ralph's records on my bedroom stereo, I was buoyed by the cutting-edge creativity of the Carmichael sound. While I loved the traditional hymns I'd learned in church, I longed for something more.

Ralph's songs we sang in youth group resembled popular music on the radio. They did more than set my feet to tapping. They gave wings to my heart. Lyrics like "There is More to Life" helped me realize that there could be more to church music than what had defined my parents' generation. In songs like "The New 23rd" I found what I wanted. I discovered a fresh culturally relevant sound that restored my soul. In the words of "Pass it On," Ralph and his collaborator, Kurt Kaiser, provided memorable word pictures of how living faith is shared one person to another, like a spark being fanned into a flame.

As I did some research on my favorite Christian composer, I discovered that Ralph had been raised in the same denomination in which I was. Like me, he was the son of a pastor, who felt a leading into church ministry. And like me, he longed for the opportunity to express the unique gifts God had given him. He wanted his creative expressions (that sometimes colored outside the traditional lines) to be accepted and celebrated.

Following studies at Southern California College (now Vanguard University), Ralph worked as a minister of music at a couple churches. But for this one who was viewed as a musical prodigy in his youth, the Christian community welcomed his virtuosity as a violinist more than his innovative arrangements of traditional hymns. It would be

Hollywood where the frustrated "preacher's kid" would initially find unconditional acceptance.

Although composing, arranging and conducting for the likes of Bob Pierce's World Vision and Billy Graham's Worldwide Pictures, Ralph made increasing inroads into the secular entertainment world. He produced albums with Nat King Cole. He also arranged music for Elvis Presley, Bing Crosby and Ella Fitzgerald as well as television shows like I Love Lucy, Bonanza and My Mother the Car. Ralph also traveled the country with the big-band sounds of his popular Ralph Carmichael Orchestra.

In his autobiography, *He's Everything to Me* (published by Thomas Nelson, 1986), Ralph confesses that his lifelong desire was to use his musical gifts to glorify the God who gave them to him. He acknowledges misspent opportunities and ego-driven pursuits that cost him his first marriage and created business nightmares. But through it all he recognizes the hand of his Heavenly Father who allowed him to leave a lasting legacy on the Evangelical world.

Through a longtime friendship with Darrel Gardner, a trumpet player in the Ralph Carmichael Orchestra, I was able reach out to Ralph and his wife, Marvella, in recent years. I wanted to express my gratitude to the man whose music had provided me a needed vocabulary of praise as a young Christian. A regular communication has developed with this dear couple who are navigating the challenges of growing older.

Five years ago, I was leading a city-wide hymnsing at a large church in Seattle. Two sons of the man who first arranged for our family to meet Ralph Carmichael back in 1968 were in attendance. It dawned on me that Ralph was about to celebrate his ninetieth birthday. I reached for my iPhone and asked Greg Tutmarc to video what I was about to do.

I invited the congregation to turn in their hymnals to "The Savior is Waiting." I explained that this wonderful invitation hymn was written by a man who had nourished my faith as a teenager. Pointing out that Ralph was about to celebrate a milestone in his life, I invited them to sing a song that had been instrumental in countless people coming into the Kingdom. While they sang, that special moment was recorded.

And then without skipping a beat I led the congregation in singing "Happy Birthday." What a joy it was to email the video to Ralph and his wife, Marvella.

As I think of Ralph Carmichael's lasting legacy on Christian music, I'm thanking the Lord for another person who inspired me to express my love for Jesus through singing. My mom, like Ralph, was born in 1927. She died three years ago. And now that the baton has been passed from them both, I want to pass it on!

Making the Most of a High School Reunion

This summer marks fifty years since I graduated high school. Although I have been to all but one reunion since 1970, this year's get together promises to be the most meaningful. Because of it being a milestone event, some former classmates will attend I haven't seen in five decades. Thank goodness for nametags.

I'm also grateful for the opportunity to revise my reputation from school days. Lest you get the wrong idea, I wasn't one of those problem kids. Quite to the contrary, I was the president of our campus Christian club. My personal faith as a high school student was hardly private. As someone who felt a call of God on my life to ministry at an early age, I was quite bold in my witness. My loyalty to the Lord was something of which I was proud. Therein is the problem.

Looking back, my fanaticism as a Christ-follower was also quite Pharisaical. My devotion bordered on self-righteousness. I kept my distance from those who smoked in the alley during lunch, experimented with pot after school or drank on the weekends. I didn't want to be corrupted by their behavior. In the process I didn't follow the Savior's lead and get to know the "outcasts" with a motive to love them into the Kingdom. I've come to see that keeping the "smokers" and "drinkers" at arm's length was just as wrong as engaging in what they were doing.

When I met up with my former classmates at reunions, I realized they had aged like I had. They showed up with more pounds and less hair. I also discovered that they were dealing with the same life issues I was. These challenges included the death of parents, the pain of unexpected unemployment, chronic health crises, concerns for adult children and regrets over lost opportunities. The rebellious behavior that had marked their adolescence was overshadowed by adult fears of the future and longings to make a difference in the world.

Getting together after going different directions in life provides an opportunity to reflect on what defined our lives as young people and what we wish hadn't. At one of our first reunions, when the mic was passed to share personal updates, I felt the Holy Spirit nudging me to publicly ask for forgiveness. I expressed how sorry I was for being a stumbling block by the way I practiced my faith in unloving ways. I confessed to wearing "goodie-two shoes" instead of slipping on the kind of sandals Jesus wore.

The reaction of my classmates to my vulnerability was obvious. Not only did they grant their forgiveness, some acknowledged their own faults. Avenues of communications were opened. Through my willingness to admit being unChristlike back in the day, the presence of Christ filled the room.

As I prepare to attend my fifty-year reunion, I am starting to contemplate who will be there ... and who won't. Sadly, of our graduating class of four hundred, nearly twenty percent have died. Reunions are a reminder that every memorial service we attend is one closer to our own. Spouses of those who've passed away will be present. I pray the Lord will use me to comfort them in their grief.

Others will be coming who have recently been given a grim diagnosis by their doctor. I want to find time in the midst of the festivities to hear their anxiety and commend to them a God who cares for them. Still others will be at our weekend of celebration looking differently than when I last saw them (and I'm not referring to their weight or wrinkles). These are they who have discovered a personal relationship with Jesus since we were in school. I look forward to hearing their stories and celebrating with them.

Of course, there will be those who verbalized faith in Jesus back in school, but who have left their first love in pursuit of other infatuations. It grieves me to see those who have abandoned ship. I am determined to not judge them but to winsomely recall times we shared when the Lord factored into our friendships. By recalling such memories I will be tossing a life preserver in their direction, all the while grateful for a God whose grace continues to pursue us.

By definition, high school reunions are not spiritual in nature. But if we are open to the whispering voice of the Holy Spirit, they can definitely have a Christian component. We can be known by more than what's written on our name tag.

Learning How to Spell Love

I met the woman who would become my wife when we were eighteen years old. We dated each other's roommates at Seattle Pacific University, but never went out with each other. Our first date was ten years after we had met when we were both settled into our careers. Wendy as a teacher, and I as a pastor.

Over the next eighteen months I became convinced I didn't want to spend the rest of my life with anyone else. When the time came to propose, I decided I would pop the question in a memorable way.

Because Wendy and I spent many Friday nights during our courtship playing Scrabble, I had an idea. I purchased a travel Scrabble board and arranged the tiles crossword-style: *"Wendy please agree to be my wife. Love Gregory."*

On a sunny afternoon I suggested we walk to a nearby park and play Scrabble on my new miniature game. I opened the board and placed it on the grass in front of her. It took a moment for Wendy to make sense of it all. Totally surprised, she shrieked in delight and hugged me. When I held out the fabric bag of letters and suggested she draw, she reached in and found a diamond ring.

The fact that Wendy and I will celebrate thirty-five years of marriage this month indicates how she answered my proposal – with a three-letter word.

Curiously, the game of letters continues to factor into our lasting relationship. On rainy spring nights we still sit by the fire, sip a glass of wine and spell words to our hearts' content. On flights to visit our oldest daughter in Chicago, we play Scrabble on our iPad to pass the time.

What is more, that old-fashioned game has found its way into a new generation of Asimakoupouloses. All three of our grown daughters love to play Scrabble on their iPads and "Words with Friends" on their smartphones.

But, beyond the joy of playing a game we love, Wendy and I see clues in Scrabble that spell out a few simple keys to commitment. Keys that can unlock resolvable conflicts in a culture where too many marriages fail.

In Scrabble as in marriage, we can't do it alone. We need each other to make it work. The essence of the game is finding ways to connect; parallel pursuits don't make it. Our relationship is strongest when both Wendy and I validate each other's contributions and seek to add to them. Occasional challenges are important for keeping each other on track.

Scrabble also reminds us we must do the best with what we have. There will always be someone who has more valuable letters or opportune places to play, just as there will always be couples who have more assets and opportunities than we do. All the same, enjoyment in Scrabble and marriage has nothing to do with possessions and everything to do with contentment.

To commemorate our thirty-fifth anniversary, we are going on a cruise to Alaska. As we start to pack, we are taking dress-up clothes for the Captain's Dinner, workout clothes for the fitness center and warm clothes for the various ports of call. But, in addition to our suitcases of appropriate apparel, you'd better believe I'll be packing a game of Scrabble. In a word, it's part of what makes our relationship special.

Let me see, if I spell *blessed*, I use all my letters and get fifty extra points.

The Class of 70 Turns 70

Two years ago, our fifty-year class reunion was canceled due to Covid. But lockdowns and social distancing can't keep the Wenatchee High School Class of 1970 from celebrating. We had a "50 + 1" gathering last fall with plans to gather for a "Class of 70 Turns 70" shindig later this year.

Upon reflection, we seventy-year-olds have more reason to celebrate than we did when we were eighteen. When we received our diplomas, we weren't really graduating with much life knowledge. What happened that warm June evening in 1970 was more accurately a commencement into the classroom-of-life experience.

Like countless gowned and capped graduates around the country this month, we heard graduation speeches. They were well-crafted messages. They were motivational calls to action. But the words were lost in the emotion of the moment. A graduation party awaited. So did one last family vacation, summer jobs and packing for college.

We could only imagine what awaited us: careers, promotions, unemployment, marriages, children, divorces, addiction, recovery, spiritual rebirth, cancer, death of parents, death of spouses, death of children. Back then we could not have imagined a global pandemic or the threat of climate change.

Now fifty-two years later, turning seventy represents more of a graduation worthy of celebrating. We are leaving behind the careers that defined our identity and entering the season most people associate with retirement. We are making peace with the fact that physical strength and beauty are fleeting and that things that matter most are not things at all. It's a season to draw near to those from whom we've been far for far too long. It is a time to celebrate jobs well done, marriages well served and friendships well invested.

But this time our parents won't be around to congratulate us. All our teachers, as well, have passed from the scene, except for one. And in the case of our class, close to one hundred have received their eternal diplomas.

Turning seventy provides an opportunity to look back and look inside. It has a way of focusing the fleeting nature of time. We have come to clearly see how fast the years have gone. A classmate recently shared that the time we've been out of high school is the same length of time between the start of the Spanish Flu in 1918 and when we took our last high school final exam. Fifty-two years is the length of time from the end of World War I until we took our first pop quiz as college freshmen. Now that's mind-boggling.

And do you know what else is mind-boggling? The threat of World War III is. After spending the majority of our lives observing how a cold war could warm to cordial relations with the Russians, we find ourselves looking at our winter wardrobe in search of what to wear as a frigid political climate looms on the horizon.

Like every other high school graduating class in modern history, the Class of 70 finds itself in search of answers that can't be found in the morning paper or the nightly news. With our forebearers, we too are called to seek Divine help even as we worship the God of our own understanding.

I take comfort from The Almighty's invitation as found in the Old Testament calling us to admit our vulnerability. *"If my people, who are called by my name, will humble themselves and pray and seek my face and turn from their wicked ways, then I will hear from heaven, and I will forgive their sin and will heal their land."* (2 Chronicles 7:14 NIV)

The White House or Our House?

Election Day has come and gone. And while some outcomes are yet to be determined, one thing is certain: No matter the winner, the "stuff" of daily life continues to confront us. You've experienced that and so have I.

Election Day twelve years ago is a case in point. That was the day the first Black man was chosen by voters to become the primary resident of the White House. While November 4, 2008 was a red-letter day for our nation, it was a rather blue day for me. That same day my eighty-two-year-old father passed away.

Looking back, the days following the election were a blur. While our nation readied itself for a peaceful transition of power, our family was consumed with the sorrowful transition death demands. We had a husband, father, uncle, and grandfather to memorialize and bury.

The evening news explained the role the Electoral College plays in formally electing our new leader. But I was not all that interested. The death of my dad found me still enrolled in another institution. The school of hard knocks and the assignments related to loss found me overwhelmed with more homework than I could have imagined.

But my situation is not unique. The "stuff of life" demands our attention long after races have been decided. No matter who works in the Oval Office or sits behind the governor's desk, we have issues to face every day that we alone must address. No wonder the first Tuesday of November pales in significance to the "choose days" that arrive with each sunrise.

Intersections

Each day we make choices. Our "choose day" choices have far-reaching consequences. What we decide to do or not to do, to say or not to say, carries weight. Because our choices impact our immediate family, colleagues at work and those in our neighborhood, they are more influential than simply voting for a candidate.

Each day we vote for the kind of person we will be. We choose between trusting or doubting, loving or hating, offering forgiveness or choosing to retaliate, being generous or stingy, becoming engaged or choosing to be apathetic. Each day we have a choice to take a risk or take a pass.

If we see each day as a "choose day," we aren't limited to voting every two years or every four years. Instead, we are continually voting our conscience and taking a stand on what we believe to be right, just and fair.

We cast our ballots by standing with family members who are going through a painful divorce, walking alongside loved ones who are battling addictions or sitting with friends who are grieving the death of a significant other. Electing to face the challenges that knock at our front door is a sign of maturity. It's a tangible way to lead by example.

It is natural to be concerned about the kind of example those in Washington, D.C., are providing. Regardless of party affiliation, we expect respect, honesty, and kindness. All the same, I've come to believe that what goes on in our homes matters even more than what takes place in the White House.

The values we embrace and the beliefs we practice have more of an impact than we might imagine. When integrity wears work clothes and interacts with those who are inclined to be dishonest or take ethical shortcuts, something happens. One choice makes another choice possible.

The kind of a world for which we long is dependent on individuals like you and me putting feet to our faith and giving voice to our values in our spheres of influence. Do I have your vote?

The Him Behind the Hymn

Recently I buried a community leader whose death unearthed a most interesting connection to a popular hymn of the last century.

At ninety-five years of age, Jack Scholfield had lived a full and rewarding life. But his faith in Christ came into focus only near the end. I met him the week I started working at Covenant Shores. Jack's wife had died six months earlier and he had just been diagnosed with inoperable cancer. I spent time getting to know this kind man. I learned that he had been a war hero in WWII and as a torpedo bomber had been awarded the Distinguished Flying Cross.

I discovered he'd become a successful lawyer. I also learned that he'd buried his twenty-eight-year-old son after a battle with bone cancer. It was a pain in his heart that never went away. Not even when he was appointed a superior court judge by Governor Dixie Lee Ray. Jack retired from the bench at the age of seventy-five when he became a pro-bono arbitrator for low-income families in our area.

Most appropriately Judge Scholfield's favorite passage in the Bible was Micah 6:8. *"He has shown you O man what is good and what the Lord requires of you, but to do justly and to love mercy and to walk humbly with your God."* All the same, Jack was quick to tell his friends and neighbors that his wife was the religious one in the family. By his own admission he was a Christmas and Easter kind of churchgoer.

An eighty-five-year-old retired CIA agent on our campus who became a believer in his fifties had a burden for this nominal Presbyterian judge. John befriended Jack and shared his faith with him. He gave him a copy of *"A Case for Christ"* and *"Evidence that Demands a Verdict."*

It paid off. As I prayed with Jack in the final days of his life, I detected living faith. I gave him a little wooden holding cross. He clutched it continuously to the end. The Lord allowed me the sacred joy of being with Jack, his son and his granddaughter when he breathed his last, "clinging to the cross."

It was a powerful image for his sixty-five-year-old son. Jim kept talking about his dad and the cross. I thought about that powerful symbol, too. In life Jack had been defined by a wooden gavel he gripped in his right hand by which he hammered out justice. In death it was a wooden cross he grasped in that same hand by which his ultimate judge dispensed mercy. A man who made a career upholding the law held on to grace at the end.

The day after the graveside service, Jack's son called me. Jim said he wanted to plan a public memorial service for his dad and was hoping it could include a hymn that his dad's dad had written.

"Your grandfather wrote a hymn?" I asked.

"Yes, and it was published," he said. Jim went on to tell me he didn't know the tune or the words. He did know the title, however. *"Saved, Saved."*

Immediately I traversed the cobweb-covered hallways of my memory and retrieved a gospel hymn I'd sung as a boy in my pastor-father's church. Could it be the one I was thinking of? Immediately went to my computer and Googled *"Saved, Saved."* Up popped a hymn written by Jack Scholfield in 1911. It was the very hymn that had come to mind when I heard the title.

"I've found a friend who is all to me. His love is ever true..."

This was amazing. It was so cool! As a hymn writer and amateur hymnologist myself, I have a collection of hymn stories. I call them "The Hims (and Hers) Behind the Hymns." I wondered why Jack had never told me about his dad or the hymn his father had written.

As I continued to Google, I discovered the rest of the story. The judge's father was twenty-nine years old in 1911. He was traveling with the Mordecai Ham Evangelist Team in Gonzales, Texas.

The evangelist was preaching on the subject, 'Christ Our Refuge.' In the audience was a man who had killed four men and had despaired of ever being saved. He listened to Mr. Ham explain that Christ is a refuge for sinners of any and every stripe and that the 'Cities of Refuge,' described in the Old Testament, are a type of Christ, who is a haven of hope and eternal forgiveness for all who will flee to Him.

Midway during the sermon this man jumped up from his seat and shouted: 'Saved! Saved! Saved!' Mr. Scholfield was so inspired that the next afternoon he sat outside the hotel, where the Ham party was residing, and composed both the words and the music for the hymn. It was sung for the first time the next night. This all took place nine years before my friend (the judge) was born.

What's even more fascinating is this. Twenty-three years later Mordecai Ham was preaching a revival in Charlotte, North Carolina when a teenager walked the center aisle and gave his heart to the Lord. That young man's name was none other than Billy Graham.

As best as I can determine, the judge had rejected his father's evangelical faith as a young man. But as he lay dying, he clung to the cross as he embraced the faith of his father. And for my friend, the words of that hymn became indicative of his eternal life.

"Life now is sweet and my joy is complete for I'm saved, saved, saved."

A few weeks later a most usual memorial service was held in an atrium without any religious flavor. A jazz guitarist played background music while people ate and drank and told stories of Jack. At the family's request, I gave the background of Jack's father's hymn that had been included in the memorial program. The message of the Gospel found wings and flew about that glass-paneled room. Accompanied by the guitarist, I sang the first verse of "Saved, Saved." I asked the gathered guests of lawyers, clerks, and friends to join me on the second and third verses. It was a holy moment.

Afterwards, Jack's son admitted that was the first time he'd ever heard his grandfather's song sung. I'm praying it won't be the last time.

Intersections

Honoring Our Spiritual Shepherds

October is Clergy Appreciation Month. It provides an opportunity to honor those who shepherd us on the journey of faith. One such shepherd in my life was Dwight Elving. Although Dwight was significantly shorter than I, he was a man to whom I looked up.

Along with his wife, Esther, Dwight moved to Mercer Island in 1980 where he became the first chaplain at Covenant Shores. In addition to being a gentleman, he was a gentle man who quietly won the confidence of those with whom he ministered.

When his wife passed away in 1988, Dwight moved to the Midwest to be near his adult children. He returned to Covenant Shores a dozen years ago where he once again involved himself in the spiritual life of the community. This time as a lay person.

I had been aware of Dwight since the beginning years of my ministry. But I really hadn't known him personally. Having served significant congregations in our denomination over seven decades, he was a patron saint of sorts. When I became chaplain at Covenant Shores two and one-half years ago, I began to spend time with Dwight. Here was a man who could relate to my challenges and opportunities as a chaplain.

On Sunday mornings prior to preaching at the worship service I conduct each week at The Shores, I would stop by Dwight's apartment. He would encourage me and pray over me. My elderly colleague was a constant source of encouragement. What the 12th Man is to the Seattle Seahawks (a source of loyalty and inspiration), Dwight Elving was to me.

This past summer Dwight informed me that he would celebrate his one hundredth birthday on October 11. How appropriate that my spiritual shepherd would reach such an amazing milestone during Clergy Appreciation Month, I thought. But without much notice my friend began to rapidly fail physically.

Sadly, Dwight died three weeks before his birthday. My sadness was softened by knowledge of how much this little giant had enriched my life. And that he had lived a full and meaningful life.

His family approached me and asked if his memorial service could be held on October 11. I smiled as I consented. How perfect, I thought. Dwight's first birthday in Heaven would be celebrated with birthday cake following the ceremony. And indeed, it was.

My favorite photograph of my dear friend is him wearing his Seahawk jersey at a Super Bowl party a year ago. It will forever be a reminder of his nonstop support.

So who is a spiritual 12th Man in your life? A rabbi? A priest? A pastor? Before this month is over, why not find a creative way to express your appreciation to them?

Intersections

Home Row of Freedom

I've had a fascination with typewriters since I was three years old. I used to sit at my pastor-father's manual Royal and pretend I was writing a sermon.

When I was in eighth grade, I audited a beginning typing class at the local community college. It was then I learned about the eight keys on the standard keyboard known as the "home row."

In case you've forgotten, the home row of keys is comprised of ASDFJKL and the semi-colon. They are the resting position for your two hands. They're like middle C on a piano. The home row serves as a foundation. It provides a perspective for your fingers as you type without having to look at the keyboard. Once your left hand and your right hand are oriented, you have a sense of security of where you are and where you're headed.

With that orientation in mind, I'd like to consider those eight keys on this Independence Day weekend. Each of those letters stands for something foundational to our identity as a nation. They underscore what sets us apart. These qualities are the home row of our freedom.

A stands for **allegiance**. Whenever we say "the pledge," we vow our allegiance to more than the flag. We promise loyalty to the republic for which it stands. As we watch the Ukrainians resisting the Russians to remain independent, we see allegiance modeled courageously. What we see inspires us to a greater patriotism.

S calls to mind **stewardship**. When we sing *America the Beautiful* we are reminded of what lies beneath our spacious skies from sea to shining sea. The beauty of our country is ours to maintain and keep beautiful. We are the stewards. We are the caretakers entrusted to guarantee a litter-free, carbon-free future for our descendants.

D is for **democracy**. My Greek ancestors introduced the concept to our planet two thousand five hundred years ago. For the last two hundred forty-six years we have carried forth the concept of self-rule. A government of the people, for the people and by the people is what makes our home sweet home as sweet as it is.

F stands for **faith**. Although we are a nation that insists on an appropriate border between church and state, we have always been a nation that has recognized a higher power and humbled ourselves with gratitude for the undeserved blessings of the Almighty. The fabric of our union frays to the degree we disregard God's presence and sovereignty.

J is for **justice**. In spite of what we promise when we place our hand over our heart and pledge allegiance to Old Glory, we have failed miserably to insure justice for all. Nonetheless, the pursuit of justice remains at the core of our corporate conscience. Equal treatment under the law is the home-field advantage our constitution guarantees.

K calls to mind **kinship**. America has always been a family of people made up of individual families. We've been called a melting pot and an ethnic gumbo. We are a quilt of diverse cultures stitched together by the thread of a common dream. But that common dream does not denigrate our unique backgrounds. Rather, it celebrates them. Kinship is at our core.

L stands for **Liberty**. The gigantic statue in New York Harbor and the cracked bell in the City of Brotherly Love will never let us forget that liberty is at the heart of our identity as a free people. We fight wars on our own behalf and on behalf of others to protect the right to vote, the right to worship, the right to protest and the right to succeed.

; The **semi-colon** reminds us of the fact that our story as a nation is still being written. According to Thomas Jefferson, the American experience is an experiment still being tested. Each Independence Day is an opportunity to reaffirm our commitment to the kind of country we desire to be as we keep our fingers on the home row.

A Wish Book Christmas

*"Over the river and through the woods to Grandmother's house we go.
The horse knows the way to carry the sleigh
through the white and drifted snow ..."*

I sang the lyrics in my head as I said goodbye to my mom and dad all the while clutching my child's-size suitcase. Like the song suggested, I was on my way to my grandmother's home some thirty miles from where I lived. But there was no snow, and I wouldn't be taking a horse-drawn sled. As an eleven-year-old, I was allowed to take the Greyhound bus all by myself to spend Thanksgiving Day with my mom's parents.

The initial nervousness I felt as the bus pulled away from the depot dissipated as the driver turned to me and smiled. I sat back and began to anticipate all that awaited me in about an hour.

Trips to Nana and Papa Birkeland's place in Seattle were magical. I loved the big picture windows in their living room that overlooked the skyline of the city. I treasured games of Chinese checkers and pickup sticks we played after dinner. I looked forward to baking cookies with her and picking wild blackberries on the side of their big house. I felt so grown up when Nana let me stay up late and listen to her favorite radio program. It was one of the first talk shows and she even helped me call in to talk on the air.

But my most favorite memory of visits to Nana's house is the one I treasure from that Thanksgiving Day visit. My grandmother carefully removed the Sears and Roebuck catalog from the kitchen cabinet where she kept it and handed it to me.

"This year I am going to let you choose your own Christmas present," she announced with a twinkle in her eye. *"Just browse through the toy section in this 'Wish Book' and make a check mark beside the gift you want. Papa and I will take it from there."*

I liked that she called the Sears catalog a 'Wish Book.' I had long since passed the age when I believed in Santa Claus and bottled-up genies who granted wishes. But I liked the idea of wishing for something you really wanted with the hope that your wishes might come true.

Collapsing in my grandfather's padded rocking chair perched in front of one of the landscape windows, I sat with the 'Wish Book' on my lap. I flipped through the clothing section and past the pages picturing appliances and furniture until I finally found the toys. I couldn't believe how many pages were devoted to things kids my age dream about.

I bypassed the model airplanes and train sets and found myself fixated on the baseball gloves like my heroes Mickey Mantle and Willie Mays used. But then my eyes drifted across the page to an interactive tabletop baseball game. According to the picture and the caption, "Bop Baseball" resembled a pinball game, but it didn't require any batteries. Since I already had a decent genuine leather mitt, I made a mark beside the picture and ran to show Nana. She nodded approvingly and gave me a hug.

I can't say I remember much about that Thanksgiving Day dinner with my cousins or my aunts and uncles. I don't really remember the next month as I went to school anxiously waiting for Christmas vacation to begin. But I do have a memory of being at my grandparents' house on Christmas Day tearing open the gift wrap on the long rectangular box beneath the tree. Just as she had promised, she ordered what I had asked for.

That Christmas I got more than a baseball game. I received the deep satisfaction that comes with someone you trust keeping their word. Whether she knew it or not, my grandmother was modeling my Heavenly Father's faithfulness. A faithfulness I would come to value in years to come. A faithfulness I will attempt to model for my grandchildren.

A Head of His Time

When I started attending an Evangelical Covenant Church in the mid-seventies, I discovered that this little Swedish-born denomination had recognition disproportionate to its size. It was the group of Christians who gave the world one of the most beloved hymns of all time: "*How Great Thou Art.*"

It was the church to which belonged such notables as Dr. Paul Rees (the Vice President of World Vision), Dr. G. Timothy Johnson (the medical editor of ABC News) and Mike Holmgren (the former head coach of the Green Bay Packers and the Seattle Seahawks).

And an unknown Chicago commercial artist who was a member of a small Covenant church gave the world the most-reproduced picture of all times. Warner Sallman had no idea that his image of Jesus would become the iconic Christian artwork that it did.

It has been estimated that this picture of Jesus (what has become known as *Sallman's Head of Christ*) has been printed and copied more than one billion times. Last year marked the eightieth anniversary of Warner Sallman's most celebrated work. But as well-known as *Head of Christ* is, how the picture came to be is anything but.

On a cold November day in 1923 as Sallman sat down to Thanksgiving dinner with his wife and three young sons, his heart was warmed with gratitude. The thirty-one-year-old Chicago illustrator had just been appointed art director for a new magazine published by his denomination. The magazine was called *The Covenant Companion*.

When the editor chose "The Christian Life" as the theme for the February 1924 issue of the new periodical, Sallman opted to come up with the cover illustration himself. He imagined the face of Jesus as an appropriate way to profile the theme. But no matter how many times he attempted to draw a close-up of Christ, he was dissatisfied.

On the night before the artwork was due at the printer, Sallman was unable to sleep. He poured out his heart to God, asking for help. At 2:00 a.m., feeling inspired, he got out of bed, hurried to his desk, and made a rough sketch. In the morning, just a few hours before his deadline, he completed two-feet by two-foot charcoal sketch. The image was titled *Son of Man*.

The popularity of the picture on the cover of the magazine was so great that requests for reprints streamed in after all seven thousand copies of the magazine were sold. Sallman agreed to a special run of one thousand additional copies of the image, which he paid for out of his own pocket. Within ten years all reprints had been sold or given away.

In 1940 he painted a colorized version of his sketch for the graduating class of the students at North Park Seminary. What had been called *"Son of Man"* became known as *"Sallman's Head of Christ."*

When the United States entered World War II in 1941, many American servicemen were given pocket-sized reproductions of Sallman's Christ. Distributed by chaplains and hometown congregations, these small cards helped spread the popularity of the painting. In the fifties and sixties Mr. Sallman started giving chalk talks at local churches and Bible camps at which he shared his faith while sketching his famous profile of Jesus.

The retirement campus where I work has one of these original charcoal sketches. It's not great art. But it is priceless. It has historical significance. Most importantly it is a glimpse of one person's impression of Jesus that for whatever reason has touched millions.

Several years ago, before my daughter and son-in-law moved to the Seattle area from Chicago, I was visiting them. I discovered that the home in which Mr. Sallman was living (and where he actually painted his famous picture of Christ) was five doors from my kids. I was bold enough to knock on the door and ask if I could see the upstairs bedroom where this most-reproduced image of all times was birthed. The current owners were more than happy to show me around.

In recent years the famous painting has become the center of some controversy because it looks too white-Evangelical and doesn't reflect a multi-cultural Jesus. Some Blacks, Asians, middle-easterners and Hispanics don't relate.

But we have to remember Warner Sallman was a Swedish-American. His painting reflects his perspective. It was an image with whom those in his sphere of influence could relate. In *"Sallman's Head of Christ"* we see an image that pictures a head of his time and his cultural milieu. (And we can't discount the fact that Sallman claimed to have had a vision in the middle of the night of the Jesus whom he proceeded to sketch.)

The Jesus we spend time with reading our Bibles and praying is the everyday Jesus to whom we relate. He meets us in our world, in our culture, in our everyday life. It's the Jesus we begin to reflect and give a face to. The fact that we are spending time with Him begins to show. Spending time with Jesus day in and day out impacts the way others see us. We become an everyday representation of who Jesus is.

Here's an interesting and curious side note. Warner Sallman's brother-in-law was a man by the name of Haddon Sundblom. Like Warner, Haddon was a commercial artist and illustrator. Like Warner Sallman, it's likely you've never heard of Haddon Sundblom. But as with his brother-in-law, you definitely are familiar with the image he painted. It was Haddon Sundblom who created the jolly needing-to-go-on-a-diet Santa Claus that Coca Cola used to market their soft drink.

People who knew Haddon were aware of something that those who didn't know the artist were blind to. Haddon Sundblom's friends couldn't help but see his face in the countenance of the Coca Cola Santa he'd created. The similarity was uncanny. When they saw Santa they saw him. I'm wondering if something similar could be said of us. That when people see us, they see Jesus.

Intersections

Life Lessons from Mister Rogers

In 2001, after three decades of entertaining little hearts and minds, Fred Rogers closeted his cardigan and removed his sneakers for the final time. A couple years later, the hero to countless children died. A recent documentary on the life of the celebrated broadcaster has reminded me how much this sweater-clad Presbyterian minister influenced my own life and ministry.

Looking back, I can say that (almost) everything I needed to know about thriving in ministry — and in life — I learned in that pre-kindergarten with my three preschoolers.

Here are just a few of the gems I've gleaned from Mister Rogers' Neighborhood.

1. Accentuate the positive

Mister Rogers always reminded his viewers that he likes them just the way they are. It was something his Grandfather McFeely used to say to him when he was a little kid. While other family members discussed young Fred's introverted nature, someone he loved and respected celebrated his praise-worthy qualities.

I needed that reminder in my first church. Early on, a few vocal critics challenged my adequacy as a spiritual shepherd. It was painful. I didn't feel loveable or loved. But when I heard Mister Rogers telling my daughters, "I like you just the way you are," it felt good — to them and to me. People could like me, just the way I was. Mister Rogers said so.

2. It takes a neighborhood

Even though it was called Mister Rogers's Neighborhood, Fred's program was not a one-man show. John Costa arranged the music and led the jazz ensemble, Betty Aberlin sang and interacted with the puppets, and Mr. McFeely delivered the mail. There were many more regulars, both on camera and off. They had much fun working—and playing—together.

The years I spent watching children's TV with my kids coincided with a time in my life when I attempted to do most of the ministry myself. As a result, I burned out.

That's when I called on my own "neighbors" to share in the ministry with me. The gifts others offered brought creativity, a shared sense of ownership and much-needed community.

3. True leaders work beneath the castle

What most kids didn't know is that during the segment of the show that featured the Neighborhood of Make Believe, Fred was under the castle supplying the hands and voices for many of the characters. He was in cramped spaces, willingly working shoulder to elbow with other puppeteers to bring fantasy to life without being recognized.

While being successful as a pastor—and in life—doesn't typically include hand puppets, it does mean getting involved up to your elbows, whether anybody knows it or not.

4. The value of ugga-mugga

One of my favorite residents in the Neighborhood is Daniel Striped Tiger, a shy, threadbare puppet with a scratchy little voice. Most viewers know there was only one person with whom Daniel confessed his fears and insecurities, and that was the lovely human Lady Aberlin. She knew the tiger's flaws and loved him anyway. Often after he unloaded his heavy heart, Lady Aberlin would rub his nose and say "ugga-mugga." I think it meant, "I care about you and you're going to be okay."

Everyone—pastor or otherwise—needs a confidant who listens but is also free to confront you with difficult truths.

5. Every day is special

It's such a good feeling to know you're alive. Mister Rogers wrapped up every show with this upbeat song. The message of the song was powerful: Every day is special and, even as one day is ending, we can anticipate with excitement what the new day will bring. And based on what I've read about Mister Rogers, he believed what he sang. He unwrapped each day's show as if it were a personal gift from God because, according to his faith, it was. Like Mister Rogers, I've learned to anticipate each new one as a "snappy new day."

Mister Rogers, thanks for all you taught me!

About the Author

Greg Asimakoupoulos is an ordained minister and freelance writer. For over four decades, Greg served congregations of The Evangelical Covenant Church in Washington, California and Illinois. Since 2013 he has been the fulltime chaplain at Covenant Living at the Shores.

Greg is the author of fifteen books including The Time Crunch, Finding God in "It's a Wonderful Life" and Sheltering in Grace. He is a regular columnist for three newspapers and a frequent contributor to Christian periodicals. His weekly poetic commentary can be accessed at: myrhymesandreasons.com

Greg and his wife Wendy have three grown daughters and two granddaughters. They live on Mercer Island in suburban Seattle.